This study throws new light on both the history of the crusades and the mendicant orders in the thirteenth century. It describes the way in which the Franciscan and Dominican orders became involved in preaching the cross and examines their contribution to the crusading movement of the thirteenth century. The availability of a large number of trained preachers from the Franciscan and Dominican orders allowed the papacy to use them in order to provide the crusades with a well-organized and efficient propaganda back-up throughout Europe unknown before the thirteenth century. The book explains how the propaganda campaigns were organized and how the recruitment of crusaders took place. It shows that the mendicant friars became the most important group of crusade propagandists recruiting crusaders for virtually all thirteenth-century crusades. The book also shows that the friars were involved in providing finance for the crusades as part of their propaganda effort, despite their vows of absolute poverty. It also challenges the traditional pacifist view of the founder saints of the two orders by showing them to be supporters of the crusades themselves.

Cambridge studies in medieval life and thought

PREACHING THE CRUSADES

Cambridge studies in medieval life and thought
Fourth series

General Editor:
D. E. LUSCOMBE
Professor of Medieval History, University of Sheffield

Advisory Editors:
R. B. DOBSON
Professor of Medieval History, University of Cambridge, and Fellow of Christ's College
ROSAMOND MCKITTERICK
Reader in Early Medieval European History, University of Cambridge, and Fellow of Newnham College

The series Cambridge studies in medieval life and thought was inaugurated by G. G. Coulton in 1921. Professor D. E. Luscombe now acts as General Editor of the Fourth series, with Professor R. B. Dobson and Dr Rosamond McKitterick as Advisory Editors. The series brings together outstanding work by medieval scholars over a wide range of human endeavour extending from political economy to the history of ideas.

For a list of titles in the series, see end of book.

PREACHING
THE CRUSADES

*Mendicant friars and the cross
in the thirteenth century*

CHRISTOPH T. MAIER

University of Basel

CAMBRIDGE
UNIVERSITY PRESS

Published by the Press Syndicate of the University of Cambridge
The Pitt Building, Trumpington Street, Cambridge CB2 1RP
40 West 20th Street, New York, NY 10011-4211, USA
10 Stamford Road, Oakleigh, Melbourne 3166, Australia

First published 1994

Printed in Great Britain at the University Press, Cambridge

A catalogue record for this book is available from the British Library

Library of Congress cataloguing in publication data

Maier, Christoph T.
Preaching the Crusades : mendicant friars and the Cross in the
thirteenth century / Christoph T. Maier.
  p. cm. – (Cambridge studies in medieval life and thought :
4th ser., 28)
  Based on the author's thesis (Ph. D.)–University of London, 1990.
  Includes bibliographical references.
  ISBN 0-521-45246-5
  1. Friars–Europe–History. 2. Crusades–Later, 13th, 14th, and
15th centuries. 3. Preaching–History–20th Century. I. Title.
II. Series
BX2820 M33 1994
270.5–dc20 93-32162 CIP

ISBN 0 521 45246 5

CONTENTS

Acknowledgements   *page* viii
List of abbreviations   ix

Introduction   1
1 The founder saints and the crusades   8
2 Pope Gregory IX and the early friars   20
3 Papal crusade propaganda and the friars   32
   Gregory IX   32
   Innocent IV   62
   The later thirteenth century   79
4 The organization of the preaching of the cross in the
   provinces of the mendicant orders   96
5 Friars, crusade sermons, and preaching aids   111
6 The friars and the financing of the crusades   123
7 The friars and the redemption of crusade vows   135
  Conclusion   161
  Appendix 1 The crusade against the Drenther and
    the Establishment of the Dominican Inquisition in
    Germany   167
  Appendix 2 A list of thirteenth century sermons
    and exempla for the recruitment of crusaders   170

Bibliography   175
Index   191

ACKNOWLEDGEMENTS

There are numerous people whose encouragement and assistance have made it possible for me to embark on, and finish, this study which in its original form was submitted for the degree of Ph.D at the University of London (UK) in 1990. I must thank those who provided me with generous financial help, namely the Schweizerische Akademie der Geisteswissenschaften, the Royal Historical Society (London), the Committee of Vice-Chancellors and Principals of the Universities of the United Kingdom, the British Council (London), and Royal Holloway and Bedford New College (University of London). I am also grateful to my parents for their generous and unconditional financial support during my time as an undergraduate and postgraduate student.

Jonathan Riley-Smith has been a better thesis supervisor than I could ever have wished for. His knowledge and enthusiasm and his relentless advice and support of all aspects of my research have given me the kind of guidance and comfort many other research students can only dream of. Among the students and scholars at the Institute of Historical Research in London whose comments and company I have enjoyed, I must especially thank Diana Greenway and Marcus Bull for advice on particular points of my thesis, and even more so David d'Avray, who more than once gave up his free time to discuss my work. During the preparation for publication Bernard Hamilton's advice has been most valuable and has helped turning my thesis into a better reading book.

Last but not least, I must thank Cathy Aitken, without whom this thesis would never have been written. Her moral support and helpful criticism were invaluable, and she more than once rescued me from the pitfalls of the English language. Thanks also to Isabel Aitken, who proof-read the final draft of my thesis.

C. T. M.

ABBREVIATIONS

Full titles are given in the bibliography

AF	*Analecta Franciscana*
AFB	'Acta Franciscana e Tabulariis Bononiensibus . . .'
AFH	*Archivum Franciscanum Historicum*
AFP	*Archivum Fratrum Praedicatorum*
Ale.IV R	*Les Registres d'Alexandre IV*
APP	*Les Actes Pontificaux Originaux . . .*
BF	*Bullarium Franciscanum*
BP	*Bullarium Ordinis Praedicatorum*
BSA	'Bullarium Pontificum quod existat . . .'
Cle.IV R	*Les Registres de Clément IV*
Delorme	Delorme, 'De praedicatione cruciatae . . .'
Doat	Ms. Paris, Bibliothèque Nationale, *Doat XVI*
ES	*Epistolae Selectae Saeculi XIII . . .*
Gre.IX R	*Les Registres de Grégoire IX*
Gre.X R	*Les Registres de Grégoire X et de Jean XXI*
Joh.XXI R	*Les Registres de Grégoire X et de Jean XXI*
Hon.III R	*Regesta Honorii Papae III*
Hon.IV R	*Les Registres d'Honorius IV*
Inn.IV R	*Les Registres d'Innocent IV*
Mar.IV R	*Les Registres de Martin IV*
MGHS	*Monumenta Germaniae Historica. Scriptores*
MGHSS	*Monumenta Germaniae Historica. Scriptores Rerum Germanicarum in usum scholarum separatim editi*
MGHS rg	*Monumenta Germaniae Historica. Scriptores Rerum Germanicarum. Nova Series*
MOPH	*Monumenta Ordinis Praedicatorum Historia*
Nic.III R	*Les Registres de Nicolas III*
Nic.IV R	*Les Registres de Nicolas IV*
PL	*Patrologiae cursus completus. Series Latina*
PUB	*Preussisches Urkundenbuch*

List of abbreviations

RISNS	*Rerum Italicarum Scriptores* (new series)
RGHF	*Recueil des Historiens des Gaules et de la France*
RHC oc.	*Recueil des Historiens des Croisades. Historiens Occidentaux*
Sevesi	Sevesi, 'Documenta Hucusque Inedita . . .'
Urb.IV R	*Les Registres de Urban IV*
Urb.IV RCam.	*Les Registres de Urban IV, i*
Verci	Verci, *Storia della Marca Trivigiana e Veronese . . .*

INTRODUCTION

During the first half of the thirteenth century, the crusade was transformed into a most sophisticated institution. By developing such aspects as recruitment, finance, liturgy, and the legal rights and duties of crusaders the Roman Curia managed to make the crusade an immensely versatile, and a potentially effective, instrument of papal politics. As a devotional activity and an expression of aggressive religious power, the crusade had kept its original momentum throughout the twelfth century, despite the set-backs in the Holy Land in the 1180s. In fact, the crusading movement was more vigorous than ever during the early 1200s. It imposed its might against the main rival of the Roman Church within Christendom by conquering Constantinople, it now fully expanded its scope into warfare against heretics and enemies of the papacy, and it achieved one of its greatest successes by defeating the Spanish Muslims in the battle of Las Navas de Tolosa in 1212. The problems facing the crusading movement at the beginning of the thirteenth century were problems of growth and expansion. There was no lack of enthusiasm, nor was there an absence of opportunity and initiative, to transform crusading zeal into positive action. And yet, the flag-ship of the crusading movement, the *negotium Terrae Sanctae*, was in dire straits. The Third Crusade had failed dismally; few elements of the Fourth Crusade ever reached Palestine. Out of this period of recurring frustration with regard to crusading efforts in the East, concerns about the nature and practice of the *negotium crucis* were bound to arise.

The success or failure of the crusade was not considered ultimately to be in the hands of its participants. The Christian defeat at the battle of Hattin in 1187 was seen as God's punishment for the sins of the wider Christian community, in the same way as the victory of Las Navas de Tolosa was viewed as having been engineered by divine will. Similarly the spiritual benefits gained by the crusader did not depend on the outcome of a campaign. The

I

crusader was a pilgrim for the good of his own soul, and a disastrous crusade was still able to provide the individual participant with a plenary indulgence. Nevertheless, the victories of the Muslims over the Christian forces were bound to cause serious concern. If Christ, as it were, gave up his patrimony, the Holy Land, to the non-believers as a sign of disapproval of the ways of his own people, how great must be the guilt of the Christian community! The crusade was a serious issue, not only because it played a role in the territorial defence and expansion of Christendom, but also because it reflected the moral constitution of Christian society as a whole.[1]

The imagination and the political will of Pope Innocent III were responsible for most of the changes which the crusading movement underwent as it entered its second century.[2] Although he was under no illusion that reforming the movement could in any way influence God's final judgement of the crusade, Innocent III was convinced that Christians were obliged by virtue of their faith to form a society organized for the defence of its religion on all fronts. This meant, among other things, creating the best conditions humanly possible for the *negotium crucis*. Innocent institutionalized such features as the redemption and commutation of crusading vows, the right to partial indulgences for material help, money collection, taxation, and a whole range of liturgical practices for the crusade. His aim was to control the crusade centrally so as to make it more effective. Since several crusades were often operating at the same time, there had to be a central agency to distribute men and money according to the most urgent needs. These resources were not only limited, but dispersed, due to the international character of the *negotium crucis*. The Roman Curia was the natural agency to take over the coordination. Only the Roman pontiff, as the head and governor of the church and as the spiritual leader of Christian society, could call for a crusade, only he could issue the indulgences and privileges pertaining to the *negotium crucis*;[3]

---

[1] For a general survey of crusading activities at the end of the twelfth and the beginning of the thirteenth centuries, see J.S.C. Riley-Smith, *The Crusades. A Short History* (London 1987), 109–45.

[2] H. Roscher, *Papst Innocenz III. und die Kreuzzüge* (Forschungen zur Kirchen- und Dogmengeschichte; Göttingen 1969), *passim*, esp. 260–91; J.A. Brundage, *Canon Law and the Crusader* (Madison 1969), *passim*, esp. 69–70, 162–3, 185–6; Riley-Smith, *Crusades*, 119–20.

[3] F.H. Russell, *The Just War in the Middle Ages* (Cambridge studies in medieval life and thought (third series), 8; Cambridge 1975), 112–26, 195–212, *passim*.

besides, the Roman Curia was the only organization that spanned the whole of Europe. Innocent III also wanted to streamline crusading armies by reducing non-combattant elements to the bare minimum, to provide sufficient finance, and to allow crusaders to be employed wherever it was considered most necessary at any one period. At the same time the home front was to provide the moral back-up for the crusade by prayers, processions, and other intercessionary practices. The bulk of these measures were incorporated into the statutes of the Fourth Lateran Council, and it was from there that all later thirteenth-century crusade bulls took their inspiration.[4] The re-shaping of the crusading movement in the early thirteenth century thus became part of a much wider reform programme, which embraced most areas of Christian society.[5]

Innocent III died shortly after the Fourth Lateran Council and was thus unable to see his high-flown, but as yet unfinished, plans through to working practice. His successor, Honorius III, was an able administrator and an unpretentious but faithful follower of the politics of his predecessor. He tried to translate Innocent's ideas regarding the crusade into reality as best as he could.[6] But the issue was not only a question of the right intention and political will. What was needed to implement these changes was an organizational structure to carry the message to the people of Europe. Following tradition, Honorius used the existing channels of crusading propaganda, the local church hierarchy, and papal legates. While the diocesan hierarchy theoretically ensured the widest possible distribution of crusading propaganda, the local clergy was not reliable. Bound by local political and social ties, the bishops and their subordinates were not always willing to comply with orders coming from Rome, which were often viewed as unwelcome outside interference in local matters. There was also no uniform level of education among diocesan clerics. Training in canon law and proficiency in preaching were accidental rather than essential to appointments within the local church, and the availability of properly trained clerics in any one diocese depended to a great extent on the outlook of the particular bishop.[7] For these reasons, the Curia always relied on a number of individuals to preach the

---

[4] *Conciliorum Oecumenicorum Decreta*, ed. J. Alberigo *et al.* (Basel 1962), 227–71, esp. 267–71.

[5] C. Morris, *The Papal Monarchy. The Western Church from 1050–1250* (Oxford 1989), 417–51.   [6] Roscher, *Innocenz III.*, 292–6.

[7] Morris, *Papal Monarchy*, 205–36, 527–41.

cross alongside the diocesan clergy. These were specially selected clerics, usually closely connected with the Curia by previous service as papal agents and chosen for their abilities with regard to the specific task of their mission.[8] Individual propagandists like Bernard of Clairvaux, Fulk of Neuilly, and Oliver of Cologne all had a great impact on the crusading movement and became legendary figures. Their success made it clear that crusading propaganda depended as much on the quality of the preachers as on their overall number. But the areas of operation of individual propagandists were limited and their impact was therefore confined. One way of getting round some of these problems was the use of members of exempt religious orders, especially the Cistercians, whose interest in the *negotium crucis* went back to the days of Bernard of Clairvaux. Their order had the advantage of being organized in a hierarchical structure which was independent of the diocesan administration. But despite the fact that learning and preaching were values fostered by the Cistercians, their readiness to apply these abilities outside the abbey was often limited, because in essence the Cistercians regarded themselves as a monastic and contemplative order.[9]

The solution to ensuring effective crusading propaganda was finally provided by Honorius III's successor, Gregory IX, who employed the mendicant friars: first, from 1230, the Dominicans for the Baltic crusade, then both the Franciscans and the Dominicans for the Holy Land crusade in the mid 1230s. The Franciscans and the Dominicans were members of the first religious orders whose main aim was preaching and they were systematically trained as preachers.[10] The mendicant orders were also organized in a strict hierarchy with provinces throughout Europe under a master- or minister-general and governed by an annual general

---

[8] P.B. Pixton, 'Die Anwerbung des Heeres Christi: Prediger des Fünften Kreuzzuges in Deutschland', *Deutsches Archiv für die Erforschung des Mittelalters*, xxxiv (1978), 166–91, here 167–72; H. Hoogeweg, 'Die Kreuzpredigt des Jahres 1224 in Deutschland mit besonderer Rücksicht auf die Erzdiözese Köln', *Deutsche Zeitschrift für Geschichtswissenschaft*, iv (1890), 54–74; J.M. Powell, *Anatomy of a Crusade, 1213–1221* (Philadelphia 1986), 67–87.

[9] L. Schmugge, 'Zisterzienser, Kreuzzug und Heidenkrieg', *Die Zisterzienser. Ordensleben zwischen Ideal und Wirklichkeit*, ed. K. Elm *et al.* (Schriften des Rheinischen Museumsamtes 10; Cologne 1980), 57–68; E. Siberry, *Criticism of Crusading 1095–1274* (Oxford 1985), 191, n. 12.

[10] D. Berg, *Armut und Wissenschaft. Beiträge zur Geschichte des Studienwesens der Bettelorden im 13. Jahrhundert* (Bochumer Historische Studien 15; Düsseldorf 1977); J.-P. Renard, *La formation et la désignation des Predicateurs au début de l'ordre des Prêcheurs 1215–1237* (Freiburg i.Ue. 1977).

chapter. Strict obedience bound the local divisions within the hierarchical structure. Compared with the Cistercians, mobility within the mendicant orders was considerable, since the principle of the *stabilitas loci* of the old-type religious orders was not part of their rules. This theoretically made the friars an ideal instrument for the controlled spread of propaganda over vast geographical areas. The mendicant friars' role as crusade propagandists has never been fully acknowledged. Until recently historians of the mendicant orders or the crusades at best described this role as marginal.[11] This was mainly due to a lack of interest in the issue, rather than an absence of relevant sources. Indeed, in the late nineteenth and the early twentieth centuries sporadic articles about individual friars and the publication of specific sources had pointed at the central role the mendicants played as crusade preachers.[12] But thereafter, with the exception of the studies by William Lunt, Valmar Cramer, and Jose Goñi-Gaztambide, which mention the friars' preaching of the cross *en passant*, the topic was dead for several decades.[13] Interest in the mendicant friars as preachers of the cross was not revived until the mid 1970s, with an article on Gilbert of Tournai by Franco Cardini.[14] Shortly thereafter, John Freed's study of the German friars in the thirteenth century for the first time gave an idea of the mendicants' central role as propagandists for the Baltic crusade and the anti-heretical and anti-Hohenstaufen crusades in Germany.[15] Around the same time, Richard Spence, in

[11] E.g., J.H.R. Moorman, *A History of the Franciscan Order from its Origins to the Year 1517* (Oxford 1968), 300–2. Moorman misdated the first use of Franciscan friars as crusade preachers by following Wadding who ascribed the bull *Rahel suum videns* to 1227 rather than its actual date 1234. See below, 35.

[12] A. Rother, 'Johannes Teutonicus (von Wildeshausen). Vierter General des Dominikanerordens', *Römische Quartalschrift für Christliche Alterthumskunde und für Kirchengeschichte*, ix (1895), 139–70; F.M. Delorme, 'Bulle d'Innocent IV pour la croisade (6 février 1245)', *AFH*, vi (1913), 386–9; Delorme, 'Bulle d'Innocent IV en faveur de l'empire latin de Constantinople', *AFH*, viii (1915), 307–10; Delorme, 'De praedicatione cruciatae saec.XIII per fratres minores', *AFH*, ix (1916), 99–117; Delorme, 'Trois bulles à frère Hugues de Turenne', *AFH*, xviii (1925), 291–5; A. Van den Wyngaert, 'Frère Guillaume de Cordelle O.F.M.', *La France Franciscaine*, iv (1921), 52–71.

[13] W.E. Lunt, *Financial Relations of the Papacy with England to 1321* (Studies in Anglo-Papal Relations during the Middle Ages 1; Cambridge, Mass. 1939); V. Cramer, *Albert der Grosse als päpstlicher Kreuzzugs-Legat für Deutschland 1263/64 und die Kreuzzugsbestrebungen Urbans IV* (Palästina-Hefte des Deutschen Vereins vom Heiligen Lande 7, 8; Cologne 1933); J. Goñi-Gaztambide, *Historia de la Bula de la Cruzada en España* (Victoriensia 4; Vitoria 1958).

[14] F. Cardini, 'Gilberto di Tournai. Un Francescano Predicatore della Crociata', *Studi Francescani*, lxxii (1975), 31–48.

[15] J.B. Freed, *The Friars and German Society in the Thirteenth Century* (The Medieval Academy of America Publications 86; Cambridge, Mass. 1977), 65–9, 91–3, 138–61, *passim*.

an unpublished Ph.D. thesis, described that same role for the crusades between 1227 and 1241 in general.[16] Since then, historians of the crusades have taken the friars' preaching of the cross more seriously.[17] Norman Housley systematically assessed the mendicants' importance as agents within the papal propaganda machinery for the Italian crusades.[18] Simon Lloyd and Christopher Tyerman made it clear that the mendicants were part of the regular crusade preaching force in England in the thirteenth century,[19] while Barrie Cook, in an unpublished Ph.D. thesis, described the importance of mendicant crusade preachers for the transmission of knowledge about the Holy Land through Europe between 1271 and 1314.[20] Many other studies on various aspects of the crusades now mention their role as crusade propagandists, without, however, dwelling on it at any length.[21]

This study intends to look at mendicant crusade preaching in its own right. It investigates the preaching of the cross by members of the two major orders of mendicant friars, the Dominicans and the Franciscans, throughout Europe between the pontificates of Gregory IX and Nicholas IV. Its overall aim is to chronicle and analyse this activity and to assess its importance for the crusading movement. The scope of the study in terms of subject matter is

---

[16] R.T. Spence, 'Pope Gregory IX and the Crusade' (unpublished Ph.D. thesis; Syracuse University 1978).

[17] C. Schmitt, 'Der Anteil der Franziskaner an den Kreuzzügen (13.-15.Jh.)', *800 Jahre Franz von Assisi. Franziskanische Kunst und Kultur des Mittelalters. Niederösterreichische Landesaustellung Krems-Stein*, ed. Amt der Niederösterreichischen Regierung (Kulturabteilung) (Katalog des Niederösterreichischen Landesmuseums. Neue Folge 122; Vienna 1982), 213–20.

[18] N. Housley, *The Italian Crusades. The Papal-Angevin Alliance and the Crusades against Christian Lay Powers 1254–1343* (Oxford 1982), 111–44 *passim*.

[19] S.D. Lloyd, *English Society and the Crusade 1216–1307* (Oxford 1988), 8–41 *passim*; C. Tyerman, *England and the Crusades 1095–1588* (Chicago and London 1988), 152–86 *passim*.

[20] B.J. Cook, 'The Transmission of Knowledge about the Holy Land through Europe 1271–1314', 2 vols. (unpublished Ph.D. thesis; Manchester University 1985).

[21] M. Purcell, *Papal Crusading Policiy. The Chief Instruments of Papal Crusading Policy and Crusade to the Holy Land from the Loss of Jerusalem to the Fall of Acre 1244–1291* (Leiden 1975); E. Christiansen, *The Northern Crusades, The Baltic and the Catholic Frontier 1100–1525* (London and Basingstoke 1980); N. Housley, 'Politics and Heresy in Italy: Anti-Heretical Crusades, Orders and Confraternities, 1200–1500', *Journal of Ecclesiastical History*, liii (1982), 193–208; Housley, *The Avignon Papacy and the Crusades 1305–1378* (Oxford 1986); E. Siberry, 'Missionaries and Crusaders, 1095–1274: Opponents or Allies', *Studies in Church History*, xx (1983), 103–10; Sibery, *Criticism*; B.Z. Kedar, *Crusade and Mission. European Approaches toward the Muslims* (Princeton 1984); A. Macquarrie, *Scotland and the Crusades 1095–1560* (Edinburgh 1985); Riley-Smith, *Crusades*; P.J. Cole, *The Preaching of the Crusades to the Holy Land, 1095–1270* (Medieval Academy Books 98; Cambridge, Mass. 1991).

determined by the available source material. Since most information for the friars' preaching of the cross comes from papal correspondence, the major part of the present work is concerned with the way in which the papacy used the mendicant friars as part of the propaganda machinery for the crusades. Papal letters have survived in most European archives. Their number is, of course, subject to chance preservation, and knowledge of them is limited by the extent and quality of archival material published. The papal registers, that is the record of letters leaving the Curia, form a more comprehensive collection, although these, likewise, have not survived in their entirety. Nor do the registers contain all papal letters. In fact, on average, only one in five was registered. There was also no consistency as to whether letters were registered before or after correction, from the final version or the draft copy. So far scholars have failed to understand how exactly, and to what end, the registers were kept.[22] Other evidence stems from narrative sources, mainly chronicles and annals. Their authors, however, usually reported only isolated snippets of information. Crusading propaganda as such was not the stuff of chronicles or of other narrative accounts of the period. It is, therefore, worth remembering that, like all medieval records, our sources can only tell part of the story. Taken together, however, the registers, the surviving copies of papal letters, and the information gathered from narrative sources probably project a fairly representative and more or less accurate overall picture of the chronology, the geography, and the nature of the mendicants' involvement in the propaganda for the *negotium crucis*.[23]

---

[22] O. Hageneder, 'Die päpstlichen Register des 13. und 14. Jahrhunderts.', *Annali della Scuola speciale per archivisti e bibliothecari dell'Università di Roma*, xii (1972), 45–76; R.C. Van Caenegem, *Guide to the Sources of Medieval History* (Europe in the Middle Ages Selected Studies 2; Amsterdam, New York, Oxford 1978), 81, 212–17.

[23] Papal letters have in many cases been edited in several collections of sources. Reference is made to the most accurate and/or most accessible editions only. Where applicable, the entries in the papal registers are added.

Chapter 1

THE FOUNDER SAINTS AND THE CRUSADES

Neither the Franciscans nor the Dominicans were instituted for the broadcasting of crusading propaganda. Both founder saints had wide-ranging ideas about the reform of Christianity as a whole which went far beyond the limited aspects of society and of the lives of individuals touched on by the crusades. Since the outlook and personality of both Dominic and Francis were of prime importance for the shaping of the two orders, the first chapter of this study explores their attitudes towards the respective crusades in which they were each involved at different times. The intention is to show that the friars' later involvement in propagating the crusade did not contradict the ideas and ideologies of the two founder saints.

Francis of Assisi's visit to Damietta during the Fifth Crusade has provoked the thoughts and comments of a great number of historians.[1] With few exceptions Francis's journey has been interpreted as a mission of peace, carried out in opposition to the war and the violence of the crusading army. By crossing enemy lines during a pause in the fighting to preach in front of Sultan al-Kamil, Francis is said by the majority of modern commentators to have attempted to promote an alternative to armed struggle: mission by preaching the word of God instead of crusading. Dominic Guzmàn, too, was in close contact with the crusading movement. Between 1205 and 1215 he was a member of the papal legation in Languedoc, which was in charge of combatting the Albigensian heresy. Initially, this was done by a combination of preaching and conducting disputations and then, from 1208, in conjunction with a crusading army. It was during this time that Dominic gathered a

---

[1] Most general histories of the crusades mention it in passing. For studies specifically concerned with this event, see *Writings and Early Biographies. English Omnibus of the Sources for the Life of St Francis*, ed. M.A. Habig (4th edn Chicago 1983), 1714–15. See also J. Powell, 'Francesco d'Assisi e la Quinta Crociata. Una Missione di Pace', *Schede Medievali*, iv (1983), 68–77; B.Z. Kedar, *Crusade and Mission, European Approaches toward the Muslims* (Princeton 1984), 116–31, which quotes more recent studies.

band of preachers, who later became the core of the Dominican order. The fact that Dominic continued his attempts to convert heretics by preaching, once the crusade against the Albigensians was operating after 1208, has again and again led historians to believe that he objected to the use of crusaders against the Albigensians.[2] Viewing both Dominic and Francis as 'anti-crusaders', however, has its problems mainly because it is based, in both cases, on the interpretation of selective evidence. In the following it will be argued that, taking into account all that is known about the two saints' involvement in the respective crusades, such a view can no longer be justified.

St Francis and the Fifth Crusade

According to his early biographers, Francis's journey to the East at the time of the Fifth Crusade was the result of his desire to become a martyr by preaching Christianity to the Muslims. It was assumed that Muslims usually killed Christian missionaries who attacked their religion as blasphemers. As early as 1212, Francis started out on a journey to the Holy Land in order to achieve martyrdom in this way. But the boat of the merchants from Ancona whom he had joined was shipwrecked off Dalmatia and Francis did not have the money to pay for a second passage. Instead he tried to reach the Muslim territories in Spain or northern Africa and set out on foot towards southern France. When he reached Spain he was, however, struck down by a serious illness and had to return to Italy.[3] Francis probably left Italy again after the Pentecost chapter of his order in May 1219 and arrived at Damietta sometime before the month of July. He may have stayed there until the autumn before returning to Italy, probably by way of Acre.[4] As for what Francis

---

[2] M.-H. Vicaire, *Histoire de Saint Dominique*, 2 vols. (Paris 1957), i, 173–358, esp. 283–93; M.-H. Vicaire, 'Les clercs de la croisade, l'absence de Dominique', *Paix de Dieu et guerre sainte en Albigeois au xiiie siècle* (Cahiers de Fanjeaux 4; Toulouse 1969), 260–80; M. Roquebert, *L'épopée Cathare*, 3 vols. (Toulouse 1970–86), i, 186–200, 206–10, 420, 491–4; W.A. Hinnebusch, *The History of the Dominican Order*, 2 vols. (New York 1965, 1973), i, 27–32. Note, however, Vicaire's qualifying remarks (*Histoire*, i, 290).

[3] Thomas of Celano, 'Vita Prima S. Francisci', *AF*, x, 1–117, here 42–3; St Bonaventure, 'Legenda Major S. Francisci', *AF*, x, 555–652, here 599–600.

[4] None of the accounts relating the journey mentioned the exact dates. Circumstantial evidence from Francis's own life and the events during the Fifth Crusade suggest this as the most likely chronological framework. See Powell, 'Francesco d'Assisi', 71–2; L. Lemmens, 'De Sancto Francisco Christum Praedicante coram Sultano Egypti', *AFH*, xix (1926), 559–78.

did at Damietta, various sources contain a number of different stories. No one, however, attempted to render a full account of Francis's journey: contemporary commentators confined themselves to the rendering of single episodes in an anecdotal fashion.

The earliest account appears in a letter of spring 1220 written by James of Vitry, who himself was with the crusading army at Damietta. James mentioned Francis's visit in passing and restricted his report to the basic facts:

When their [the Franciscans'] master, who is also the founder of their order, came to stay with our army, he was not afraid to go into the camp of our enemy burning with zeal for the faith; for several days he preached the word of God to the Saracens, but with little success. However, the sultan, the king of Egypt, secretly begged him to pray to the Lord for him so that, by divine inspiration, he might adhere to that religion which was more pleasing to God.[5]

Like all subsequent writers, James of Vitry reported that Francis's mission was unsuccessful and that he returned unscathed from the Muslim camp. But James of Vitry does not appear to have had any detailed information about what exactly happened between Francis and Sultan al-Kamil. A number of commentators who wrote towards the end of the 1220s seem to have had the same problem. Thomas of Celano in his *Vita Prima*, Julian of Speyer in his *Vita S. Francisci*, and the lengthy verse life of St Francis ascribed to Henry of Avranches all chose as a narrative framework for Francis's encounter with al-Kamil a *topos* which was part of literary tradition.[6] It runs as follows: a Christian envoy to a Muslim court tries to forge an alliance between a Christian and a Muslim ruler, on the basis that the latter converts to Christianity with his whole people. The envoy is, in turn, tempted by offers of rich gifts to betray his fellow Christians, which he subsequently does or refuses to do, depending on the context in which the *topos* is used. This set story appears, for example, in the tenth-century *Vita* of the Bl. John of Gorze who spent three years at the court of the caliph of Cordobà as an envoy of Emperor Otto I between 953 and 956. John's biographer, Abbot John of St Arnulf, probably found

---

[5] James of Vitry, *Lettres*, ed. R.B.C. Huygens (Leiden 1960), 132–3. For the date of the letter, see page 131, note to l. 248. James used the same basic story again in his *Historia Occidentalis* [ed. J. Hinnebusch (Specilegium Friburgense 17; Freiburg i.Ue. 1972), 161–2].

[6] Thomas of Celano, 'Vita Prima', 43–4; Julian of Speyer, 'Vita S. Francisci', *AF*, x, 333–71, here 352–3; Henry of Avranches, 'Legenda S. Francisci Versificata', *AF*, x, 405–521, here 457–61. For the date of these lives, see the introduction to *AF*, x.

himself in the same position as the early commentators of Francis's visit at Damietta. Since he did not know in any great detail what really happened during John of Gorze's stay at Cordobà, he reverted to an acceptable element of literary (and/or oral) tradition which he elaborated to suit the historical events. Thus John of Gorze was also said to have tried to convert the Muslims, attended disputations on the validity of the Christian faith, and resisted the offers of rich gifts in return for apostasy.[7] The best-known use of this *topos*, however, comes from the *Chanson de Roland*. Here it is used with a negative outcome when Ganelon accepts King Marsile's offer and betrays Charlemagne's army.[8] The Chronicle of Ernoul and Bernard the Treasurer, which is roughly contemporary with the early lives of St Francis, uses the same basic story about Francis's visit to Damietta as Thomas of Celano and the other early biographers, but told in a much more elaborate way. It is this version, therefore, which will be discussed in more detail. Here Francis and a fellow Franciscan – who are not identified by name but simply referred to as two clerics – first asked the papal legate for permission to go to the sultan's camp. The legate warned them of the danger of being put to death, but finally let them go after he had become aware of their determination. After crossing enemy lines, the two were brought in front of al-Kamil, who assumed that they were defectors and asked if they wanted to become Muslims. But the two told al-Kamil that they had come as messengers sent by their God in order to pray for the sultan's soul and to make him accept the Christian faith. Al-Kamil, so the story went on, called upon his *imams* to face the challenge of the two missionaries, who had offered to prove the nullity of the Muslim religion. The *imams*, however, refused to take part in a disputation and instead demanded of the sultan that, in accordance with Muslim law, he killed the two Christians. But al-Kamil was said to have been touched by the two missionaries' sincere concern for his soul, for which they had even been prepared to die. He, therefore, offered them his hospitality and rich gifts. The two friars, however, refused and returned to the Christian camp.[9]

New material for Francis's visit to Damietta only appeared in the

---

[7] John of St Arnulf, 'Vita Johannis abbatis Gorzensis', *MGHS*, iv, 335–77, here 370–5.
[8] *La Chanson de Roland*, ed. J. Bédier (Paris 1922), 29–53.
[9] *Chronique d'Ernoul et de Bernard le Trésorier*, ed. M.L. de Mas Latrie (Paris 1871), 431–4. For the date and the authorship of the chronicle, see M.R. Morgan, *The Chronicle of Ernoul and the Continuations of William of Tyre* (London 1973).

mid 1240s when more information about the saint's life in general was made available. At the general chapter of the Franciscan order at Genoa in 1244 a decision was taken to collect all that was known about the life of the founder saint so that it could be preserved in writing. These stories were to be sent to Leo, Rufino, and Angelo, three of the early friars who had known Francis well. The material was kept by Brother Leo at Assisi in the form of *rotuli*, that is single quires. Some of the information gathered in this way subsequently served as the basis for Thomas of Celano's *Vita Secunda* and the group of collections of anecdotes about the life of St Francis variously known as *Scripta Leonis*, the Legend of Perugia, and the Legend of the Three Companions.[10] As a result of the appeal of 1244, Thomas of Celano seems to have been able to introduce into his *Vita Secunda* a story of how Francis preached to the crusaders at Damietta on the eve of a battle. Francis tried to dissuade them from engaging the Muslims on that specific day, since he had had a vision that the battle would end in a disaster for the Christian army. But no-one took his warning seriously, and after the saint's premonition had come true, Francis was said to have mourned the valiant Christian soldiers who had been killed.[11] Thomas of Celano, however, left out the story of Francis's preaching before the sultan. This may suggest that, when he wrote the *Vita Secunda* in 1246–47, more information about the latter episode had not yet come to light.

After 1247, however, the appeal of 1244 seems to have produced further information about the visit to Damietta. Three new episodes about Francis's preaching in front of al-Kamil had come forward by 1260. One of them was used by Bonaventure in his *Legenda Major*, two other ones appeared in an *exempla* collection of the mid thirteenth century, also claiming Bonaventure as their source. For all three stories Bonaventure quoted Illuminatus, Francis's companion to the Muslim camp, as his informant. Illuminatus, in turn, was also one of the principal sources of the Legend of the Three Companions, which was to a large extent compiled from the *rotuli* collected after 1244.[12] In his *Legenda Major*, which was commissioned by the general chapter of 1260,

[10] See the introduction to: *Scripta Leonis, Rufini et Angeli Sociorum S. Francisci, The Writings of Leo, Rufino and Angelo Companions of St Francis*, ed. and trans. R.B. Brooke (Oxford 1970), 17–25.

[11] Thomas of Celano, 'Vita Secunda S. Francisci', *AF*, x, 127–268, here 149. The earlier *Estoire de Eracles* confirmed that Francis did preach to the crusaders. See 'L'Estoire de Eracles Empereur', *RHC oc.*, ii, 1–481, here 348–9.   [12] *Scripta Leonis*, 86.

Bonaventure took over the story of Francis preaching to the crusaders from Celano's *Vita Secunda*.[13] But in contrast to the *Vita Secunda*, he re-introduced the encounter with al-Kamil. In doing so, Bonaventure hung on to the narrative framework which had so far been used by Ernoul, Celano in his *Vita Prima*, and the other early biographers. He was, however, the first writer to report details which were obviously not part of the set story. Apart from naming Francis's companion as Brother Illuminatus, he elaborated on the meeting with the sultan. Francis, according the *Legenda Major*, challenged the sultan and his *imams* to an ordeal by fire, in order to establish which religion was the more powerful. He suggested that he and the most worthy of the sultan's *imams* enter a bonfire in order to find out which faith would protect its believer. When the Muslims refused to do so, Francis offered to undergo the ordeal by himself, on the condition that al-Kamil would convert to Christianity if he left the fire unharmed. But the sultan refused to agree to this, allegedly because he would never dare to become a Christian even if he felt impelled to. Again the story is concluded by al-Kamil offering rich gifts to Francis, who declined them and left the Muslim camp.[14] This story, with its powerful visual image of the ordeal by fire, became the favourite version of later medieval hagiographers and mural painters, by whom it was repeatedly elaborated with a good deal of fantasy.[15]

In a Franciscan *exempla*-collection two more episodes from Francis's meeting with the sultan were recorded.[16] The two *exempla* belong to the earliest section of the collection, which seems to have been written during the generalate of Bonaventure between 1256 and 1273.[17] The first *exemplum* begins by stating its

[13] Bonaventure, 'Legenda Major', 606. For the date see the introdution in *AF*, x.

[14] Bonaventure, 'Legenda Major', 600–1. Bonaventure used the same story in one of his sermons. See St Bonaventure, *Opera Omnia*, 10 vols. (Ad Claras Aquas (Quaracchi) 1882– 1902), ix, 579–80.

[15] For the later medieval sources, see G. Golubovich, *Biblioteca Bio-bibliographica della Terra Santa e dell'Oriente Francescano* (1st ser.), 5 vols. (Ad Claras Aquas (Quaracchi) 1906–27), i, 1–84, ii, 280–3. There is only one tenuous and inconclusive reference in an Arab source which might refer to Francis's meeting with al-Kamil. See M. Roncaglia, 'Fonte Arabo-Muselmana su San Francesco in Oriente?', *Studi Francescani*, l (1953), 258–9. For the later medieval pictorial representations, see J.W. Einhorn, 'Franziskus und der "Edle Heide"', *Text und Bild. Aspekte des Zusammenwirkens zweier Künste in Mittelalter und früher Neuzeit*, ed. C. Meier and U. Ruberg (Wiesbaden 1980), 630–50.

[16] See below, 174, nos. 45, 46.

[17] See the introduction by Oliger in: 'Liber Exemplorum Fratrum Minorum Saeculi XIII (Excerpta e cod. Ottob. lat. 522)', ed. L. Oliger, *Antonianum*, ii (1927), 203–76, here, 206, 209–10.

source as Bonaventure having been told the story by Brother Illuminatus.[18] It reports how the sultan wanted to test Francis's faith. Al-Kamil had a piece of cloth put in front of him, which was decorated all over with the sign of the cross. He then decided to call Francis and see whether or not the saint, when approaching him, would walk across the cloth. If he did, so the sultan thought, it would mean an insult to God, which the saint then would have to justify. Francis, in fact, did step on the crosses, and when asked how he could do so without offending God, he replied:

You must know that along with Our Lord thieves were crucified. We in fact have the cross of God and Our Saviour Jesus Christ, and it is this cross which we worship and embrace with all our devotion. The holy cross of God has been given to us, whereas the crosses of the thieves were left as your share; this is why I was not afraid to walk over the signs of the thieves. Nothing of the sacred cross of the Saviour belongs to you or is amongst you.[19]

Francis's reasoning may sound odd, but the topic of the discussion fitted well the context of the Fifth Crusade. During the peace negotiations between the crusaders and the Muslims in summer 1219, the sultan had offered not only to cede the Holy City and the lands west of the Jordan, but also to return the largest existing part of the relic of the True Cross, which had been lost to Saladin at the battle of Hattin in 1187. There were, however, rumours among the crusaders at Damietta that the sultan was not in possession of the relic because Saladin was suspected of having lost it soon after the battle of Hattin.[20] Francis doubtless knew these rumours and this explains his allegation that al-Kamil was not in possession of the cross of Christ. Following his own peculiar way of reasoning, Francis suggested that the crosses on the piece of cloth could not, therefore, represent the True Cross. And since the crusaders had, in fact, brought other pieces of the True Cross to Damietta,[21] Francis was to some extent justified in saying that the Christians had the cross of Christ.

[18] Ms. Vatican, Biblioteca Apostolica, *Ottob.lat.522*, f.243r(92r): 'Referebat generalis minister quod socius beati Francisci qui eum comitatus fuit quando ivit ad soldanum Babylonie talia narrare consueverat.' The general minister was Bonaventure. See 'Liber Exemplorum', 206–10.
[19] Ms. Vatican, Biblioteca Apostolica, *Ottob.Lat.522*, f.243r(92r): 'Debetis, inquit scire quod cum domino nostro crucifixi fuerunt et latrones. unde crucem dei et Salvatoris nostri ihesu christi nos habemus et illam adoramus totaque devotione complectimur. Data igitur nobis Sancta dei cruce; vobis latronum cruces relicte sunt. Et ideo super latronum signacula non sum veritus transire. Ad vos enim aut inter vos nihil de sacra cruce Salvatoris.' [20] James of Vitry, *Lettres*, 124–5. [21] Powell, *Anatomy*, 143.

The second *exemplum* does not directly quote its source, but a marginal note in the manuscript underneath the first *exemplum* suggests that the two belong to the same context.[22] Here al-Kamil challenged Francis to justify the present crusade. Quoting from Matthew Chapter 5, the sultan asked him how it was possible for the Christians to invade the Muslims in their own lands when God taught them in the Gospels that evil must not be repaid with evil. Replying to the sultan that he obviously had not read the whole of the Gospels, Francis quoted from the same chapter:

'If your eye causes you scandal, tear it out and throw it away.' Through this [God] wanted to teach us that no fellow human being, even if so dear to us as the apple of our eye, could ever be so dear and so near to us that we would not have to eradicate him and cast him away if he tried to keep us away from the faith and the love of our God. And because of this it is just that the Christians invade you and the land you occupy because you blaspheme the name of Christ and you try to alienate people from worshipping Christ. But if you want to recognize our creator and redeemer, to confide in him and worship him, [the Christians] will love you as they love their fellow believers.[23]

There is nothing surprising in Francis's argument. As a matter of fact, it merely portrays him as a strict adherent of the contemporary doctrine commonly used to justify the crusades. Francis's first argument was that the Muslims blasphemed the name of Christ and that they hindered the practice and propagation of the Christian religion in their lands. This constituted an insult to the Christian people, which, according to canon law, allowed Christians to wage just war in order to punish the offence done to them.[24] His second argument was that the access of Christians to

---

22 Ms. Vatican, Biblioteca Apostolica, *Ottob.lat.522*, f.243r(92r). The note reads: 'Quere in eximo folio infra.' This is followed by an asterisk which appears again on the margin next to the second *exemplum*. See also f.250v(99v).

23 Ms. Vatican, Biblioteca Apostolica, *Ottob.lat.522*, f.250v(99v): 'Aliam questionem idem Soldanus fecit ei dicens: Deus vester docuit in evangeliis suis malum pro malo vos non debere reddere, non deffendere pallium, etc. Quanto magis ergo non debent christiani terras nostras invadere? etc. Vos, inquit beatus franciscus, non videmini totum legisse christi domini nostri evangelium. Alibi enim dicit: Si oculus tuus scandalizat te, erue eum et prohice a te, etc. per quod quidem docere nos voluit, nullum hominem esse ita carum nobis, vel ita propinquum, etiam si carus nobis fuerit quasi oculus capitis, quin separare, eruere et penitus eradicare debeamus, si nos a fide et amore dei nostri conetur avertere. Unde propter hoc christiani vos et terram quam occupastis iuste invadunt, quia blasphematis nomen christi, et ab eius cultura quos potestis avertitis. Si autem velletis creatorem et redemptorem cognoscere, confiteri et colere, diligerent vos quasi se ipsos. mirantibus quoque astantibus in responsionibus eius.'

24 Gratian's principle 'iusta bella ulciscuntur iniurias' was still one of the principal arguments among early thirteenth-century decretalists. See Russell, *Just War*, 131–8.

Jerusalem, and their worship at the holy places there, was restricted by the Muslim occupation. Both Egypt and Palestine, the conquest of which was the crusaders' aim, had been Christian at an earlier stage and had Christian inhabitants. It was a common argument in justifying the crusade that its purpose was the reconquest of former Christian lands.[25] Francis thus accepted the crusade as both legitimate and ordained by God and he was quite obviously not opposed to the use of violence when it came to the struggle between Christians and Muslims. This also becomes clear in another story told by Brother Leo, in which Francis praised Charlemagne and the heroes of Roncesvalles for their victory against the enemies of the Christian faith, even though, they too, slaughtered scores of Muslims in the process of defending the Christian faith.[26]

The two *exempla* have for a long time been disregarded by historians. Their exclusion from any discussion of Francis's attitude towards the crusade cannot, however, be justified. As has been shown, the only three stories which provide detailed information about the meeting of Francis and al-Kamil and which are not obscured by the imposition of a literary *topos* come from the same source, that is from Illuminatus through Bonaventure, and were recorded around the same time, that is during the latter's generalate. Of course, neither the evidence from saints' lives nor from *exempla* collections can be taken at face value in every detail, and it is on those grounds that some historians have preferred to reserve final judgment on the matter altogether.[27] But if anything at all can be said about the visit to Damietta, the conclusion, on balance, must be that Francis did not come to Damietta to stop the Fifth Crusade. On the contrary, his overall objective was the same as that of the crusaders. Francis, like the crusaders, wanted to liberate the holy places in Palestine from Muslim rule. What was different was his strategy: Francis went beyond the idea of simply expelling the

---

25 Russell, *Just War*, 195–201.

26 *Scripta Leonis*, 214: 'Cui beatus Franciscus tale responsum dedit dicens: "Carolus imperator, Rolandus et Oliuerius et omnes paladini et robusti uiri qui potentes fuerunt in prelio prosequentes infideles cum multo sudore et labore usque ad mortem habuerunt de illis gloriosam et memorialem uictoriam et ad ultimum ipsi sancti martures mortui sunt pro fide Christi in certamine, et multi sunt qui sola narratione eorum que illi fecerunt uolunt recipere honorem et humanam laudem".'

27 E.g., Kedar, *Crusade*, 129–31, 157; F. Cardini, 'Nella presenza del Soldan superba: Bernardo, Francesco, Bonaventura e il superamento spirituale dell'idea di crociata', *Studi Francescani*, lxxi (1974), 199–250; G. Wendelborn, *Franziskus v. Assisi. Eine historische Darstellung* (Leipzig 1977), 255–7.

Muslims from where they interfered with Christian life. He wanted their total submission to the Christian faith. Short of this total submission there would be no peace; short of this, for Francis too, was the necessity, if not the duty, to crusade against the enemies of the faith.

St Dominic and the Albigensian Crusade

Dominic did not, of course, preach the cross for the Albigensian crusade. At least, there is no evidence to suggest that he did. And there were good reasons why Dominic should not have become a crusade propagandist. He had just taken over the leadership of a new religious community at Prouille, which he himself had founded as a sanctuary and school for former female heretics. At the same time Prouille served as the operational base for the preachers around Dominic.[28] Leaving Prouille in order to preach the crusade would have jeopardized the development of the new community. In addition, while there was still no actual fighting in Languedoc, conversion by preaching and debate would still have been possible, especially for so gifted a preacher as Dominic. There is, however, no indication that Dominic shunned the crusaders once the military campaign against the Albigensians had started. The passage in Jordan of Saxony's *Libellus* which is usually quoted as evidence for Dominic's negative attitude towards crusading does not warrant the conclusion that he dissociated himself from either the participants or the methods of the Albigensian crusade. In Chapter 34 of the *Libellus*, Jordan told how the saint fearlessly approached the heretics, despite the fact that the crusade had brutalized the Albigensian conflict. But Jordan said nothing about Dominic's attitude towards the activities of the crusaders:

During the time when people there were signed with the cross, Brother Dominic remained a dedicated preacher of the word of God until the death of the count of Montfort. How many insults against him by the unjust did he bear in those days, and against how many insidious attacks did he defend himself![29]

---

[28] Vicaire, *Histoire*, i, 235–74; Roquebert, *L'épopée*, i, 189–92.

[29] Jordan of Saxony, 'Libellus de Principiis Ordinis Praedicatorum', *MOPH*, xvi, 1–88, here 41–2: 'Eo tempore, quo ibi cruce signati fuerunt, mansit frater Dominicus usque ad obitum comitis Montisfortis verbi divini sedulus predicator. Quantas in illis diebus pertulit ab iniquis iniurias, sprevit et insidias!' See also Peter Ferrand, 'Legenda S. Dominici', *MOPH*, xvi, 195–260, here 222–4; Humbert of Romans, 'Legenda S. Dominici', *MOPH*, xvi, 353–433, here 384–5.

Dominic seems, in fact, to have stayed with the crusading army at certain times. One of Simon of Montfort's charters suggests that Dominic was present at the siege of Toulouse in 1211.[30] Gerard of Fracheto confirmed his presence there in one of his stories about the saint.[31] It thus need come as no surprise that Bernard Gui indicated that Dominic, amongst other clerics, was with the crusaders praying for their victory at the battle of Muret in 1213, even though the account was written over a hundred years after the event.[32] It seems that Bernard Gui was following the account in Peter of Vaux-de-Cernai's chronicle, adding Dominic's name to the list of clerics there.[33] Since Peter of Vaux-de-Cernai himself hardly referred to Dominic at all and certainly never by name, the fact that he omitted Dominic in this case does not necessarily mean that he was not at Muret. Dominic must, in fact, have been in frequent contact with the papal army, since between June 1211 and June 1219 he obtained various donations for the endowment of Prouille from a number of Albigensian crusaders.[34]

Even more indicative of Dominic's attitude is his relationship with the military leader of the Albigensian crusade. It may have been a coincidence that Simon of Montfort established himself at the strategically important stronghold of Fanjeaux in 1209, where Dominic was the chaplain of the adjacent village.[35] But out of this geographical proximity, a relationship of mutual assistance and appreciation was formed between the two members of the papal party in Languedoc, on which almost all of Dominic's early biographers commented.[36] Simon granted a number of endowments to the community at Prouille, which was in the immediate vicinity of Fanjeaux.[37] Dominic in turn baptized Simon of Montfort's daughter in early 1211 and, while standing in as spiritual vicar for the absent bishop of Carcassonne, he officiated at the count's son's marriage in June 1214.[38] Both these events were public statements at the time, openly associating Dominic with the

[30] 'Monumenta Diplomatica S. Dominici', *MOPH*, xxv, no.12.
[31] Gerard of Fracheto, 'Vitae Fratrum ordinis Praedicatorum necnon cronica ordinis', *MOPH*, i, 68–9.
[32] *Cartulaire ou Histoire Diplomatique de S. Dominique*, ed. F. Balme *et al.*, 3 vols. (Paris 1893–1901), i, 415.   [33] Roquebert, *L'épopée*, ii, 178.
[34] 'Monumenta Diplomatica', nos. 12, 31, 38, 40, 50, 51, 53, 55, 59, 65, 71, 100; Roquebert, *L'épopée*, ii, 356–60.   [35] Vicaire, *Histoire*, i, 285–8; Roquebert, *L'épopée*, i, 298–307.
[36] Jordan of Saxony, 'Libellus', 43–4; Peter Ferrand, 'Legenda', 228–9; Humbert of Romans, 'Legenda', 389; Gerard of Fracheto, 'Vitae', 322.
[37] 'Monumenta Diplomatica', nos. 10, 38, 45.
[38] Gerard of Fracheto, 'Vitae', 322; Vicaire, *Histoire*, i, 288–9.

leader of the crusade. If Dominic had been opposed to the crusade, he would certainly have avoided such close public contact with its leader.

Unfortunately, no reliable contemporary source directly reveals Dominic's attitude to the crusade. Only one late and unreliable source actually called Dominic a crusader.[39] But his relationship with Simon of Montfort and members of his army, makes it seem unlikely that he was altogether against the crusade. This comes as no surprise at all because Dominic could reasonably have considered the crusade an appropriate means of combatting the Albigensians, since preaching alone had not been successful. Again, only one late and inaccurate source makes this point explicitly.[40] Still, Dominic would probably have subscribed to Gerard of Fracheto's words, who said that 'during this time the count of Montfort fought against the heretics with the material sword and the Blessed Dominic with the sword of the word of God'.[41] Two ways, one aim: the eradication of unorthodox religious belief. This, after all, was the reason why Dominic had come to Languedoc.

[39] Galvagno de la Flamma, 'Cronica Ordinis Praedicatorum', *MOPH*, ii, 3.: 'Et post duos annos [episcopus Didacus] beatum Dominicum suum vicarium et caput omnium crucesignatorum ordinavit.' The chronicle was written in the first half of the fourteenth century. In this instance the chronicle is very inaccurate, indeed, since it mentions Bishop Diego, Dominic's erstwhile superior and companion, who died almost certainly in September 1207, i.e., before the crusade was operating. See Vicaire, *Histoire*, i, 273
[40] Stephen of Salagnac, 'De quatuor in quibus Deus praedicatorum ordinem insignivit', *MOPH*, xxii, 15–16. For the factual errors of this passage, see Vicaire, *Histoire*, i, 292, n. 72.   [41] Gerard of Fracheto, 'Vitae', 322.

Chapter 2

POPE GREGORY IX AND THE EARLY FRIARS

Plans to use the mendicant orders as preachers of the cross in a systematic manner could not have been made until the late 1220s, when the two orders had become established throughout the whole of Christendom; in addition, Pope Gregory IX does not seem to have been convinced of the friars' usefulness and reliability as papal agents until after they had shown themselves to be faithful followers of the papacy during the struggles between the pope and the emperor in Italy at the end of the 1220s. This chapter, therefore, investigates the crucial role which Gregory IX, then Cardinal Ugolino of Ostia, played in supporting the two orders' international expansion during the late 1210s and early 1220s and how, as pope, he began to involve the friars as papal agents against Frederick II during the emperor's first excommunication.

Gregory IX and the growth of the Franciscan order

Until 1217 the Franciscans had hardly stuck their noses outside the Italian peninsula.[1] Some friars had been on a pilgrimage to Santiago de Compostela in the early 1210s, during which they may have founded a few small communities in Northern Spain, but that was all.[2] Nevertheless, the leaders of the order began to develop plans to capitalize on the growing popularity they had acquired on

---

[1] The following Italian communities of Franciscan friars may have been founded before 1217: Assisi, Bologna, Cairo Montenotte, Castelvecchio, Celano, Cesapolombo, Cortona, Fabriano, Messina, Milan, Siena, and Teramo. Although many others were said to have been founded by this time, there is no evidence to confirm these claims. See J.R.H. Moorman, *Medieval Franciscan Houses* (Franciscan Institute Publications. History Series 4; New York 1983) (*s.v.*).

[2] Moorman (*Medieval Franciscan Houses* (*s.v.*)), lists as possibly founded before 1217: Arevalo, Ayllon, Barcelona, Burgos, Ciudad Rodrigo, Compostela. Many other convents in the Hispanic Peninsula claimed to have been founded by Francis himself when he was in Spain. Few of these claims, however, seem to be supported by sound historical evidence. See also A. Lopez, *La Provincia de España de los Frailes Menores. Apuntes Històrico-Crìticos sobre los orìginos de la Orden Franciscana en España* (Santiago 1915), 1–27.

home ground by starting a conscious policy of international expansion. At the Franciscan general chapter of 1217, it was decided to send contingents of friars to Spain, France, Germany, Hungary, and the Holy Land.[3] Francis himself wanted to join the brothers who went to France, but was stopped from going there by Cardinal Ugolino of Ostia, who was later to become Pope Gregory IX. Their meeting in Florence in 1217 was a mile-stone in the history of the order. Ugolino seems to have welcomed the plans to spread the friars throughout Europe and, probably as a result of this meeting, accepted Francis's invitation to become the first cardinal-protector of the new order. In turn, Ugolino dissuaded Francis from leaving Italy at this stage, probably because he foresaw that the planned expansion would put an enormous strain on the inner fabric of the Franciscan community, particularly over the question of leadership. So far it had mainly been the founder's charismatic authority which held the order together.[4]

Despite the abortive missions of those friars sent to Germany and Hungary in 1217,[5] the foundation of several Franciscan houses in France, Spain, and the Holy Land almost doubled the number of Franciscan convents between 1217 and 1219.[6] But as yet no institutional structure existed within the order to ensure cohesion between those scattered communities. When Francis went to the Levant in 1219, his absence, in fact, provoked the first serious crisis amongst the other leaders of the order. This made clear that the survival of the order on a international level would only be guaranteed if based on a strict hierarchy under an efficient, authoritative government and on a well-defined common code of conduct. Around this time Ugolino began to take a strong personal interest in the affairs of the order, based on his office of cardinal-protector. His decisive influence on the formation of the Franciscan

[3] Moorman, *History*, 46–7.
[4] Neither the meeting between Francis and Ugolino nor the formal appointment of Ugolino to the office of cardinal-protector can be dated conclusively. The former probably took place in 1217 or 1218, the latter probably in winter 1220–1. See R.B. Brooke, *Early Franciscan Government. Elias to Bonaventure* (Cambridge Studies in Medieval Life and Thought [new series] 7; Cambridge 1959), 61–7, 286–91.
[5] Moorman, *History*, 67–8; Freed, *Friars*, 26.
[6] According to Moorman (*Medieval Franciscan Houses* (*s.v.*)), the following convents were probably founded between 1217 and 1219: Ancona, Cosenza, Farneto, Monte Luco, and Poggiobustone in Italy; La Bastida, Calatayud, Coimbra, Guimeraes, Lerida, Lisbon, and Toledo in the Spanish Peninsula; Damietta in the Levant; Paris in France. For the last two, see also R.W. Emery, *The Friars in Medieval France. A Catalogue of French Mendicant Convents 1200–1500* (London and New York 1962), 109. Again many more houses claimed foundation during this time, but without sound evidence.

order during the 1220s, and later on as pope, has been traced by a number of historians, whose findings need not be repeated in every detail here.[7] The cardinal himself presided over the general chapter of 1220, at which the decision was taken to subdivide provinces into custodies. Under his influence the first papal bulls of recommendation of the Franciscans were sent to the secular clergy of Europe in June 1219 and in May 1220.[8] A year later, at Pentecost 1221, a number of bishops and members of other religious orders attended the general chapter. These were the first indications that the Franciscans were beginning to grow into an institutionalized body within the church and were slowly gaining the support and respect of the church hierarchy. In the following two years Ugolino, together with a group of friars, worked hard to hammer out a definitive constitution of the order. In 1223 the *Regula bullata* was finished. A consensus regarding the new structure and the nature of the order and its leadership had not been established easily, but the new rule provided a suitable instrument for the government of an international order. Having achieved a viable degree of internal cohesion as a community backed by papal support, the Franciscan order was set for further expansion during the following years. By the end of Honorius III's pontificate the order had rapidly spread throughout Europe. Counting only those convents for which there seems to be some kind of sound historical evidence concerning the date of their foundations, just over one hundred new houses had been established between 1220 and 1227.[9]

---

[7] The most important and most recent studies are: L. Zarncke, *Der Anteil des Kardinals Ugolino an der Ausbildung der drei Orden des hl. Franz* (Beiträge zur Kulturgeschichte des Mittelalters und der Renaissance 42; Berlin and Leipzig 1930); K.-V. Selge, 'Franz von Assisi und die Römische Kurie', *Zeitschrift für Theologie und Kirche*, lxvii (1970), 129–61; K.-V. Selge, 'Franz von Assisi und Ugolino von Ostia', *S. Francesco nella ricerca storica degli ultimi 80 anni* (Atti del Centro di studi sulla spiritualità medievale 9; Todi 1971), 157–222; J.M. Powell, 'The Papacy and the Early Franciscans', *Franciscan Studies*, xxxvi (1976), 248–62; E. Pasztor, 'San Francesco e il Cardinale Ugolino nella "questione Francescana"', *Collectanea Francescana*, xlvi (1976), 209–39.

[8] *BF*, i (Hon.III), nos. 2, 4.

[9] Fifty in Italy and Sicily: Agropoli, Alcamo, Angarano, Bari, Bisignano, Capua, Carmignano, Castrovillari, Cefalù, Cesi, Colfano, Colombaia, Corigliano, Cotrone, Cuneo, Curtarolo, Fara, Ferrara, Florence, Fonte Colombo, Gemona, Gioia, Gorizia, Gubbio, Lecce, Lentini, Mantua, Marsala, Massa Maritima, Modena, Montebaroccio, Nicastro, Oria, Padua, Palermo, Piano, Poggiobonsi, Ragusa, Rossano, S. Geminiano, S. Miniato, Siracusa, Spoleto, Subiaco, Trapani, Trento, Vercelli, Verona, Veruccbio, Vicenza; seventeen in Germany: Augsburg, Brunswick, Cologne, Eisenach, Erfurt, Goslar, Gotha, Halberstadt, Hildesheim, Magdeburg, Mainz, Regensburg, Speyer, Strasbourg, Trier, Worms, Würzburg; thirteen in France (*Francia* and *Provincia*): Auxerre, Avignon, Besançon, Bordeaux, Castres, Châtillon, Le Puy, Lille, Limoges,

Gregory IX and the growth of the Dominican order

When Dominic travelled to Rome to obtain papal confirmation for his new order in November 1215, his request was initially referred to Cardinal Ugolino of Ostia. What exactly Ugolino's role was during the period between then and the final approval of the Dominican order in January 1217 is not quite clear. But since he was Dominic's contact at the Curia, his influence on the nature of the new order's constitution was probably not inconsiderable.[10] The cardinal's personal stamp on the development of the order was most noticeable during the following three years. Because of the strong emphasis on education within the Dominican order, one pre-condition for international expansion was the recruitment of a sufficient number of well-educated friars and the establishment of suitable training facilities for future recruits. Given the geographical location of the early Dominican convents of southern France and northern Italy, the obvious places to find new recruits and to obtain training facilities were the universities at Paris and Bologna.[11] Cardinal Ugolino was instrumental in helping to set up the Dominicans in both centres of learning and thus in creating the basis of the order's European expansion.

The Dominican community at Bologna had been founded by Dominic himself in late 1217, but its growth and prosperity seem to have progressed at a slow pace. Only with the arrival of Reginald of Orleans a year later did its fortunes and popularity increase significantly. Reginald, dean of St Aignan at Orleans and a former master of canon law at the University of Paris, was passing through Italy on his way to Palestine on the Fifth Crusade in spring 1218. While he was at Rome, Cardinal Ugolino arranged a meeting with Dominic. According to the legend Reginald fell ill and became a friar after Dominic's prayers had procured a miraculous recovery and the Blessed Virgin, in a vision, had

Narbonne, Toulouse, Valenciennes, Ypres; nine in England: Cambridge, Canterbury, Hereford, London (2), Northampton, Norwich, Oxford, Worcester; four in Spain: Muros, Teruel, Vich, Zaragoza; three in Hungary (including Dalmatia): Eger, Sebenico, Zara; one in Bohemia, Ireland, Greece, and Northern Africa and Palestine: Prague, Youghal, Constantinople, Ceuta, Acre. See Moorman, *Medieval Franciscan Houses* (*s.v.*); Freed, *Friars*, 182–209; Emery, *Friars*, 32, 47, 52, 61, 64, 66, 70, 97, 98, 114, 118, 123; D. Knowles and R.N. Hadcock, *Medieval Religious Houses. England and Wales* (London 1971), 222–3; A. Gwynn and R.N. Hadcock, *Medieval Religious Houses.* Ireland (London 1970), 241.
[10] Vicaire, *Histoire*, ii, 7–75, esp. 20, 63, 69; R. Manselli, 'S. Domenico, I Papi e Roma', *Studi Romani*, xix (1971), 133–43. [11] Berg, *Armut*, 38–43, 85–7.

suggested that Reginald join the new order.[12] Although the legend obscures the exact circumstances of his entry into the Dominican order, it appears that Cardinal Ugolino, Dominic, and Reginald had a clear idea about the latter's future role. The reasons for recruiting Reginald must have been his prestige as a former master of Paris University and his charisma as a preacher. After his return from the East, he stayed at the Dominican convent in Bologna for almost a year, before returning to Paris some time during the second half of 1219. With the collaboration of Cardinal Ugolino, then papal legate in Lombardy, Reginald finalized the transfer of the church of St Nicholas to the Dominicans of Bologna. This provided the friars with a large house and, more importantly, with sufficient income to allow them to spend their time studying at the university rather than begging for alms.[13] During Reginald's short stay at Bologna, the Dominican convent was turned into a highly respectable scholarly community. His preaching attracted a great number of new recruits, among whom were two canon lawyers, Clarus of Sesto and Paul of Hungary, and two teachers of the liberal arts, Roland and Moneta of Cremona. Paul later became the first provincial prior of Hungary, Roland the first Dominican master of theology at Paris University.[14] During the following two years, the Dominican community at Bologna enjoyed an increasing popularity amongst students and scholars of the university. Another canon lawyer, Conrad of Höxter, joined the order and played an important role during its period of expansion when he became provincial prior of Germany from c.1225 to 1234.[15] The first Scandinavian Dominicans, Simon of Sweden and Nicholas of Lund, also joined the order at Bologna around that time,[16] as did John of Vicenza and Ceslaus of Cracow, the latter being the founder of the first Polish convent at Prague.[17] It is also possible that Reginald's preaching influenced Raymond of Penyafort's decision to become a friar; Raymond left Bologna in 1221 and became a Dominican friar in Spain in 1222.[18]

[12] Vicaire, *Histoire*, i, 111–12; Hinnebusch, *History*, i, 59–60.

[13] Vicaire, *Histoire*, ii, 150–9; Hinnebusch, *History*, i, 57–67 *passim*.

[14] Hinnebusch, *History*, ii, 38, 101, 238, 246.

[15] Freed, *Friars*, 123, n. 46; Hinnebusch, *History*, ii, 238.

[16] J. Gallen, *La province de Dacie de l'ordre des Frères Prêcheurs. I. Histoire générale jusqu'au Grand Schisme* (Dissertationes Historicae: Institutum Historicum Fratrum Praedicatorum Romae ad Sa. Sabina 12; Helsingfors 1946), 3– 11.

[17] M. Goodich, *Vita Perfecta: The Ideal of Sainthood in the Thirteenth Century* (Monographien zur Geschichte des Mittelalters 25; Stuttgart 1982), 154.

[18] Hinnebusch, *History*, ii, 248.

The Dominican community at Paris had been established in 1216, but did not do particularly well during the first two years of its existence. It consisted, in the words of one commentator, of 'youthful and simple-hearted' friars, and came into frequent conflict with the local clergy. Cardinal Ugolino's initiative again seems to have been decisive in bringing about change. In 1217 he arranged contacts between Dominic and William of Montferrat, then probably a member of the cardinal's household. William became a Dominican friar in 1219 while studying at Paris. His entry into the order coincided with a series of papal recommendations of the new order to the secular clergy.[19] From then onwards the public face and the intellectual fabric of the Parisian community improved steadily throughout 1219. The Dominicans were now benevolently received at the university and promoted by John of St Albans, a master of theology, royal chaplain and dean of St Quentin. In February 1219 a Parisian nobleman and his wife granted them the chapel and houses of St Jacques, which, as at Bologna, provided the friars with a sufficient material base, allowing them to devote their time to learning and preaching. Two of the Benedictine monasteries in Paris now also allowed the friars to preach in their churches, thus providing a public forum which had been denied to them in the past. In late 1219 and early 1220, the pope finally decreed that the friars should be allowed to celebrate mass, to preach, and to have a cemetery at their own convent.[20] During this time Dominic himself recruited three well-known members of Paris university, namely Jordan of Saxony, Henry of Cologne, who was a former canon at Utrecht, and a certain Leo. Two of these later assumed influential roles within the order: Jordan became Dominic's successor as master-general and Henry, between 1221 and 1229, was prior of Cologne, which was the most important of the early German houses.[21] The collaboration between Cardinal Ugolino, Dominic, and Reginald of Orleans thus effected a most remarkable success for the new order at Bologna and Paris in the short period between 1218 and 1220. The impact of those years became obvious during the early and mid 1220s, when the Dominicans had as spectacular an expansion

---

[19] *BP*, i (Hon.III) nos. 8–10.
[20] Vicaire, *Histoire*, ii, 106–11, 135–49, 266–7, 373–6; Hinnebusch, *History*, i, 50–66.
[21] Freed, *Friars*, 82, 232; H.C. Scheeben, *Beiträge zur Geschichte Jordans von Sachsen* (Quellen und Forschungen zur Geschichte des Dominikanerordens in Deutschland 35; Vechta i.O. 1938), 34–41, 157–68.

throughout Europe as the Franciscans. Although the establishment of Dominican houses has not been studied as systematically as that of the Franciscans, no less than sixty convents are known to have been founded throughout Europe and the Levant during the decade following 1218.[22]

Papal politics in Italy and the Mendicant friars 1228–30

The Franciscans

In July 1228 Gregory IX, the former Cardinal Ugolino of Ostia, solemnly canonized Francis at Assisi. At the same time he laid the foundation-stone of the new church of St Francis which he provided with the right to grant between one and three years indulgence, a privilege few pilgrimage centres could surpass at the time.[23] Both the canonization and the building of a shrine of St Francis stood as monuments to the rapid success and growing reputation of the Franciscan order. They were also signs of the close association between the Curia and the new, popular force in the religious life of Italy. As early as 1216, James of Vitry noted the good rapport between the Curia and the Franciscans.[24] Francis was widely known and an immensely popular figure. The frequent

---

[22] Sixteen in France (*Francia* and *Provincia*): Narbonne, Bayonne, La Rochelle, Besançon, Le Puy, Limoges, Montpellier, Orleans, Angers, Reims, Metz, Lille, Clermont, Lyons, Rouen, Poitiers; eight in Germany and Austria: Magdeburg, Bremen, Friesach, Cologne, Strasbourg, Trier, Vienna, Worms. Seven in Poland and Bohemia: Cracow, Wroclaw (Breslau), Sandomierz, Kamien Pomorski (Cammin), Gdansk (Danzig), Prague, Olomouc (Olmütz); seven in Italy: Bergamo, Rome, Milan, Florence, Verona, Piacenza, Brescia; five in Ireland: Dublin, Drogheda, Kilkenny, Limerick, Waterford; four in England: Oxford, London, Norwich, York; four in Spain and Portugal: Segovia, Palencia, Santarem, Zamora; four in Scandinavia: Lund, Ribe, Visby, Nidaros; two in Hungary and Dalmatia: Szkesfehervar (Stuhlweissenburg), Ragusa; one each in Greece, Palestine, and Cyprus: Constantinople, Nicosia, Acre. Hinnebusch, *History*, i, 66, 78, 89–90, 92; Emery, *Friars*, 32, 37, 44, 52, 66, 70, 74, 84, 88, 90, 95, 97, 103, 105, 112, 121. Freed, *Friars*, 56, 210–22; V.J. Koudelka, 'Zur Geschichte der Böhmischen Dominikanerprovinz im Mittelalter II. Die Männer- und Frauenklöster', *AFP*, xxvi (1956), 127–60, here 133–41; J. Kucynski, *Le Bienheureux Guala de Bergame de l'Ordre des Frères Prêcheurs. Évêque de Brescia, Pacaire et Légat Pontifical (†.1244)* (Estavayer 1916), 22–3; Gwynn and Hadcock, *Medieval Religious Houses*, 220; Knowles and Hadcock, *Medieval Religious Houses*, 213–17; Gallen, *Province*, 21–2; N. Pfeiffer, *Die Ungarische Ordensprovinz von ihrer Gründung 1221 bis zur Tatarenverwüstung 1241–42* (Zürich 1913), 28–9, 42; B. Altaner, *Die Dominikanermissionen des 13.Jahrhunderts* (Breslauer Studien zur historischen Theologie 3; Habelschwerdt 1924), 9–11, 21–3. In addition, as many as seven houses may have already been founded in Latin Greece by 1228. See Altaner, *Dominikanermissionen*, 9–10.

[23] Moorman, *History*, 85–6. For the indulgence, see *Gre.IX R*, no. 449; N. Paulus, *Geschichte des Ablasses im Mittelalter vom Ursprung zur Mitte des 14. Jahrhunderts*, 3 vols. (Paderborn 1922, 1923), ii, 4–5.   [24] James of Vitry, *Lettres*, 75.

meetings between him and Cardinal Ugolino would not have passed unnoticed. Then there was Ugolino's participation as cardinal-protector at the general chapters of the order, which were attended by great numbers of friars and increasingly also by non-members of the order.[25] From the early 1220s on, the Franciscans doubtless appeared in the public eye as especial *protégés* of the papacy. The decision to proceed with the canonization of Francis of Assisi was taken at a time when Gregory IX's authority was at a critically low point in his conflict with the emperor. The pope had excommunicated Frederick II in September 1227 for having failed to fulfil his crusading vow as promised, but the ban did not seem to have damaged the emperor's position in any serious way, nor did it effectively limit his scope for action. In March 1228 the pope repeated the excommunication and also put the places where Frederick stayed under interdict. In spite of this, however, the latter was able to proceed with his crusading plans and left for the East at the end of June. To make matters worse for Gregory, the citizens of Rome supported Frederick and forced the pope to flee the town. In the face of the emperor's successful defiance of papal authority Gregory was hard pressed to restore the papacy's credibility and authority.[26] Francis's canonization was one way of doing so. The canonization procedure was hurriedly planned and was finished within a few days in an unprecedented hurry. A few miracles of the saint were read out before a papal commission, but no *Vita*, usually the mainstay of any canonization, existed yet.[27] The canonization ceremonial itself, on 16 July 1228, was a carefully stage-managed public event, attended by representatives of all tiers of the church hierarchy and by members of the secular nobility.[28]

Among the guests at Assisi was John of Brienne, the former king of Jerusalem, who was to become the leader of the papal army which invaded the southern Italian parts of the *Regno* during Frederick II's absence.[29] To support the military efforts of the papal army, Gregory IX enlisted the Italian Franciscans to spread papal

[25] Moorman, *History*, 48, 52, 55–6.
[26] T.C. Van Cleve, *The Emperor Frederick II of Hohenstaufen. Immutator Mundi* (Oxford 1972), 194–207; J. Felten, *Papst Gregor IX.* (Freiburg i.Br. 1886), 66–73, 89–95; D. Abulafia, *Frederick II. A Medieval Emperor* (London 1988), 164–202.
[27] Thomas of Celano, 'Vita Prima', 97–103; M. Goodich, 'The Politics of Canonization in the Thirteenth Century: Lay and Mendicant Saints', *Church History*, xliv (1975), 294–307, here 301.   [28] Moorman, *History*, 86.
[29] L. Böhm, *Johann von Brienne, König von Jerusalem, Kaiser von Konstantinopel* (Heidelberg 1938), 85–8; Van Cleve, *Emperor Frederick II*, 208–13, 228–30.

propaganda in the *Regno*. Already in May 1228, the pope had sent two Franciscan friars to Frederick II in order to protest about the maltreatment of clerics in Apulia and Sicily.[30] It seems that the pope was trying to stop the excommunicate emperor from using church funds to finance his crusade.[31] Other Franciscan friars acted as secret papal messengers in the *Regno* during 1228–9. Richard of S. Germano reported that they were sent to the heads of town governments reminding the latter about their duties towards the pope.[32] By 1228 there were at least twenty-one Franciscan convents in the *Regno*, which suggests that the new order was enjoying an immense popularity in that region.[33] The great number of convents would also have provided ideal conditions for Franciscan messengers travelling *incognito*. The fact that Raynald of Spoleto, the imperial vicar in the *Regno*, went as far as evicting all the Franciscan friars from the Kingdom of Sicily shows that their efforts were, at least to some extent, damaging to the imperial cause.[34]

The suggestion that the Franciscans supported the pope during this time out of gratitude for the canonization of Francis has been proposed long ago.[35] It would, however, be misleading to lay too much stress on this single event. The service the Franciscans performed for the papacy must be seen against the decade of support and sympathy which the order had received from Cardinal Ugolino. Supporting the papacy against the excommunicate emperor was, in any case, not only a matter of honour and gratitude. As faithful followers of the Roman Church, it was the Franciscans' duty. The *Regula bullata* expressed most forcefully the concept of the all-embracing obedience of the order towards the pope in its opening and closing lines:

The rule and life of the Friars Minor is this, namely to observe the Holy Gospel of our Lord Jesus Christ by living in obedience, without property, and in chastity. Brother Francis promises obedience and reverence to his holiness the Pope Honorius and his lawfully elected successors and to the Church of Rome. The other friars are bound to obey Brother Francis and his successors. [...]

---

[30] *ES*, i, no. 372 (= *Gre.IX R*, no. 193).
[31] Richard of St Germano, 'Chronica', *MGHS*, xix, 321–84, here 349.
[32] Richard of St Germano, 'Chronica', 353.
[33] Moorman, *Medieval Franciscan Houses (s.v.)*: Agropoli, Alcamo, Bari, Capua, Castrovillari, Cefalù, Cosenza, Cotrone, Gallipoli, Gioia, Isérnia, Lecce, Lentini, Marsala, Messina, Nicastro, Oria, Palermo, Ragusa, Rossano, Siracusa, Trapani. Only claims, but no sound evidence exist for thirty other convents.   [34] See above, n. 32.
[35] E. Winkelmann, *Kaiser Friedrich II.*, 2 vols. (Leipzig 1889, 1897), i, 50.

The ministers, too, are bound to ask the Pope for one of the cardinals of the holy Roman Church to be governor, protector, and corrector of this fraternity, so that we may be utterly subject and submissive to the Church. And so, firmly established in the Catholic faith, we may live always according to the poverty, and the humility and the Gospel of our Lord Jesus Christ, as we have solemnly promised.[36]

In his testament Francis echoed the rule even more forcefully by saying that God had inspired him with so much faith in the Roman Church that, even if she was persecuting him, he would still turn to her for aid.[37]

The Dominicans

The late 1220s also saw the Dominicans' entry on to the political stage of Italy. When Frederick II in July 1225 finally agreed to fulfil his crusading vow and go to the Holy Land in summer 1227, the conflict between the emperor and the Lombard League still seemed to be a major obstacle to a successful imperial crusade. Following the experiences on the eve of the Fifth Crusade, the Curia was well aware that peace in northern Italy was necessary, and the pope was prepared to use his political influence in order to mediate between Frederick II and the Lombard cities.[38] It was during the peace negotiations in preparation of Frederick's crusade that the first Dominican friars appeared as papal agents.

Guala of Bergamo was first mentioned in 1219 as sacristan of the Dominican convent at Bologna.[39] Despite the seemingly lowly office which he initially held, Guala quickly assumed a leading role in the order. On his initiative the Dominican convent at Brescia was founded around 1220 and, a year later, he was presiding over the Dominican general chapter. During these years he came into close contact with Cardinal Ugolino, who as papal legate in Lombardy promoted the Dominican order's establishment at Bologna and later also at Brescia.[40] Guala and Ugolino were again working together during the mid 1220s when the cardinal defended the foundation of a female Dominican convent at Rome against the reservations of Pope Honorius III.[41] From May 1226 Guala became one of the papal negotiators at the peace talks

---

[36] *Opuscula S. Patris Francisci*, ed. L. Lemmens (Bibliotheca Franciscana Ascetica 1; Ad Claras Aquas (Quaracchi) 1909), 63, 74.

[37] *Opuscula*, 78.

[38] Van Cleve, *Emperor Frederick II*, 179–93; Abulafia, *Frederick II*, 151–63.

[39] Kucynski, *Bienheureux Guala*, 11–12.   [40] Kucynski, *Bienheureux Guala*, 22–5.

[41] Kucynski, *Bienheureux Guala*, 18–20.

between the Lombard League and Frederick II.[42] After this conflict had been settled by the end of the year, Guala was also involved in supervising the implementation of the terms of the agreement in the spring of the following year.[43]

When Honorius III suddenly died in March 1227, Guala's mission was immediately reconfirmed by the new pope.[44] He was also present as the papal representative at Brescia when the League finally ratified the treaty with the emperor and, in July 1227, Gregory IX sent Guala as his envoy to Frederick in order once more to remind the emperor of his duties with regard to the approaching crusade.[45] After Frederick's excommunication and his return from crusade Guala remained one of the principal papal negotiators during Gregory IX's attempt to maintain a unified anti-Hohenstaufen front in support of his military campaign in the *Regno*.[46] In fact, Guala was probably one of the most active papal diplomats in Northern Italy between 1227 and 1229. During the peak of his diplomatic activity to enlist military support in Lombardy for the papal war in the *Regno*, Gregory IX had made Guala a member of his household. In autumn 1229 Guala was referred to for the first time as a *familiaris papae* and was acting with the full legatine powers.[47] The Dominican friar finally crowned his diplomatic career as papal envoy during the concluding stages of the peace talks between the pope and the emperor by arranging the final conciliatory meetings between Gregory and Frederick at St Germano and Ceprano at the end of August 1230.[48] The value the pope attached to Guala's services was reflected by the fact that, after these achievements, he was made bishop of Brescia. As bishop, Guala remained a close confidant of Gregory IX and continued to play an important diplomatic role during the disputes between the pope, the emperor, and the Lombard League throughout the 1230s.[49]

Although Guala of Bergamo was the most prominent Dominican friar in papal service, there were other fellow-members of his

[42] *Acta Imperii Selecta. Urkunden deutscher Könige und Kaiser 928–1398*, ed. J.F. Böhmer (Innsbruck 1870), no. 290. Kucynski, *Bienheureux Guala*, 37–50.

[43] *ES*, i, no. 342 (= *Hon.III R*, no. 6280); *Hon.III R*, no. 6282.

[44] *ES*, i, no. 350 (= *Gre.IX R*, no. 29).

[45] *Historia Diplomatica Frederici Secundi*, ed. J.L.A. Huillard-Bréholles, 6 vols. (Paris 1852–61), iii, 3–6 (= *ES*, i, no. 344; *Gre.IX R*, no. 12); *ES*, i, no. 365 (= *Gre.IX R*, no. 142).

[46] *Gre.IX R*, nos. 6121, 6122; Kucynski, *Bienheureux Guala*, 53–68.

[47] *ES*, i, no. 405 (= *Gre.IX R*, no. 352).   [48] Kucynski, *Bienheureux Guala*, 70–5.

[49] Kucynski, *Bienheureux Guala*, 79–135.

order who took on minor tasks as papal envoys during the second half of the 1220s. Several Dominican friars appeared alongside Guala during his mission to Northern Italy.[50] But the pope also began to employ Dominican friars as papal agents elsewhere. In September 1227, three friars were appointed on an independent mission as visitors of exempt monasteries in the cities and dioceses of Padua, Venice, and the March of Treviso,[51] and, during the following two years, several other Dominicans were commissioned as judge delegates by the pope in France and northern Italy.[52]

It was during the excommunicate emperor's crusade in the Holy Land that Gregory IX for the first time enlisted friars from both mendicant orders to propagate papal policy alongside each other. After the imperial fleet left for the Holy Land, the pope dispatched two Franciscans to the patriarch of Jerusalem with orders to excommunicate Frederick II publicly throughout the Kingdom of Jerusalem.[53] At the same time, one English Dominican, Brother Walter of St Martin, was given a papal commission as preacher to accompany the crusading army which left for the Holy Land in 1228. Walter seems to have executed his anti-imperial mission faithfully since he is known to have rallied papal supporters among the crusaders for the celebration of divine services outside the city walls during Frederick II's coronation in Jerusalem, which had been put under interdict.[54] Following this, friars from both mendicant orders denounced the excommunicate emperor and were attacked by members of the imperial party during the Palm Sunday celebrations 1229.[55] By then there was no longer any doubt that the members of both mendicant orders were faithful followers of the pope and adept executors of the Curia's policies.

[50] Kucynski, *Bienheureux Guala*, 43, 65–6.
[51] *BP*, i (Gre.IX) no. 14 (= *Gre.IX R*, no. 153).
[52] *Gre.IX R*, nos. 183, 253, 274, 316.   [53] 'L'Estoire de Eracles', 370.
[54] Matthew Paris, *Chronica Majora*, ed. H.R. Luard, 7 vols. (Rolls Series 47; London 1872–83), iii, 177.   [55] Matthew Paris, *Chronica Majora*, iii, 183.

Chapter 3

PAPAL CRUSADE PROPAGANDA AND
THE FRIARS

The fact that the mendicant orders could make available resources of trained preachers almost anywhere in Europe, accounted for the omnipresence of the friars on all levels of the propaganda machinery for the crusade after 1230. Mendicants preaching the cross appeared in various capacities in the thirteenth century: (i) as preachers personally commissioned by the pope, (ii) as propagandists within a province of their order commissioned through their superiors, who had received orders from the Curia, (iii) as members of papal legations, and lastly (iv) as preachers within the dioceses appointed to support the propaganda efforts of local bishops.

GREGORY IX

The first mendicant friar known to have been involved in crusading propaganda was John of Wildeshausen, who later became the fourth master-general of the Dominican order. He seems to have joined the Dominicans some time in the early 1220s.[1] The earliest, firmly datable evidence concerning his life, in fact, shows John as a crusade preacher for Frederick II's crusade to the Holy Land. Several chronicles mentioned a certain Dominican, Brother John, having preached the cross alongside the papal legate, Conrad of Urach, in south-western Germany between 1225 and 1227.[2] Gerard of Fracheto, in his *Vitae Fratrum*, confirmed his identity as that of the later Dominican master-general.[3] A papal commission has survived from early 1227 in which John of Wildeshausen is

---

[1] Rother, 'Johannes Teutonicus', 143.

[2] 'Annales Gotwicenses. Continuatio Sancrucensis I', *MGHS*, ix, 626–8, here 626; 'Annales Gotwicenses Continuatio Claustroneoburgensis III', *MGHS*, ix, 628–37, here 636; Conrad of Scheirn, 'Annales', *MGHS*, xvii, 629–33, here 632; 'Annales Scheftlarienses Maiores', *MGHS*, xvii, 335–43, here 338.

[3] Gerard of Fracheto, 'Vitae', 229.

mentioned among several other crusade preachers in Germany.[4] Humbert of Romans later described John as 'a companion of many cardinals and a penitentiary in papal legations'.[5] He appeared in this double function for the first time as a member of the papal legation led by Cardinal Otto of St Nicholas in Germany between 1229 and 1231; during this time he also became involved in the preliminaries to the crusade against the Stedinger.[6] John was subsequently sent to Hungary by the pope and temporarily became bishop of Bosnia. In 1234 he received orders from the Curia to preach the cross against Hungarian heretics and in 1237–8 he joined the papal legation which had been set up to organize the crusade in the Balkans for the defence of the Latin Empire.[7] The second Dominican friar known to have been commissioned to preach the cross was Raymond of Penyaforte. Raymond was a doctor of law at Bologna University until 1221, when he left for his native Spain and soon after took the Dominican habit.[8] In 1228–9 Raymond, who at the time was prior of the Dominican convent at Barcelona, appeared as penitentiary to the papal legate in the Kingdom of Aragon, Cardinal John of Sta. Sabina.[9] One of the tasks of the legation was to organize King James I of Aragon's crusade for the conquest of Majorca.[10] At the end of the legation Raymond was told by the pope to organize the preaching for King James's crusade in the Archdioceses of Arles and Narbonne.[11] Later Raymond was called to Rome by Gregory IX and became a papal chaplain and penitentiary, a position which he held until his death in 1275. In addition, he was master-general of his order between 1238 and 1240. In the sources, he appeared only once more in direct connection with the crusade in 1237, when he was ordered by the pope to oblige the heretic Robert, lord of Château Roussillon, to go on crusade as a sign of penance.[12]

The first Franciscan crusade preacher known by name was also a papal penitentiary. Brother William of Cordelle was mentioned

---

[4] *Hon.III R*, no. 6157. John was called *Johannes Argentinensis ordinis Predicatorum*, which seems to refer to the fact that he was staying at the Dominican convent in Strasbourg at the time. See Rother, 'Johannes Teutonicus', 144.

[5] J. Quétif and J. Echard, *Scriptores Ordinis Praedicatorum Recensiti*, 2 vols. (Paris 1719, 1721), i, 111.   [6] Rother, 'Johannes Teutonicus', 145–7; see also below, 53.

[7] Rother, 'Johannes Teutonicus', 152–4; see also below, 38.

[8] Hinnebusch, *History*, ii, 248.   [9] *Gre.IX R*, no. 628 (III).

[10] P. Linehan, *The Spanish Church and the Papacy in the Thirteenth Century* (Cambridge Studies in Medieval Life and Thought (3rd series) 4; Cambridge 1971), 20–34, 49.

[11] 'Raymundiana seu Documenta quae pertinent ad S. Raymundi de Pennaforti Vitam et Scripta', 2 fasc., *MOPH*, vi, no. viii (= *Regesta Pontificum Romanorum*, ed. A. Potthast, 2 vols. (Berlin 1874, 1875), no. 8471).   [12] *Gre.IX R*, nos. 3480–2, 3584, 3589.

for the first time in this office in 1234 during a papal mission to Tuscany.[13] During the second half of the 1230s, he was put in overall charge of organizing the propaganda and finance in the French kingdom for the crusades to the Holy Land and to the Latin Empire.[14] William was French and had been chosen for the task because he knew some of the crusaders personally and was familiar with their lands and customs.[15] He was also said to have been a gifted crusade propagandist and preacher to the crusading army which he accompanied to the Holy Land in 1239–40.[16] The three first mendicant friars known to be individually appointed as crusade preachers were thus all closely connected to the household of Pope Gregory IX. All of them were papal penitentiaries and all of them were involved in various diplomatic missions for the papacy. This indicates that Gregory continued the tradition of appointing as crusade propagandists individual clerics who were known to be reliable papal agents because of services rendered earlier to cardinals or the popes themselves. Equally important, however, seems to have been the crusade preachers' familiarity with the people and conditions of the areas in which they were supposed to preach the cross. John of Wildeshausen first preached in Germany, Raymond of Penyaforte in his native Catalonia and William of Cordelle in France.

During the early 1230s Gregory IX also started using the mendicant orders *en bloc* to broadcast propaganda for all major and most minor crusades. The crusade to the Holy Land was the flagship of the crusading movement. It was usually given the greatest possible support by the papacy when it came to crusading propaganda and finance. Orders to preach the cross were sent to the secular clergy and the mendicant orders and often also to selected members of other religious orders throughout Europe. Depending on the leadership of a specific crusade, the papacy, in addition, marked out areas where preaching efforts were to be concentrated, either because the crusading potential seemed particularly promising or because recruitment was difficult owing to a lack of enthusiasm.

[13] Van den Wyngaert, 'Frère Guillaume', 58, 68–71.
[14] See below, 39–41.
[15] *Gre.IX R*, no. 3903; Van den Wyngaert, 'Frère Guillaume', 57.
[16] Philippe Mouskes, *Chronique rimée*, ed. [F.] de Reiffenberg, 2 vols. (Brussels 1836, 1838), ii, 606–7, 620; *AF*, i, 416; 'Continuation de Guillaume de Tyr', *RHC oc.*, ii, 489–639, here 550.

Gregory IX very early on started organizing a crusade to the Holy Land in view of the end of the ten-year truce of 1229 between Frederick II and al-Kamil. The basis for the preaching of the cross was the bull *Rahel suum videns* issued at the beginning of September 1234.[17] Although this bull authorized the crusade and contained information concerning the indulgence and the privileges, it was another letter, *Pium et sanctum*, which actually commissioned the preaching. *Pium et sanctum* was sent to the Franciscan minister of Lombardy and to the Dominican provincial prior of Tuscany in October.[18] The letter required them to select two reliable friars to preach the cross throughout their provinces in accordance with *Rahel suum videns*. The same letter has survived in another copy sent to the Franciscan minister of the Province of Ireland.[19] Matthew Paris later also confirmed that the mendicant friars preached the cross in England.[20] But even though no papal correspondence is available for other parts of Europe, there is little doubt that Gregory IX tried to involve the mendicants throughout Europe in propagating the new crusade to the Holy Land.

It has been said that during the first year the preaching of the cross was extraordinarily successful.[21] This assumption appears to be based upon Gregory IX's letter of September 1235 in which he told the bishops of France, England, Germany, and Hungary to prevent crusaders from leaving for Palestine before the general passage, the date of which had not yet been fixed.[22] The pope's instructions to the crusade preachers earlier in the same year do not, however, point in that direction. It rather seems that Gregory IX was forced to enhance their powers in order to make the preaching more attractive. New instructions, set out in the letter *Quantum nos urgeat*, were sent to the Franciscans of Ireland, Austria and probably elsewhere in July 1235. This allowed them to grant between ten and thirty days indulgence to people who attended their crusade sermons twice a week. In addition, the friars could absolve those excommunicated for arson or violence against clerics in return for

---

[17] Matthew Paris, *Chronica Majora*, iii, 280–7; *BF*, i, 139, n.(d); *Gre.IX R*, nos. 2200–2. See also Cole, *Preaching*, 161–2.

[18] *BF*, i (Gre.IX) no. 146 (= AFB, no. 4); *BP*, i (Gre.IX) no. 112.

[19] *Pontifica Hibernica. Medieval Papal Chancery Documents concerning Ireland (640–1241)*, ed. M.P. Sheeny, 2 vols. (Dublin 1962, 1965), ii, no. 214.

[20] Matthew Paris, *Chronica Majora*, iii, 287–8.

[21] S. Painter, 'The Crusade of Theobald of Champagne and Richard of Cornwall 1239–41, *A History of the Crusades*, ii, 463–85, here 465; Riley-Smith, *Crusades*, 154.

[22] *Gre.IX R*, nos. 2786–9.

taking the cross.[23] An earlier version of *Quantum nos urgeat* was listed in the papal registers as early as May 1235. It was addressed to the German Dominicans with additional powers granted to absolve those who had been excommunicated because they had not paid the crusading twentieth, had supported heretics and Muslims, or had visited the Holy Sepulchre despite the papal interdict and the ban imposed during Frederick II's crusade in 1229.[24] This letter, however, bears a deletion mark and was almost certainly never sent, probably because Gregory IX was anxious not to interfere with Frederick II's attempts – undertaken in accordance with the Curia – to crush the rebellion of his son Henry VII that summer.[25] By taking advantage of the terms of the original version of *Quantum nos urgeat*, Frederick's enemies could have claimed exemption from imperial jurisdiction under the legal privileges of a crusader. This interpretation is supported by the fact that the scaled-down July version of *Quantum nos urgeat* was not sent to Germany until September 1235 after Henry VII's submission to Frederick.[26] It seems that by the end of the summer 1235 all crusade preachers were furnished with the additional powers of *Quantum nos urgeat*. If Matthew Paris can be believed, it was, in fact, the granting of indulgences to those attending crusade sermons that rendered the preaching of the cross in the mid 1230s so successful. His astonishment and outrage at the effectiveness of the friars' preaching was clearly connected with their lavish dispensation of indulgences to their audiences.[27] The enthusiastic response to the preaching campaign as a whole was thus not the result of the first year of the preaching campaign but followed the enhancement of the preachers' powers in the summer of 1235. A number of other chroniclers confirmed that the use of the friars as preachers of the cross for the Holy Land crusade in the mid and late 1230s was a success.[28] As a result, Pope Gregory IX and his successors continued to employ them as the principal preaching force alongside the local clergy in all major propaganda campaigns for the crusades to the Holy Land throughout the thirteenth century.

[23] *Pontifica Hibernica*, ii, no. 228; *Bullarii Franciscani Epitome et Supplementum Quattuor Voluminum Priorum Olim a Johanne Hyacinthio Sbaralea Editorum*, ed. C. Eubel (Ad Claras Aquas (Quaracchi) 1908), 233, no. vii.   [24] *ES*, i, no. 640 (= *Gre.IX R*, no. 2586).

[25] Van Cleve, *Emperor Frederick II*, 377–88; Abulafia, *Frederick II*, 239–48.

[26] *ES*, i, no. 664 (= *Gre.IX R*, no. 2790).

[27] Matthew Paris, *Chronica Majora*, iii, 287–8, 312, 373–4.

[28] 'E mari historiarum auctore Johannis de Columpna OP', *RGHF*, xxiii, 106–24, here 109–10; William of Nangis, 'Chronicon', *RGHF*, xx, 543–82, here 548; Philippe Mouskes, *Chronique*, ii, 606–7.

While the Holy Land crusade was being preached, the precarious situation of the Latin Empire made it necessary to raise a quick relief force of crusaders to come to the aid of Emperor John of Brienne. The lack of men and money necessary for the defence of the Latin Empire had been a source of worry ever since the conquest of Constantinople in 1204 during the Fourth Crusade, in particular because the Latins were faced with frequent attempts by the rulers of Epirus and the exiled Byzantine emperors at Nicaea in Asia Minor to re-establish Greek rule. At the end of the 1220s another threat was added. John Asen, the Vlach ruler of Bulgaria, had been frustrated in his hopes of becoming regent for the young Latin emperor Baldwin II after the death of Robert of Courtenay in 1228. After conquering most of the Epirote realm from his former ally Theodore Dukas, Asen conducted long diplomatic negotiations throughout the early 1230s for an alliance with the Nicaean government. The Greek emperor John Vatatzes was, however, holding out for the result of a papal mission to the exiled Orthodox patriarch of Constantinople in the hope of regaining his former empire by diplomacy. But the talks with the papal envoys came to nothing and shortly thereafter, in 1235, a treaty between Asen and Vatatzes was concluded which posed a serious threat to the Latin Empire.[29] Realizing this, Pope Gregory IX sent calls for crusading support to Hungary and France. Hungary was already supplying the Latin Empire with crusaders. Between 1231 and 1234, Gregory IX had been urging the Hungarian church hierarchy to induce the nobility of their own countries to come to the aid of John of Brienne, the new regent emperor, also by commuting the vows of Holy Land crusaders to the defence of Constantinople.[30] This suggests that there may have been a steady stream of crusaders from Hungary to Constantinople during the early 1230s.[31] When the threat of a renewed attack on the Latin Empire became very real during the second half of 1235, Gregory IX in December asked King Bela IV of Hungary, who had taken the cross for the Holy Land some time before, to crusade to the Latin Empire instead.[32] The same appeal was sent to the Ruthenian King Coloman, while

---

[29] R.L. Wolff, 'The Latin Empire of Constantinople, 1204–61', *A History of the Crusades*, ii, 187–233, here 217–22; R. Spence, 'Gregory IX's attempted expeditions to the Latin Empire of Constantinople: the crusade for the union of the Latin and Greek churches', *Journal of Medieval History*, v (1979), 163–76, here 169–70.

[30] *Vetera Monumenta Historica Hungariam Sacram Illustrantia*, ed. A. Theiner, 2 vols. (Rome 1859, 1860), i, no. 171 (= *Gre.IX R*, no .657); *Gre.IX R*, no. 1957.

[31] *Gre.IX R*, no. 1957.   [32] *Gre.IX R*, no. 2872.

the bishops of Hungary were ordered to recruit crusaders for the two kings' campaign.[33] In addition, Gregory IX sent the Cistercian abbot of St Thomas in Torcello to Hungary to help organize the crusade.[34]

King Bela of Hungary reacted cautiously to the pope's request for him to join the crusade. He was seemingly unwilling to antagonize John Asen of Bulgaria, who was his brother-in-law and was by no means irretrievably lodged in the enemies' camp. Asen, in fact, renounced his alliance with John Vatatzes in 1237 and negotiations between the pope and the Bulgarian ruler about the security of the Latin Empire took place. These were conducted in early summer of that year on behalf of the pope by two former bishops of Bosnia: the bishop of Perugia, now papal legate, and John of Wildeshausen, who at that time was the provincial prior of the Hungarian Dominicans. They were told to start recruiting crusaders as soon as a treaty between the two rulers was established.[35] The negotiations with John Asen, however, came to nothing. Instead, Asen renewed his alliance with John Vatatzes, which provoked Gregory IX to redirect Bela IV's crusade against the ruler of Bulgaria. In 1238 the pope commissioned the preaching of the cross for this new crusade first to the bishops of Hungary, and later also to the Dominicans in Hungary and the Franciscans in the Archdiocese of Gran.[36] But the crusade never took place, since the threat seems to have been enough to force John Asen back into an alliance with Bela IV. Although a joint Bulgaro-Hungarian force attacked Tzurulum in 1239, Hungarian commitment to crusading in the Latin Empire was never strong enough to play a decisive role. In March 1240 the Hungarian Dominicans were given renewed orders to preach the cross for the defence of the Latin Empire and to commute the vows of Holy Land crusaders, but the Mongol invasions during the following years probably prevented Hungarians from crusading abroad.[37] No evidence has survived

---

[33] *Gre.IX R*, nos. 2873–6.

[34] *Gre.IX R*, no. 2911. The abbot was presumably chosen because he was expected to be well informed about the Latin Empire, since St Thomas of Torcello was the mother monastery of the Cistercian abbey of St Stephen near Constantinople. See B.K. Panagopulos, *Cistercian and Mendicant Monasteries in Medieval Greece* (Chicago 1979), 6–7.

[35] *Gre.IX R*, no. 3695; *Vetera Monumenta Historica*, i, nos. 277–8 (= *Gre.IX R*, nos. 3716–17); Rother, 'Johannes Teutonicus', 152–4.

[36] *Gre.IX R*, nos. 4056–64; *BF*, i (Gre.IX) no. 273 (= *Gre.IX R*, nos. 4484–5).

[37] *BP*, i, no. 200 (= *Gre.IX R*, no. 5123).

for any later Hungarian involvement, or papal attempts to campaign for such involvement, in defence of the Latin Empire.

When Gregory IX envisaged the dispatch of a quick relief force of crusaders to come to the aid of John of Brienne in 1235, the most obvious area for the recruitment of such a relief force was the emperor's home land in central France. This was, however, also a primary recruitment ground for the crusade to the Holy Land, which was to be led by Count Thibald IV of Champagne. In order to coordinate the distribution of crusading aid between the two crusades, Gregory IX dispatched one of his penitentiaries, the Franciscan William of Cordelle, some time between mid 1234 and late 1235. In December 1235 the pope told him to commute the vows of 400 crusaders from Palestine to Constantinople,[38] while Count Thibald of Champagne and the archbishop of Sens were asked to induce Herard of Chacenai and other blood relations of the emperor to take the cross without delay.[39] One month later, a papal appeal to recruit crusaders and commute more vows was also sent to the French bishops, and they and William of Cordelle were informed that the doge of Venice had offered free transport for the crusaders.[40] Gregory IX must have been aware of his precarious situation in trying to recruit a quick relief force for the Latin Empire in an area where a new crusade to the Holy Land had only just begun to be preached. On the one hand, this had the advantage that prospective participants were already preparing to go on crusade and could, therefore, be expected to leave within a relatively short time. On the other hand, disagreements and rivalries over the distribution of resources for the two crusades were bound to arise. This is why Gregory IX from the very beginning tried to involve Thibald of Champagne in the recruit-ment of crusaders for the Latin Empire. The pope was most certainly expecting him to give an example by re-directing resources, which might have benefited his own crusade, to a project which obviously needed support much more quickly and urgently. But Gregory IX also wanted to make it quite clear that he wanted the recruitment for the Holy Land crusade to continue.

---

[38] *BF*, i (Gre.IX) no. 185 (= *Gre.IX R*, no. 2879).   [39] *Gre.IX R*, nos. 2877, 2878.
[40] *Gre.IX R*, nos. 2909–10. At the beginning of the letter no. 2909, William of Cordelle is wrongly addressed as one-time bishop of Modena. This constitutes an error by the scribe who initially, though not in the remainder of the letter, confused him with another papal penitentiary called William who at that time was the papal legate in Prussia.

William of Cordelle himself was given orders to preach the cross for Thibald's crusade, and he did so with great success.[41]

William's principal task, however, seems to have been the supervision of vow redemptions and commutations and the distribution of money to individual crusaders since these were the most likely causes for quarrels between the participants of the two crusades. In May 1237 he was advised to organize the collection of vow redemptions of all crusaders and pilgrims in the Archdiocese of Rheims; only the lands of Thibald of Champagne were excluded from this order because the vow redemption money had been promised to him in person.[42] The pope allowed William to use some of this money to induce Count Henry of Bar-le-Duc and his followers to commute their vows from the Holy Land crusade to the defence of the Latin Empire.[43] Although Henry refused to do this, Gregory IX later instructed William of Cordelle to pay him 10 per cent of the money for his crusade to the Holy Land.[44] In the case of Count Amalric of Montfort, his crusade was to be financed from vow redemptions in the count's own territories and in the remaining parts of the Archdiocese of Sens, except the lands of other crusaders.[45] Late in 1238 the Franciscan crusade preacher was given orders to select two French dioceses in which vow redemptions were not yet promised to any other crusader in order to finance the bishop of Nevers's crusade.[46] For the last time, before Thibald of Champagne's army left for the East, William of Cordelle was mentioned in connection with the concession of vow redemptions to crusaders in late November 1238, when he was told to confirm the grant of such money to Humbert of Beaujeu from his lands in the Diocese of Mâcon.[47] William of Cordelle did not have full legatine powers. But since he was responsible for the allocation of money to crusaders, his lack of legatine powers made it necessary to collaborate with the local clergy. The papal orders for the collection of money were, therefore, always addressed to William and the bishop or archbishop in whose territory the subsidy was to be raised, such as, for example, the archbishop of Rheims in the case of Henry of Bar-le-Duc or the archbishop of

[41] *BF*, i (Gre.IX) no. 232 (= *Gre.IX R*, no. 3643); see also *Gre.IX R*, no. 3327 and above, 33–4.   [42] *Gre.IX R*, no. 3632.
[43] *BF*, i (Gre.IX) no. 229 (= *Gre.IX R*, no. 3633).
[44] *BF*, i (Gre.IX) nos. 246, 247 (= *Gre.IX R*, nos. 4105, 4106).
[45] *Gre.IX R*, nos. 3923, 3924.   [46] *BF*, i (Gre.IX) no. 279 (= *Gre.IX R*, no. 4585).
[47] *BF*, i (Gre.IX) no. 281 (= *Gre.IX R*, no. 4627).

Sens for Amalric of Montfort.[48] If, on the other hand, William was ordered to distribute money that had already been collected, and thus belonged to the Curia, as in the cases of Geoffrey of Argentan and Humbert of Beaujeu, the pope would address the letter to him alone. But despite the patchiness of the evidence, there is no doubt that William was in overall charge of the distribution of the money from vow redemptions. The bishop of Le Mans, who in 1237 had also been appointed to collect money for crusaders to Palestine and the Latin Empire, was told by the pope to distribute subsidies in accordance with William's precepts.[49] By the same token, the pope issued a special permit to allow the same bishop and the Dominican William of Oléron to overrule William of Cordelle's powers regarding the assignment of crusading funds for Peter of Brittany.[50] And when, towards the end of 1238, several archbishops, bishops, and abbots were given renewed orders to collect testaments and other donations in the Archdioceses of Rheims, Bourges, and Tours and in the Diocese of Le Puy, the pope reminded them that this had to happen in coordination with William of Cordelle's chosen strategies.[51]

There is no evidence to say whether Gregory IX's appeals for a quick relief force for the defence of the Latin Empire were effective. However, a series of surprise victories by a small force under John of Brienne over the Bulgaro-Nicaean forces in the summer of 1236 and a truce between the Latin emperor and John Vatatzes helped temporarily to alleviate the pressing situation in Constantinople.[52] When the new emperor Baldwin II came to France in 1237, the pope supported his efforts to raise money and gather an army by stepping up crusading propaganda for the Latin Empire. Baldwin's departure was scheduled for August 1238.[53] But the fact that many northern French knights had already taken the cross for Thibald of Champagne's crusade to the Holy Land made the task difficult. The attempts to encourage the counts of Brittany and Bar-le-Duc to commute their vows to help Baldwin

---

[48] See also *BF*, i (Gre.IX) no. 267 (= *Gre.IX R*, no. 4437).
[49] *Gre.IX R*, no. 3903. For the bishop of Le Mans's commission see *ibid.*, nos. 3726, 4029, 4265, 4316, 4527.
[50] *Gre.IX R*, nos. 4265, 4266; for William of Oléron see also below, 42.
[51] *BF*, i (Gre.IX) no. 277 (= *Gre.IX R*, nos. 4519–22).
[52] Wolff, 'Latin Empire', 219. Nevertheless, the call for vow commutations was re-issued to the French and Hungarian bishops in December 1236; they were now also allowed to let Holy Land crusaders redeem their vows for money paid in aid of the crusade in the Latin Empire. See *Gre.IX R*, nos. 3395, 3396.   [53] *Gre.IX R*, no. 3939.

failed;[54] only Humbert of Beaujeu and Thomas of Marly are known to have followed the pope's request and went on crusade to the Latin Empire.[55] What was needed was a speedy propaganda campaign to attract additional crusaders, without depriving the Holy Land crusade of too many of its resources.

The Dominicans in the northern Province of *Francia* were ordered to preach the cross in support of the Latin Empire some time before May 1237.[56] In the autumn of the same year the Dominicans in Paris were told to make sure that those who had taken the cross left with Baldwin or else redeemed their vows before the general passage, provided they had legitimate reasons.[57] Over the following months the secular clergy in Gascony, Burgundy, Lotharingia, Flanders, and England were also commissioned to preach the cross.[58] But in central and northern France, where most of the Holy Land crusaders around Thibald of Champagne came from, Gregory IX only commissioned the Dominican friars. As the date for the departure was approaching, the Dominicans' powers were further enhanced by permission to absolve knights who were excommunicated for having taken part in tournaments, provided they took the cross.[59] In addition, a personal commission was given to the Dominican William of Oléron in November 1237 in connection with the attempt to make Peter of Brittany commute his Holy Land vow to a crusade for the defence of the Latin Empire. Like other friars commissioned to deal with crusading matters in a specific area, William was a local coming from the Ile d'Oléron off the Atlantic coast of Poitou, though nothing else is known about him. He was told to preach the cross to the Latin Empire, to compel weak and poor Holy Land crusaders to redeem their vows for the defence of the Latin Empire, and to make sure that no crusaders left before the general passage. The area assigned to William was Brittany and the Dioceses of Poitiers and Angers.[60] The Franciscan friars and the secular clergy of central and northern France were presumably meant to continue concentrating their propaganda efforts on the Holy Land crusade during this time. What may have led the pope to prefer the Dominicans to the Franciscans was their relatively early establish-

---

[54] *Gre.IX R*, nos. 3363, 3633, 4027; see also S. Painter, *The Scourge of the Clergy. Peter of Dreux, Duke of Brittany* (Baltimore 1937), 105–6.

[55] *Gre.IX R*, no. 4219; Painter, 'Crusade of Theobald', 466–8.

[56] *APP*, i, no. 400.   [57] *BP*, i (Gre.IX) no. 175 (= *Gre.IX R*, no. 3936).

[58] *Gre.IX R*, nos. 3937, 3944, 3946, 4209–17.

[59] *Gre.IX R*, no. 4206.   [60] *Gre.IX R*, no. 3945.

ment in Latin Greece. Judging from the prominent role the Greek Dominicans played in raising money for the defence of Constantinople in the early 1240s, they must already have been well established in Greece by the late 1230s.[61] The pope also tried to promote their presence there by offering plenary indulgences to French Dominicans who went to live in Constantinople.[62] As with the abbot of Torcello's commission to Hungary in the early 1230s,[63] good access to first hand information may have been regarded as an advantage to successful crusade propaganda, a point which incidentally was stressed thirty years later in general terms in Humbert of Romans' *De predicatione sancte crucis*.[64] The pope's aim must have been to control and at the same time guarantee the preaching of the cross to the Latin Empire by assigning it to the Dominicans only and by restricting the propaganda to the northern French territories. There is evidence that the recruitment efforts had fulfilled some of the pope's objectives since a great number of crusaders were said to have gone to fight for the defence of the Latin Empire.[65] In summer 1238 Baldwin II sent a small force under John of Béthune to Constantinople; he himself left France with the remainder of the army one year later.[66] But even after this, the French Dominicans were ordered to continue preaching the cross in early 1239, presumably to keep up a certain level of support for John's continued efforts in defending the Latin Empire.[67]

A similar propaganda strategy to that for the crusades in the Latin Empire was adopted by Gregory IX after 1230 for the crusades in the coastal lands of the Baltic. Initially only the Dominicans, later both mendicant orders and selected secular clerics, were commissioned to preach the cross. In addition, recruitment areas were strictly limited to parts of Germany, Bohemia, Poland, and Scandinavia in an attempt to control and channel crusading into the hands of the Teutonic Order. This strategy was mainly the result of the papacy's propagation of the Teutonic Order's leading role in the colonization and christianiza-

[61] Evidence for the first Dominican houses in Greece is, however, scarce. See Altaner, *Dominikanermissionen*, 9–12.

[62] *Gre.IX R*, no. 4206. Salimbene de Adam ('Cronica', 185), however, reported the same for the Franciscans. He himself was asked by the Franciscan minister of Greece to settle in his province. [63] See above, 38. [64] See below, 115.

[65] Albert of Trois-Fontaines, 'Chronicon', *MGHS*, xxiii, 631–950, here 946; 'Annales Erphordenses Fratrum Praedicatorum', *MGHSS*, xlii, 72–116, here 96–7.

[66] Wolff, 'Latin Empire', 221–2. [67] *BP*, i (Gre.IX) no. 188.

tion of the Baltic lands, which strictly speaking started in 1230, after the peace of S. Germano and Ceprano between Gregory IX and Frederick II.

Since their revival in the 1190s the crusades in the coastal lands of the Baltic had largely been organized by a circle of northern German noblemen and *ministeriales* around Archbishop Hartwig II of Bremen and his nephew, Bishop Albert of Üxküll, and later Riga. In the long run, however, their project for the colonization and christianization of Livonia (=Latvia) met with serious problems. Conflicts between the Danish kings and sectors of the northern German nobility intermittently hampered the recruitment of crusaders and seriously disrupted the supply lines to the area. In Livonia itself, the German crusaders first struggled against the Danes. Later on the newly constituted Order of the Sword Brothers opposed Bishop Albert's bid for political control. From about 1217 Albert began losing his grip on the situation and a revolt of the newly converted Livonians in 1222 made clear not only that the colonization was threatened by the colonists' weakness but also that the efforts to christianize the native population had so far been unsuccessful.[68] The conquest and christianization of Prussia underwent a similar development before 1230. Since 1217 Bishop Christian of Prussia had been engaged in a crusade aided by German and Polish armies. But Christian, too, lacked control over the crusaders and failed to protect the rights of the newly converted Prussians. He faced competition from Polish noblemen and, like Albert with the Sword Brothers in Livonia, had to deal with the grossly understaffed and underfinanced military order of the Knights of Dobrin. But the difficulties in establishing a Christian community were even greater than in Livonia, primarily because the military resistance of the native non-Christian population was much stronger.[69]

When his quarrels with the Danish king and the Sword Brothers had led to stalemate by the mid 1220s, Bishop Albert of Riga himself approached Honorius III in a bid to remedy the situation. But it was only after the first legatine mission of the papal vice-

[68] These matters are discussed in greater detail in: G. Gnegel-Waitschies, *Bischof Albert von Riga. Ein Bremer Domherr als Kirchenfürst im Osten* (1199–1229) (Hamburg 1958); Christiansen, *Northern Crusades*, 93–6; W. Urban, *The Baltic Crusade* (De Kalb 1975), 33–123.

[69] W. Urban, *The Prussian Crusade* (Lanham 1980), 74–83; Christiansen, *Northern Crusades*, 100–1; D. Rüdebusch, *Der Anteil Niedersachsens an den Kreuzzügen und Heidenfahrten* (Quellen und Forschungen zur Geschichte Niedersachsens 80; Hildesheim 1972), 168–77.

chancellor William of Modena to Livonia in 1225 and 1226 that the Curia gained sufficient knowledge of the situation in the Baltic to be able to start formulating a consistent policy towards that region.[70] Earlier, popes had confined themselves to issuing crusading bulls to Bishop Albert and his deputies. This had obviously contributed to the factionalism in Livonia, since it allowed Albert to control the recruitment of crusaders on his annual propaganda campaigns through northern Germany.[71] The ruthless exploitation of the native population by the Sword Brothers had partly been caused by their inability to obtain sufficient finance from elsewhere. The Brothers needed money badly for the payment of mercenary troops in order to complement their own ranks, which never exceeded 180 knights.[72] This had become very clear to William of Modena during his first mission and one of the principal measures he took was the negotiation of the just distribution of crusaders between the bishop, the town of Riga and the Sword Brothers.[73] In addition, the pope declared all newly christianized territories to be subject to the Roman Church.[74] Gregory IX, however, was well aware that papal pronouncements alone could not remedy the situation. Greater political stability in Livonia required the reorganization of military defences. The opportunity to take first steps towards major changes finally came in 1229 with the death of Bishop Albert. A solution also seemed to emerge in Prussia. Duke Casimir of Masovia, one of the main secular propagators of the colonization of Prussia, had already approached the Teutonic Order at the beginning of the 1220s. With its predominantly German origin and membership, the order could well be expected to show an interest in the Baltic lands. Indeed, the Knights responded positively after their order obtained from Frederick II the status of an imperial prince in Culmerland and Prussia in 1226. A small number of knights finally arrived in Prussia in 1228, but the order was in no position to send larger contingents

---

[70] R. Spence, 'Pope Gregory IX and the Crusade on the Baltic', *The Catholic Historical Review*, lxix (1983), 1–19, here 1–4; G.A. Donner, *Kardinal Wilhelm von Sabina. Bischof von Modena 1222–1234. Päpstlicher Legat in den Nordischen Ländern (t.1251)* (Societas Scientiarum Fennica. Commentationes Humaniorum Litterarum ii, 5; Helsingfors 1929), 73–142.

[71] Urban, *Baltic Crusade*, 33–123 *passim*; Roscher, *Innocenz III.*, 198–211.

[72] F. Benninghoven, *Der Orden der Schwertbrüder. Fratres Milicie Christi de Livonia* (Cologne und Graz 1956), 75–193, *passim*, esp. 82–5, 121–3.

[73] *Liv-, Esth- und Curländisches Urkundenbuch nebst Regesten*, ed. F.G. v.Bunge, 12 vols. (Reval 1852–1910), i, no. LXXXIII.   [74] Spence, 'Pope Gregory IX', 8.

to north-eastern Europe until after the emperor's crusade to the Holy Land was over.[75]

Gregory IX was aware that the death of Bishop Albert of Riga had opened the way to tackling the fundamental issues in Livonia and it is likely that he saw the potential to stabilize the situation in Prussia if the Teutonic Knights could be convinced to put a major effort into that area. This was a move Frederick, in turn, seemed to support. From the point of view of the papacy's wider crusading policies, the time also seemed right to give more attention to the struggling Baltic Crusades, since the Albigensian war had been ended successfully in 1229 and the Holy Land had been secured, at least temporarily, by the conclusion of a ten years truce between Frederick II and al-Kamil.[76] In addition, William of Modena had just come back from his second legatine mission to northern Europe and may have urged the pope to go ahead with changes in that area.[77] It seems that during the negotiations leading up to the peace of St Germano and Ceprano the pope and the emperor also discussed the Baltic situation. Hermann of Salza, the grand-master of the Teutonic Order, was the emperor's chief negotiator, and there is evidence from as early as January 1230 that Gregory and Hermann conferred about the Teutonic Knights' position in Prussia.[78] Since few details are known about the peace talks in 1229 and 1230, it is impossible to say in exactly what way the Baltic crusade became part of the negotiations. However, there is evidence that Hermann of Salza and William of Modena met during the final stages of the peace talks.[79] Only two weeks after the reconciliatory meeting between the pope and the emperor at Ceprano, Gregory IX issued the official papal approval which guaranteed the Teutonic Order's right to possess the territories which they conquered, and thus matched the emperor's golden bull of 1226.[80]

The day after the issue of the papal privileges for the Teutonic Order in Prussia, according to the papal registers, or five days later

[75] H. Boockmann, *Der Deutsche Orden. Zwölf Kapitel aus seiner Geschichte* (Munich 1981), 66–92; Urban, *Prussian Crusade*, 83– 107; Christiansen, *Northern Crusades*, 79–80.
[76] Roquebert, *L'epopée*, iii, 297–429; Van Cleve, *Emperor Frederick II*, 213–20.
[77] Donner, *Kardinal Wilhelm von Sabina*, 143–58.
[78] *PUB*, i, 1, no. 72 (= *ES*, i, no. 411; *Gre.IX R*, no. 387); H. Kluger, *Hochmeister Hermann von Salza und Kaiser Friedrich II. Ein Beitrag zur Frühgeschichte des Deutschen Ordens* (Quellen und Studien zur Geschichte des Deutschen Ordens 37; Marburg 1987), 141–64.
[79] Donner, *Kardinal Wilhelm von Sabina*, 55–6.
[80] *PUB*, i, 1, no. 80 (= *Gre.IX R*, no. 494).

according to one of the surviving copies, the Dominicans of northern Germany received the first papal bull, *Cum misericors*, ordering them to recruit crusaders for the Teutonic Knights in Prussia.[81] According to the bull, Hermann of Salza himself had requested that the Dominicans take on the task of preaching the cross in support of the Teutonic Order. There was a variety of reasons for choosing the Dominicans. Hermann of Salza may have been informed by William of Modena that they were showing a keen interest in the Baltic mission. As early as 1220, the papal vice-chancellor had supported St Dominic himself, who, shortly before his death, was showing a renewed interest in the Baltic mission, stemming from his early journeys in north-eastern Europe.[82] On his first Baltic journey William had encouraged Duke Swietopelk of Pomerania to found a Dominican convent at Gdansk (Danzig) as a missionary centre, which he did in 1227.[83] By 1230 the order had, in fact, founded convents at Wroclaw (Breslau), Kamien Pomorski (Cammin), Chelmno (Culm), Gdansk (Danzig), and Tallinn (Reval).[84] At a more general level, there was a sense of common purpose between the Teutonic Order and the Dominicans which was symbolized by their strong devotion to the cult of the Virgin Mary. The Virgin was the Teutonic Order's patron, and her cult played an overwhelmingly important role in the life and politics of the Baltic lands both before and after the arrival of the Knights.[85] The Dominican master general in 1230, Jordan of Saxony, had also done much to propagate the devotion to the Virgin Mary: on his initiative the *Salve Regina* was introduced into the Dominican liturgy in the mid 1220s.[86] Another factor which may have encouraged Hermann of Salza and Gregory IX to favour the Dominicans was that two of the leaders of the Dominican order

---

[81] See below, 49.

[82] Vicaire, *Histoire*, ii, 197–9; Donner, *Kardinal Wilhelm von Sabina*, 15, 155–6.

[83] Altaner, *Dominikanermissionen*, 161–3; Freed, *Friars*, 58, 67.

[84] Freed, *Friars*, 222. The Dominican house at Tallinn (Reval) was founded in 1229 and destroyed by the Swordbrothers in 1233 before being re-established in 1246. See G. von Walther-Wittenheim, *Die Dominikaner in Livland im Mittelalter. Die Natio Livoniae* (Institutum Historicum Fratrum Praedicatorum Romae ad S. Sabinam Dissertationes Historicae 9; Rome 1938), 8–11. Later, in 1234, William of Modena lobbied the bishop of Riga to provide the Dominicans with better lodgings, arguing that they might be particularly able to propagate the Christian faith in Livonia. See Freed, *Friars*, 69.

[85] B. Rosenberg, 'Marienlob im Deutschordenslande Preussen. Beiträge zur Geschichte der Marienverehrung im Deutschen Orden bis zum Jahre 1525', *Acht Jahrhunderte Deutscher Orden in Einzeldarstellungen*, ed. K. Wieser (Bad Godesberg 1967), 321–37; M. Dygo, 'The Political Role of the Virgin Mary in Teutonic Prussia in the fourteenth and fifteenth centuries', *Journal of Medieval History*, xv (1989), 63–80. [86] Scheeben, *Beiträge*, 42–4.

came, like Hermann himself, from ministerial families attached to noble dynasties of northern Germany who were known to be enthusiastic supporters of the crusades.[87] Jordan of Saxony was born into a ministerial family attached to the counts of Dassel while his parents were on a *peregrinatio* in the Holy Land; John of Wildeshausen, another prominent Dominican in papal service in 1230, who later also became master general, came from a ministerial family attached to the counts of Oldenburg-Wildeshausen.[88] The counts of Dassel were crusaders of long-standing tradition, and Jordan's former lord, Count Adolf II, was on the Fifth Crusade and went to Livonia in 1221.[89] John's former lord, Count Henry II of Oldenburg-Wildeshausen, twice went to the Holy Land, with Frederick Barbarossa in 1189 and with Henry VI in 1197.[90] His successor, Count Burchard, had a particular inclination towards the Baltic crusades. He had been to Livonia in 1214–15 and 1224–5 and he appeared in the company of William of Modena at Riga in 1226.[91] Both Jordan of Saxony and John of Wildeshausen could thus be expected to be familiar with, and favourably disposed towards, the Baltic crusades.

It has been argued that the German Franciscans did not get involved in the propagation of the Baltic crusades at this early stage because they had not yet managed to attract great numbers of friars from noble and ministerial backgrounds, who might have been able to spread propaganda amongst potential supporters by personal contacts.[92] But even if their social origins made it more difficult to gain access to the more powerful of the potential crusaders, this does not prevent that their propaganda would have been inefficient. The Baltic crusades were popular amongst many lesser knights and burghers, who were in a position to raise the money to crusade in the Baltic but could not afford to participate in the more expensive expeditions to the Holy Land. In addition, there were many middling knights and people of low social standing who went to the Baltic as crusaders in the hope of raising their social status by settling there.[93] It must not be forgotten either that the preaching of the cross in the thirteenth century was also

---

[87] Hermann came from a ministerial family of the Landgraves of Thuringia. See E. Maschke, 'Die Herkunft Hermann von Salzas', *Zeitschrift des Vereins für Thüringische Geschichte. Neue Folge*, xxxiv (1940), 372–89. [88] Freed, *Friars*, 123–4, n. 47.
[89] Rüdebusch, *Anteil Niedersachsens*, 117–20, 230–1.
[90] Rüdebusch, *Anteil Niedersachsens*, 25, 34.
[91] Rüdebusch, *Anteil Niedersachsens*, 107–8, 123–4, 230.
[92] Freed, *Friars*, 128. [93] Rüdebusch, *Anteil Niedersachsens*, 236–8.

partly aimed at raising money by way of vow redemptions. This the Franciscans could have done even more effectively than the Dominicans, because they had at least thirteen convents in the area of Germany where the Baltic crusade was initially preached in 1230, compared to the Dominicans' five.[94] Nevertheless, it should not come as a surprise that the Franciscans did not get involved in the preaching of the cross to the Baltic in 1230. Their involvement in anti-Hohenstaufen propaganda in the *Regno* most certainly made them *personae non gratae* with the emperor. To employ them as propagandists for the Teutonic Knights' crusade in the Baltic, which was to some extent a result of the politics of reconciliation between Gregory IX and Frederick II, may have seemed inopportune. From the pope's point of view there was, however, another reason to refrain from enlisting the Franciscans for the Baltic crusade. At the translation of St Francis's body in early summer 1230, the order had been thrown into a crisis. The new sumptuous church at Assisi, which had been built in honour of the founder saint, was seen by many friars as a betrayal of Francis's ideal of absolute poverty being one of the cornerstones of the new religious community. During the subsequent general chapter, the governing heads of the order were deeply divided over the issue. The rift was not remedied until Gregory IX's authoritative pronouncement of September 1230 in the bull *Quo elongati*, which ascribed the possessions of the order to the pope or the cardinal protector.[95] Although this eventually reconciled the factions within the order for some time to come, the Franciscans seemed hardly fit to take on another major propaganda task in late summer 1230.

The earliest surviving commission to the Dominicans for the preaching of the cross dates from September 1230. The bull *Cum misericors* was sent to the Dominicans in the Archdioceses of Magdeburg and Bremen.[96] The cross was to be preached in these two provinces and in Holstein, Gotland, Pomerania, Poland, Moravia, and Suravia. The crusaders were told to fight under the leadership of the Teutonic Order and they were granted full remission of their sins in return for one year's service or if they died

---

[94] The Franciscans had houses at Erfurt, Eisenach, Gotha, Nordhausen, Halberstadt, Brunswick, Hildesheim, Goslar, Hamburg, Bremen, Lübeck, Magdeburg, and Oschatz; the Dominicans at Magdeburg, Bremen, Lübeck, Erfurt, and Leipzig. See Freed, *Friars*, 182–6, 210.

[95] M.D. Lambert, *Franciscan Poverty. The Doctrine of the Absolute Poverty of Christ and the Apostles in the Franciscan Order* (London 1961), 76–88.

[96] Gre.IX R, no. 493 (= ES, i, no.417); PUB, i, i, no. 81.

while on crusade. In summer 1231 the pope also allowed the commutation of crusading vows from the Holy Land to Prussia and the redemption of the vows of weak and poor crusaders.[97] With the papal ban against joining Frederick II's crusade of 1228, a considerable number of crusaders might indeed have wanted to fulfil their vows in the Baltic. At the beginning of the following year the preaching was extended to the Kingdom of Bohemia; the Dominicans there received a new papal bull describing the recent attacks of the Prussians.[98] Shortly thereafter the powers of the Dominican crusade preachers were still further enhanced. They were given permission to absolve those excommunicated for arson and violence against clerics if they joined the crusade. In addition, they could grant twenty days indulgence for attending a crusading sermon. The pope's new instructions also included provisions against false crusade preachers who fraudulently enriched themselves by collecting vow redemptions; the Dominican friars were told to proceed against them with ecclesiastical censures.[99] Although progress was made in the first years of the Prussian crusade, with Christian bases established at Chelmno (Culm) and other strongholds along the Vistula, there was no foreseeable end to the hostilities and still more demand for crusaders.[100] After the capture of Bishop Christian by renegade Prussian converts in 1233, the Dominicans were urged to go on preaching the cross against the Prussians in order to counteract their protracted hostility to Christianity. The master-general, Jordan of Saxony, was requested by the pope to make an urgent appeal to his friars concerning the seriousness of this matter.[101] When the Teutonic Knights took over from the Sword Brothers in Livonia in 1236, the Dominicans also became involved in the Teutonic Order's fight against the Livonians. From now on they preached the Livonian crusade alongside that to Prussia, as a new papal bull was issued in early 1236.[102] During this time a prominent Polish Dominican appeared among the crusade propagandists of his order. Jacek of Ople, better known as St Hyacinth, was referred to as 'Jazco tunc in ministerio crucis constitutus' in a witness-list of one of Duke Wladislaw of

[97] *PUB*, i, 1, no. 85.   [98] *ES*, i, no. 460 (= *Gre.IX R*, no. 754).
[99] *PUB*, i, 1, no. 89; *Diplomatarium Danicum*, i, 6, no. 132.
[100] Christiansen, *Northern Crusades*, 101.
[101] *PUB*, i, 1, no. 98 (= *Gre.IX R*, no. 1534).
[102] *PUB*, i, 1, nos. 121, 123; see also *BP*, i (Gre.IX) no. 145.

Poland's privileges granting free passage to crusaders and Teutonic Knights.[103] But no other information about his preaching of the cross has survived.[104]

One of the key factors of papal crusading policy in the Baltic after 1230 was the attempt to channel all the resources into the hands of the Teutonic Order in Prussia and, after the collapse of the Sword Brothers in 1236, also in Livonia. The aim seems to have been to concentrate as much military power as possible with the Teutonic Knights in order to minimize the rivalries between the Christian powers in the Baltic and thus create better conditions for the christianization of north-eastern Europe. Throughout the remainder of the thirteenth century, popes earmarked financial support for the Baltic crusade for the exclusive use of the Teutonic Knights, and time and again during the following decades the Baltic crusaders were ordered to collaborate with the Knights and act in strict accordance with their advice.[105] In order to ensure that this policy was adhered to, the recruitment of crusaders was strictly reserved to the Dominicans of northern Germany, Bohemia, Poland, and Scandinavia, whom the papacy seemed to trust to execute orders in strict accordance with the precepts of the crusading bulls. In addition, it appears that the Baltic crusades were generally very popular in northern Germany and Scandinavia and that there was no immediate need to extend the propaganda efforts beyond the Dominican friars. Only in the 1260s, when the Christian Baltic came under unusually serious threat, were first the Franciscans, and then also members of other orders and the Baltic bishops, drafted into preaching the cross.[106] Even in Scandinavia, crusaders were normally recruited by the Dominicans for the Teutonic Knights in Prussia and Livonia. Only in 1237 were some Swedish bishops allowed to recruit crusaders for a campaign against the Tavistians of Finland and in 1240 the archbishop of Lund and his suffragans were given powers to preach the cross for the defence of Estonia.[107] Unauthorized preaching of the cross was not tolerated. Thus, in 1234, Bishop Nicholas of Riga was disciplined by the pope after, amongst other transgressions, rec-

---

[103] *PUB*, i, 1, no. 127.
[104] R.-J. Loenertz, 'La vie de S. Hyacinthe du lecteur Stanislas envisagée comme source historique', *AFP*, xxvii (1957), 5–38. [105] E.g., *PUB*, i, 1, nos. 81, 102, 115, 150.
[106] See below, 89f.
[107] *Diplomatarium Suecarum*, i, no. 298; *ES*, i, no. 796 (= *Gre.IX R*, no. 5326); Christiansen, *Northern Crusades*, 112.

ruiting crusaders without papal authority.[108] A similar case was Bishop Christian of Prussia, who, after his release from Prussian captivity between 1233 and 1239, was faced with the situation in which the Teutonic Knights were undoubtedly dominating the political scene in Prussia to the detriment of his archiepiscopal authority. When Christian demanded crusading resources for his own use in defiance of papal orders, Innocent IV ordered the Dominican prior of Magdeburg in 1243 to stop the archbishop from issuing bogus indulgences and from depriving the Knights of their financial aid by collecting crusade vow redemptions.[109]

While the great and more permanent crusading projects to the Holy Land, the Latin Empire, and the Baltics were underway, other more localized conflicts between the church and its enemies within Christendom were also given the status of a crusade by Pope Gregory IX. Foremost amongst these were the campaigns against heretics in Germany and Hungary. The conflict between Archbishop Gerhard II of Bremen and the Stedinger peasants, his subjects on the Unter-Weser, had been going for many years, when in 1229 his brother Count Hermann II of Lippe was defeated and killed by the Stedinger.[110] This murder greatly exacerbated the long-standing conflict and Archbishop Gerhard decided to take decisive action. He excommunicated the Stedinger, probably shortly before Christmas 1229.[111] This turned out to be the prelude to a crusade. The archbishop's hopes of obtaining the status of a crusade for his projected war against the Stedinger were almost certainly founded on the fact that Bishop Willibrand of Utrecht had managed to do just that a few years earlier in his conflict with the Drenther peasants.[112] On *Laetare Jerusalem* (21 March) 1231 a diocesan synod declared the Stedinger to be heretics, probably because of their recalcitrant disregard of the excommunication.[113] Gerhard may have asked the pope in person for the grant of a crusading indulgence.[114] Gregory IX, however, seems to have

---

[108] *Gre.IX R*, no. 2287; Spence, 'Pope Gregory IX', 11–15.   [109] *PUB*, i, 1, no. 149.

[110] H.A. Schumacher, *Die Stedinger. Beitrag zur Geschichte der Weser-Marschen* (Bremen 1865), 51–76.

[111] R. Köhn, 'Die Verketzerung der Stedinger durch die Bremer Fastensynode', *Bremisches Jahrbuch*, lvii (1979), 15–85, here 75–80. The author convincingly argued for a new chronology of the conflict between the Stedinger and Archbishop Gerhard between late 1229 and summer 1231, which has been adopted in the following.

[112] See below, 167–9.   [113] Köhn, 'Verketzerung', 76–81.

[114] W. von Bippen, *Geschichte der Stadt Bremen*, 3 vols. (Bremen 1892–1904), i, 136; *cf.* Schumacher, *Stedinger*, 89, n. 22.

been concerned to make sure that the allegations were investigated properly before a crusade might begin. In July 1231 he ordered the bishop of Lübeck, the prior of the Dominican convent in Bremen and a Dominican papal penitentiary, John, to investigate the alleged heresy of the Stedinger.[115] The papal penitentiary was almost certainly John of Wildeshausen, who at this time was a member of Cardinal Otto of St Nicholas's legation to Germany and Denmark. As deputy of the cardinal, John of Wildeshausen had carried out administrative reforms in the Diocese of Bremen in 1230.[116] The cardinal had also appointed the Dominican prior and the dean and *scholasticus* of Bremen as general visitors in the Diocese of Bremen.[117] The intimate knowledge of the diocese which John of Wildeshausen and the prior of the Dominicans at Bremen thus acquired must have recommended these two friars for the inquest into the alleged heresy of the Stedinger. In addition, the German Dominicans were already designated as inquisitors by July 1231. But since the powers of the Dominican inquisition had not yet been confirmed, it may have seemed wise to have the inquiry assisted by a local bishop.[118] The papal order required the three addressees to investigate the reasons for the excommunication of the Stedinger; it also already contained powers to approach the neighbouring nobility for military assistance against the peasants should the archbishop's allegations of heresy turn out to be justified. Since the accusations, judging from subsequent developments, seem to have been confirmed by the papal delegates, one may well ask if John of Wildeshausen had contacted his former lords already at this stage about joining the crusade against the Stedinger.[119] Count Burchard of Oldenburg-Wildeshausen died fighting against the Stedinger in 1233 and his successor Henry III met the same fate in the following year.[120] The participation of the counts of Oldenburg-Wildeshausen was ultimately crucial since they, in turn, seem to have caused their in-laws, the counts of Breda

---

[115] *Bremisches Urkundenbuch*, ed. D.R. Ehmck, 5 vols. (Bremen 1863–1893), i, no. 166; see also Köhn, 'Verketzerung', 72–3.

[116] Rother, 'Johannes Teutonicus', 145–7; Freed, *Friars*, 146–7.

[117] This is mentioned in *Gre.IX R*, no. 1365.

[118] See below Appendix 1. Köhn ('Verketzerung', 81–3) with due caution, owing to the lack of detailed information, suggested that the Bremen Dominicans and John of Wildeshausen might have been instrumental in bringing the charges of heresy against the Stedinger at the Lent synod.   [119] For John's origins, see above, 48.

[120] Schumacher, *Stedinger*, 111, 116–20.

and Schoolen, to join the crusade against the Stedinger.[121] In the final battle of the crusade at Altenesch on 27 May 1234, Bishop Gerhard also received substantial assistance from the counts of Holland, Guelders, and Cleve, as well as from the duke of Brabant, who all had direct or indirect family ties with the counts of Oldenburg-Wildeshausen.[122]

The preaching of the cross against the Stedinger was not authorized until October 1232. This suggests that the pope actually waited for the results of the inquest. The commission to preach the cross did not, however, go to the archbishop of Bremen himself, but to the bishops of Lübeck, Minden, and Ratzeburg.[123] Thus Gerhard II would have been free to organize the military campaigns without having to spend time travelling in order to recruit crusaders, as Willibrand of Utrecht had done four years previously for the crusade against the Drenther.[124] To help them carry out their assignments, the bishops were told to call on any Dominican friar they saw fit for the job, even if he should claim exemption on the grounds of a papal privilege.[125] In January 1233, Gregory IX confirmed the commission and asked for support for the appointed preachers from the five bishops of Paderborn, Hildesheim, Verden, Münster, and Osnabrück, in whose dioceses, along with that of Bremen, the preaching of the cross was to take place.[126] In June 1233 Gregory IX upgraded the crusade against the

---

[121] H. Oncken, 'Studien zur Geschichte des Stedingerkreuzzuges', *Jahrbuch für die Geschichte des Herzogtums Oldenburg*, v (Schriften des Oldenburger Vereins für Altertumskunde und Landesgeschichte 14; Oldenburg 1896), 27–58, here 30–41.

[122] 'Emonis Chronicon', *MGHS*, xxiii, 465–523, here 516–17; 'Historia Monasterii Rastedensis', *MGHS*, xxv, 495–511, here 506; Schumacher, *Stedinger*, 117–22, 246–8.

[123] *ES*, i, no. 489 (= *Gre.IX R*, no. 940). Freed (*Friars*, 147) is misleading about the nature of the indulgence. The areas in which the cross was to be preached were the Dioceses of Paderborn, Hildesheim, Verden, Minden, Münster, Osnabrück, and Bremen. The bull allowed the bishops to grant five years indulgence to those crusaders who served in person and at their own expense and three years to those who were in somebody else's pay. The length of service was to be determined at the preachers' own discretion and in accordance with the exigencies of the campaign. All those who died while fulfilling their vows were to enjoy a plenary indulgence. A proportional indulgence was to be given to those who assisted the business in any other way according to the size of the aid. In addition, attendance at a crusade sermon was rewarded with twenty days indulgence. The crusade preachers were also allowed to use ecclesiastical censures against anyone who obstructed the business of the cross.

[124] See below, 167.

[125] This refers to a papal privilege granted to the Dominicans for the first time in 1225. See below, 66.

[126] Schumacher, *Stedinger*, 99–100 (= *Regesta Pontificum*, no. 9076). There is, however, no indication that these five bishops were meant to preach the cross themselves. *Cf.* E.T. Kennan, 'Innocent III, Gregory IX, and Political Crusades: A Study in the

Stedinger by granting the same full indulgence as was given to Holy Land crusaders. By doing this the pope acknowledged the concern of the bishops of Minden, Lübeck, and Ratzeburg, who had informed him that the response to the preaching had not been as great as expected. People were said to have been reluctant to fight against such a strong enemy in a country which they considered unconquerable, because it was naturally fortified by so many rivers. The pope had also been told of the victories of the Stedinger in the winter of 1232–3 and in particular of their conquest of the archbishop's fortress at Slutter.[127] Offering the full crusading indulgence for the Stedinger crusade also put this on an equal footing with the parallel crusade preached against other heretics in Germany, and avoided the diversion of resources from the Stedinger campaign.[128] The upgrading of the indulgence seems to have had some success. The recruitment of crusaders peaked in early 1234, significantly with the support of the friars. Emo reported that the Dominicans travelled all over the Rhineland, Westphalia, Holland, Flanders, and Brabant and recruited a great number of crusaders.[129]

One group of Dominican crusade preachers were, however, less successful, according to Emo.[130] When two friars from Bremen came to Fivelgo in early January 1234 to recruit crusaders at Appingdam, they were attacked by a crowd and only just escaped to Groningen. What had caused the hostile reaction is not quite clear from Emo's report. But once they were in Groningen, the Dominicans excommunicated the people of Appingdam and started preaching against the Fivelgonians, whom they also accused of disobedience to the church authorities. Not surprisingly, very few took the cross against the Stedinger in those parts. In fact, the people of Appingdam were difficult to reconcile, and finally had to be forced to do penance for their attacks against the friars. Later, at Stets, the preachers used their inquisitorial powers against a monk who disturbed their sermons. They accused him of blasphemy and had him imprisoned in the monastery at Rottum. The inquisitorial procedure and the sentence passed on the repentant monk was in

---

Disintegration of Papal Power', *Reform and Authority in the Medieval and Reformation Church* ed. G.F. Lytle (Washington 1981), 15–35, here 26.

[127] *ES*, i, no. 539 (= *Gre.IX R*, no. 1402); *Bremisches Urkundenbuch*, i, no. 176; 'Annales Stadenses', *MGHS*, xvi, 271–379, here 361–2.

[128] See below, 56–8.   [129] 'Emonis Chronicon', 516.

[130] 'Emonis Chronicon', 515–16.

strict compliance with the imperial provisions of 1232.[131] The harsh measures adopted by the Dominicans, however, were sharply criticized by Emo and he accused the two Dominicans of abusing their papal authority in an irresponsible manner.

While the crusade against the Stedinger was still under way, the papal inquisitor Conrad of Marburg was joined by other mendicant friars when he preached the cross against a number of German heretics in 1233. Conrad had been involved in the investigation of heresy in Germany at least since 1227.[132] Gregory IX's re-affirmation of his inquisitorial powers in October 1231 allowed Conrad to appoint assistants.[133] His collaboration with individual mendicant friars started in or even before 1231. The Franciscan Gerhard Lützelkolb appeared in his company before Elizabeth of Thuringia's death in November 1231.[134] The *Annales Wormatienses* report that, as early as 1231, Conrad was also joined by the Dominican lay-brother Conrad Tors and his one-eyed and one-armed companion John.[135] The annalist of Worms added that Conrad of Marburg received assistance from local Dominican and Franciscan friars who were not his constant companions; he suggested that this happened without papal authority, but was obviously mistaken.[136] After hearing about the spread of heresy in Germany from the archbishop of Mainz and the bishop of Hildesheim, Gregory IX in June 1233 allowed Conrad of Marburg to recruit crusaders with the same indulgences and privileges as those to the Holy Land in order to help him in his inquisitorial investigations.[137] Conrad is known to have preached the cross

---

[131] H. Köhler, *Die Ketzerpolitik der deutschen Kaiser und Könige in den Jahren 1152–1254* (Jenaer Historische Arbeiten 6; Bonn 1913), 36–7. The Dominicans apparently also conducted inquisitions against the Stedinger around the same time. One friar was said to have been beheaded by the Stedinger when he demanded that they pay tithes and other dues. See 'Historia Monasterii Rastedensis', 506.

[132] A. Patschovsky, 'Zur Ketzerverfolgung Konrads von Marburg', *Deutsches Archiv für die Erforschung des Mittelalters*, xxxvii (1981), 641–93; here 642–89; see also below appendix 1.

[133] *Analecta Hassiaca*, ed. J.P. Kuchenbecker, 6 vols. (Marburg 1728–1742), iii, 73–5.

[134] Caesar of Heisterbach, 'Epistola in Vitam Sancte Elyzabeth Lantgravie', *Die Wundergeschichten des Caesarius von Heisterbach*, ed. A. Hilka, 3 vols. (Publikationen der Gesellschaft für Rheinische Geschichtskunde 43; Bonn 1933–7), iii, 341–81, here 353, 375. Freed (*Friars*, 144, n. 40) suggested that Gerhard Lützelkolb could have come from a knightly family from Magdeburg and thus may have been Conrad of Marburg's kinsman. There is, however, no definite proof of this.

[135] 'Annales Wormatienses', *MGHS*, xvii, 34–73, here 38–9. Conrad Tors and John may have been former heretics. See 'Gesta Treverorum Continuata', *MGHS*, xxiv, 368–488, here 400.   [136] 'Annales Wormatienses', 39.

[137] *ES*, i, no. 533 (= *Gre.IX R*, no. 1381).

against the counts of Sayn and Arnsberg and the countess of Looz, whom he suspected of heresy. In order to avoid a crusade, members of the German episcopate and nobility decided to convene in order to inquire into their alleged heresy at a diet in Mainz which began on 25 July 1233. The allegations were not considered to be convincing by the majority of the bishops and princes, who referred the matter to the pope directly. But despite this, and despite repeated warnings from the archbishops of Mainz, Cologne, and Trier, Conrad of Marburg went ahead with the preaching of the cross in Mainz immediately after the council. As a result he was murdered by a number of noblemen when he left Mainz on 30 July. He was accompanied at the time by Gerhard Lützelkolb who was killed with him. A little later Conrad Tors and his companion John were also murdered.[138] On hearing about the killings, Gregory IX reacted furiously by re-confirming the crusade against the German heretics. All prelates in Germany were ordered to excommunicate the murderers of Conrad of Marburg, and Archbishop Siegfried of Mainz, Bishop Conrad of Hildesheim, and Conrad of Höxter, the Dominican provincial prior of Germany, were told to resume the preaching of the cross in the whole of Germany in October 1233.[139] At the same time, the pope approached Landgrave Conrad of Thuringia personally, asking him to take the cross.[140] By February 1234 Count Henry of Thuringia, Duke Otto of Brunswick, Marquess Henry of Minden, and Counts John and Otto of Brandenburg had joined him.[141] But although there is evidence that Conrad of Hildesheim, at least, carried out the papal orders,[142] the crusade never got under way. The matter was settled peacefully by another diet at Frankfurt at the beginning of February 1234.[143] As in the case of the crusades to the Latin Empire and the Baltics, Gregory IX successfully used the mendicant friars to boost, and at the same time control the

---

[138] 'Annales Erphordenses', 84–6; Albert of Trois-Fontaines, 'Chronicon', 931–2; 'Annales Wormatienses', 39–40; Patschovsky, 'Ketzerverfolgung', 685–7. Albert of Trios-Fontaines reported that two Franciscans were killed with Conrad, whereas the *Annales Erphordenses* stated that Conrad Tors first went to Rome to inform the pope about the murder.

[139] *ES*, i, nos. 558, 561 (= *Gre.IX R*, nos. 1541, 1581); 'Annales Erphordenses', 86; Freed, *Friars*, 144.   [140] *ES*, i, no. 557 (= *Gre.IX R*, nos. 1556, 1558).

[141] *ES*, i, nos. 572, 573 (= *Gre.IX R*, nos. 1785–91). Siberry (*Criticism*, 168) seems to be mistaken when putting these letters in the context of the crusade against the Stedinger.

[142] 'Annales Erphordenses', 84.

[143] L. Förg, *Die Ketzerverfolgung in Deutschland unter Gregor IX. Ihre Herkunft, ihre Bedeutung und ihre rechtlichen Grundlagen* (Historische Studien 218; Berlin 1932), 85–90.

propaganda for the crusades against the German heretics. While individual friars like John of Wildeshausen were given more prominent tasks because of their good knowledge of local matters, the bulk of the Dominicans were called upon to support the local clergy, who were in charge of organizing these crusades. Although the pope acknowledged the urgency of these localized conflicts, he was quite clearly not wanting to channel more crusading resources than was absolutely necessary away from the more laborious crusades overseas.

Germany was not the only country where the Dominicans were involved in anti-heretical crusades in the 1230s. From around 1234 and into the fourteenth century, alleged heretics and schismatics in Bosnia were the subject of a continuous, drawn-out crusade which was mainly organized by the Hungarian nobility and episcopate. The sources for this crusade are scarce and reveal few details. There are, in fact, more questions asked than can be answered about the nature of the heresies and the conditions and the organization of the crusades.[144] The Dominicans played a role in its preaching, although the extent of their involvement is difficult to assess.

In 1232 Pope Gregory IX commissioned an inquiry by the bishops of Kolocsa and Zagreb into the suspected unorthodoxy of the Bosnian church. This ended with the dispatch of Cardinal Jacob of Praeneste as papal legate to Bosnia and the removal, in October 1233, of the bishop of Bosnia, who was accused of incompetence and a lack of knowledge of Catholic practices.[145] The pope appointed in his stead John of Wildeshausen who, shortly after his appearance as papal delegate in the preparatory stages of the Stedinger crusade, had become the provincial prior of the Hungarian Dominicans.[146] But with the Bosnians seemingly resentful of the appointment of a foreigner as their spiritual leader, John's attempts to reform the Bosnian church were frustrated. In consequence, the pope authorized a crusade against them in 1234 under the leadership of Duke Coloman of Croatia, king of Ruthenia and brother of King Andrew II of Hungary, which was to be preached by John himself and the new papal legate, Bartholomew of Trisulto.[147] Later, when John had resigned his bishopric in order to

---

[144] J.V.A. Fine, *The Bosnian Church: A New Interpretation. A Study of the Bosnian Church and its Place in State and Society from the 13th to the 15th Centuries* (East European Monographs 10; London and New York 1975), 137–55. [145] Fine, *Bosnian Church*, 137–8.

[146] Pfeiffer, *Die Ungarische Dominikanerprovinz*, 63–4.

[147] *ES*, i, no. 574 (= *Gre.IX R*, no. 1798); Pfeiffer, *Die Ungarische Dominikanerprovinz*, 65–7.

resume his career within the Dominican order, his role was taken over by the new bishop of Bosnia, Ponsa, himself a former Dominican friar.[148] Throughout the following four decades the crusade seems to have lingered on, but almost nothing is known about it.[149] When Honorius IV renewed the preaching of the cross against a variety of non-Christians, heretics, and schismatics in Hungary and the neighbouring areas in the late 1280s, he generally addressed the secular and regular clergy, including the friars.[150] But when his successor Nicholas IV re-confirmed the commission a year later, he expressly ordered the mendicants to assist the archbishop of Gran in preaching the cross only if asked to do so.[151] It seems that the minor role played by the friars in the organization of these crusades was due to the fact that the Hungarian kings had taken on the leadership of the wars against heretics and non-Christians in conjunction with the Hungarian nobility and church hierarchy. Since these crusades were always connected with the conquest of new lands, strict control over their organization was important in order to determine the distribution of such lands. As in the Baltic, where the Teutonic Knights were profiting from the well controlled and exclusive propaganda by the Dominican crusade preachers, the Hungarian kings probably considered the local episcopate as their natural allies in controlling the crusade and its resources.

Out of Hungary, also, came the last call for crusading support during Gregory IX's pontificate. At the beginning of the year 1241, it seemed almost certain that the Mongols, after having attacked Hungary, would soon also threaten Germany. Because of this, a number of German nobles, led by King Conrad IV, were planning a military campaign against them in the spring of 1241.[152] There was a need for organizing support quickly and, in the absence of positive action from the Curia, the German bishops decided to commission the preaching of the cross in support of Conrad's efforts by themselves.[153] They must have been aware that the authorization of a crusade was a strictly reserved papal

---

[148] Fine, *Bosnian Church*, 139–43, 147–8; Pfeiffer, *Die Ungarische Dominikanerprovinz*, 71–4.
[149] Fine, *Bosnian Church*, 145–53.
[150] *Vetera Monumenta Historica*, i, nos. 573–5 (= *Hon.IV R*, no. 761).
[151] *Nic.IV R*, no. 197; Fine, *Bosnian Church*, 153–5.
[152] The most recent account is: P. Jackson, 'The Crusade Against the Mongols (1241)', *Journal of Ecclesiastical History*, xlii (1991), 1–18.
[153] 'Annales Wormatienses', 46–7; Matthew Paris, *Chronica Majora*, iv, 109–11. Jackson, 'Crusade', 6.

privilege, but the Mongols progressed at such a staggering pace that the bishops decided to issue their own crusading bull without waiting for a reaction from the pope.[154] Some German bishops and friars of both mendicant orders were said to have been preaching the cross as early as March 1241, on the instigation of Landgrave Henry of Thuringia.[155] In April 1241 Bishop Henry I of Constance ordered Anselm, the head of the Franciscan Custody of Lake Constance, and his friars to preach the cross against the Mongols in accordance with the bull issued by the archbishop of Mainz.[156] A similar commission by Bishop Siboto of Augsburg to the Franciscans of his diocese survived from June 1241.[157] It is likely, therefore, that the German friars were already preaching the cross when, in June of the same year, Gregory IX finally sent a papal crusading bull to all mendicant friars in Germany, the Dominicans at Vienna, and the Cistercian abbot of Heiligenkreuz in Austria.[158] Some Polish and Hungarian Dominicans and Franciscans were also reported to have preached the cross in Germany, having fled their own territories after the first Mongol attacks.[159] It seems that the news of the ravaging and ferocious conquest of Hungary and the fear of the Mongols crossing the Danube created such a panic in Germany that within weeks crusade preachers easily recruited scores of crusaders and collected huge amounts of money.[160] But the Mongols did not cross the Danube after all and Conrad's crusade never took place.

From around 1230 Pope Gregory IX thus used the mendicant friars, both individually as specially commissioned preachers or envoys and collectively as a pool of propagandists, to broadcast the propaganda for practically all crusades. Proven diplomatic and preaching skills, reliability of service and familiarity with the

---

[154] *Historia Diplomatica*, v, 1209–13. The instructions were more detailed than any extant papal crusading bull, specifying for example the payment of vow redemptions in local currency and exact liturgical precepts. But on the whole the bull conformed with papal practice, relying on the *Corpus juris canonici* concerning the absolution of excommunicates. See also Jackson, 'Crusade', 16–17.

[155] Matthew Paris, *Chronica Majora*, iv, 110.

[156] *Historia Diplomatica*, v, 1209–13; for the dating, see page 1213, n. 1; see also *Das Archiv der Oberdeutschen Minoritenprovinz im Staatsarchiv Luzern*, ed. A. Gössi (Luzerner Historische Veröffentlichungen, Archivinventare 2; Lucerne and Munich 1979), 83. Jackson, 'Crusade', 6, n. 18.

[157] *Die Goldene Chronik von Hohenschwangau*, ed. J. (Frhr. von) Hormayr-Hortenburg (Munich 1842), ii, 71 (no. 12).   [158] *ES*, i, no. 822 (= *Gre.IX R*, nos. 6072–5).

[159] 'Annales S. Pantaleonis', 535.

[160] 'Annales Wormatienses', 47; 'Annales S. Pantaleonis', 535–6; Matthew Paris, *Chronica Majora*, vi, 81–4.

recruitment grounds were among the principal criteria for the appointment of individual friars as crusade preachers. This followed a well-known tradition from earlier times and was continued throughout the remainder of the thirteenth century. But whereas before 1230 preachers directly appointed by the papacy were the mainstay of crusading propaganda, their function now changed. They were usually dispatched to areas where the preaching of the cross proved difficult or where special recruitment efforts were thought to be necessary. As the principal preaching force, Gregory IX now employed the mendicant orders *en bloc* alongside the local church hierarchy. As a rule, the friars were better trained than local clerics and they were not tied down by matters of church government. This point was made explicit by the papal legate in France, Cardinal Simon of Sta. Cecilia, in December 1267, when he ordered the Franciscan guardian of Anduze to support the recruitment efforts for the Holy Land crusade in the Archdiocese of Narbonne. He explained that the secular clergy had many other things to attend to and did not have sufficient time to broadcast the crusade themselves.[161] But although the mendicant orders provided the papacy with an unprecedented number of propagandists, the crusading resources themselves, in terms of both men and money, were limited and there was a very real danger of overexploiting these resources unless crusading propaganda was planned carefully. During the mid and later 1230s, as later on in the 1240s and 1260s, the papal propaganda machinery was coming under pressure because several crusades were being preached at the same time. In certain areas, the preaching of two parallel crusades could at times result either in the channelling of crusading aid to one crusade exclusively or in creating a situation where neither crusade attracted adequate support because the resources were divided. Gregory IX was well aware of this and tried to deal with these problems by strictly limiting recruitment for specific crusades to certain areas and by distributing the available preaching force carefully. In implementing these strategies the mendicant orders played a decisive role because they provided a pool of proficient preachers all over Europe and because their status as exempt orders put them under the direct command of the papacy. One may well ask whether Gregory IX could have provided the various crusades which took place during his pontificate with adequate support, had

161 *Layettes du Trésor des Chartes*, A. Teulet *et al.*, 5 vols. (Paris 1863–1909), iv, no. 5339.

it not been for the availability and reliability of the mendicant preaching force.

INNOCENT IV

After Gregory IX's death, Innocent IV continued his predecessor's propaganda strategies for the crusades without major changes. He did well to do so because he, too, had to manage an exceptionally strong demand for crusading aid from all over Europe. The earliest evidence for the preaching in support of King Louis IX's first crusade to the Holy Land dated from February 1245, when Innocent IV ordered the Franciscan general minister, all provincial ministers and guardians to preach the cross on the basis of the papal bull *Terra Sancta*, issued one month earlier.[162] Later in the year, at the First Council of Lyons, the encyclical *Afflicti corde* confirmed the preaching of the cross everywhere in Europe. This would have been passed on to the participants of the council, including the representatives of the mendicant orders.[163] A number of French chronicles indeed confirm that in 1245 the cross was preached and that many clerics and laymen took the cross.[164] Until Louis IX's departure in August 1248 the preaching of the cross was masterminded by the papal legate, Cardinal Eudes of Châteauroux.[165] There is evidence that he reconfirmed the order to preach the cross to the Dominican provincial prior of the Province of Provence, Brother Ponce.[166]. Salimbene reported that Eudes was in close contact with the French mendicants during this time. The Franciscan chronicler himself accompanied an unnamed Franciscan preacher of the cross on his recruitment tour through the Diocese of Autun in Spring 1248.[167]

Evidence from elsewhere in Europe is not as readily available. A year after the initial appeal, in November 1246, Innocent IV told Eudes of Châteauroux to re-commission the preaching of the crusade in England, Scotland, Denmark, Germany and Bra-

---

[162] Delorme, 'Bulle d'Innocent IV pour la croisade', 387–9.
[163] *Conciliorum Oecumenicorum Decreta*, 297–301.
[164] 'E Chronicon Normanniae', *RGHF*, xxiii, 212–22, here 214; 'E Chronicon Sanctae Catharinae de Monte Rothomagi', *RGHF*, xxiii, 397–410, here 400; 'E Mari Historiarum', 114.   [165] Matthew Paris, *Chronica Majora*, iv, 488.
[166] Delorme, 'Bulle d'Innocent IV en faveur de l'empire latin', 307–8. The document as a whole is discussed in more detail below, 101–2.
[167] Salimbene de Adam, 'Cronica', *MGHS*, xxxii, 218, 223.   [168] *Inn.IV R*, no. 2229.

bant.[168] King Henry III of England had not been very enthusiastic about the idea of joining a crusade under the leadership of the French king. Already in 1245 Innocent IV had tried to change Henry's mind but without success. Henry was adamant and excused himself by saying that his realm was under threat from rebels within and enemies outside.[169] In England, the cross was probably not preached successfully until after William Longsword and several other English noblemen had taken the cross.[170]

In Germany the preaching seems to have had especially little impact after the crusade against Frederick II was announced. Gregory IX's project of a crusade against Frederick II, following the emperor's second excommunication in 1239, had come to an end during its preparatory stages when the old pope died in 1241, and in Germany, in particular, plans to raise a crusading army against the threat of a Mongol invasion took precedence over an anti-Hohenstaufen crusade between 1240 and 1242.[171] In 1239, the German friars had been ordered to announce Frederick's excommunication, but there is no evidence to establish to what extent they complied with the papal directives. Gregory IX's death and the ensuing two year period without a pope may have caused uncertainty as to what the papacy's long-term strategy concerning Frederick would be. This uncertainty more than anything else probably made the German friars adopt a position of neutrality between pope and emperor during the early 1240s. Some Austrian Dominicans were even known to have opposed the militant anti-Hohenstaufen diplomacy of the papal legate Albert Behaim, archdeacon of Passau, in 1240.[172]

The new pope, Innocent IV, was in no way less determined than his predecessor to force Frederick II back into line with the Roman Church. After ascending to the papal throne in 1243, Innocent entered diplomatic negotiations with the excommunicate emperor, but he also conducted secret talks with certain nobles in the *Regno* in an attempt to put pressure on Frederick II from within his own power base in the south of Italy.[173] Again, as in 1228–9, it

---

[169] Matthew Paris, *Chronica Majora*, iv, 488–9; Lloyd, *English Society*, 29–30, 210–11.

[170] *Inn.IV R*, nos. 2959–63.

[171] J.R. Strayer, 'The Political Crusades of the Thirteenth Century', *A History of the Crusades*, ii, 343–75, here 350–3.   [172] Freed, *Friars*, 147–50.

[173] C. Rodenberg, *Innocenz IV. und das Königreich Sizilien 1245–1254* (Halle 1892), 41–9. This must be read with: K. Hampe, 'Papst Innocenz IV und die sizilianische Verschwörung von 1246' (Sitzungsberichte der Heidelberger Akademie der Wissenschaften. Phil.-hist. Klasse 8; Heidelberg 1923), *passim*, esp. 11–19.

was the Franciscans who acted as the pope's messengers in the *Regno*. Once more very little is known about the details of the friars' activities, but it seems that the pope had given them powers to grant crusading indulgences to anti-Hohenstaufen rebels.[174] As early as 1243, two Franciscans paid for their services to the pope with their lives when Frederick II had them hanged.[175] By the same token, Frederick's son Conrad punished friars in Germany for delivering money or letters to and from the Curia.[176] Public preaching for a crusade against the emperor was not reinstituted until the First Council of Lyons had formally deposed Frederick II in July 1245. Only after the election of Landgrave Henry Raspe of Thuringia as king of the Romans at the end of May 1246 was there a realistic chance of organizing a crusading army against Frederick II and his supporters in Germany.[177] At the end of June 1246 the archbishop of Mainz and his suffragans were issued with orders to preach the cross in order to recruit an army for Henry Raspe.[178] The commission included powers to appoint crusade preachers from among the secular and the regular clergy. Because there seemed to be little response to Louis IX's project in many other parts of the Empire anyway, the papal legate Cardinal Eudes of Châteauroux was advised, in July 1246, to order preachers of the cross to the Holy Land in certain parts of Germany including the mendicant friars to preach against the emperor instead.[179] In some parts, however, the parallel preaching campaign for Louis IX's Holy Land crusade made it necessary to demarcate areas of recruitment. Frisia, in particular, was an area where recruitment of crusaders was contested between the two crusades. Despite the well-known enthusiasm of the Frisians for the crusade to the Holy Land, there must have been many crusaders who would have been prepared to join either crusade and might quite naturally have chosen the cheaper option, given the fact that both crusades offered the same spiritual rewards. Nevertheless, the pope told the bishops in Frisia to continue recruiting for Louis IX's crusade after the preaching against Frederick II had been authorized, adding that crusaders who had already taken the cross to the Holy Land were, if

---

[174] Matthew Paris, *Chronica Majora*, iv, 573.

[175] Matthew Paris, *Chronica Majora*, iv, 256

[176] Matthew Paris, *Chronica Majora*, iv, 278.

[177] O. Hintze, *Das Königtum Wilhelms von Holland* (Historische Studien 15; Leipzig 1885), 138–9.   [178] *ES*, ii, no. 199 (= *Inn.IV R*, no. 1993).

[179] *Inn.IV R*, no. 2935.

necessary, to be compelled by ecclesiastical censures to accompany the French army to Palestine.[180]

The sudden death of Henry Raspe in mid February 1247 was a blow to the papal party in Germany. As a result, Innocent IV dispatched new papal legates to Germany, Denmark and Poland, northern Italy, and Spain in March 1247, whose task seems to have been to enlist crusaders by diplomatic negotiation rather than public preaching; according to Matthew Paris, the mendicant friars supported the legates actively in this.[181] All through the summer of 1247, however, the confusion over the future of the papal party in Germany seems to have made the task of recruiting crusaders difficult. It was not until the beginning of October that William of Holland was elected the new anti-king. William's power base was in the Low Countries and his political influence extended into north-western Germany and the imperial lands west of the Rhine. William's main supporters in this area were the counts of Guelders and Brabant and the bishop of Louvain.[182] It appears that William of Holland himself determined the recruitment strategy to a great extent. He asked for Archbishop Albert of Prussia and Livonia, a native of Cologne, to be sent to Frisia to preach the cross and to be allowed to commute the vows of Palestine crusaders.[183] William of Holland specifically requested the commutation of five Holy Land crusaders in the Kingdom of France and of fifteen in the Empire.[184] Innocent IV agreed to his request, despite the fact that he had shortly before forbidden the commutation of crusading vows already made in favour of the Holy Land in the Dioceses of Louvain, Metz, Verdun, Cambrai, and Toul, where the crusade against Frederick was now preached.[185] In fact, it seems that both in Frisia and in the northern borderlands between the French kingdom and the Empire, the response was overwhelmingly in favour of William's crusade.[186] In spring 1248, Innocent IV also appointed the absentee bishop of Courland, the former Franciscan Henry of Lützelburg, to preach the cross.[187] It appears that the choice of a bishop of local origin whose episcopal authority was based on a remote bishopric was deliberate, as in the case of Archbishop Albert. For advocating a crusade which was embed-

---

[180] *Inn.IV R*, no. 2054
[181] *ES*, ii, nos. 292, 309, 313 (= *Inn.IV R*, nos. 2964, 2999, 3002); Matthew Paris, *Chronica Majora*, iv, 612–13.   [182] Matthew Paris, *Chronica Majora*, iv, 653–4.
[183] *ES*, ii, no. 453 (= *Inn.IV R*, no. 4070); see also no. 462 (= *Inn.IV R*, no. 4068).
[184] *Inn.IV R*, no. 4060.   [185] *Inn.IV R*, no. 3384.   [186] Menko, 'Chronicon', 540.
[187] *ES*, ii, no. 504 (= *Inn.IV R*, no. 3646). For Henry, see also below, 90.

ded in a local political conflict, knowledge of the area combined with the absence of direct personal involvement would have been an advantage. Still, the major propaganda effort for William of Holland's army before and during the siege of Aachen came from the friars. There is ample evidence from chronicles that it was they who recruited most of the crusaders.[188]

In order to rescue at least some of the Frisian crusaders for Louis IX's crusade, Innocent IV appointed a Franciscan, Brother Willibrand, to preach the cross there. Menko reported that Willibrand had originally been commissioned in 1246 by Archbishop Siegfried of Mainz to preach the cross against Frederick II. Willibrand had apparently been extraordinarily successful, although his Franciscan superiors – Menko did not specify who they were – accused him of disobedience and tried to stop him from preaching the cross. The appointment by the archbishop of Mainz might have been viewed as unlicensed outside interference with the order. Papal privileges permitted Franciscan ministers (and Dominican priors) to reject such appointments. The popes repeatedly issued privileges which allowed the mendicant orders to refuse any request for service by any members of the church hierarchy unless they had obtained a papal commission which named a friar, or friars, specifically.[189] Mendicant friars thus could normally not be forced by their bishops to preach the cross on their behalf. But in this case Willibrand himself seems to have contradicted his superiors. He decided to visit the papal Curia at Lyons in order to have his commission as crusade preacher confirmed by the pope personally. On the instigation of the French king, who had heard about Willibrand's earlier success, Innocent IV, however, ordered the Franciscan friar to abandon the preaching for the anti-Hohenstaufen crusade and start recruiting for Louis IX's campaign to the Holy Land. In order to avoid renewed friction between the Franciscan friar and his superiors, the pope dispatched Archbishop Albert of Prussia and Livonia, who was leading the recruitment of

---

[188] 'Annales Sancti Pantaleonis Coloniensis', *MGHS*, xxii, 529–47, here 543; Matthew Paris, *Chronica Majora*, iv, 653–4, v, 17.

[189] The indult was issued to the Dominicans as early as 1225. See H.C. Scheeben, 'De Bullario quodam Ordinis Praedicatorum saeculi XIII', *AFP*, vi (1936), 217–66, no. 93. For subsequent issues, see nos. 94–101, 103–5; D. Planzer, 'De Codice Ruthenensi miscellaneo in Tabulario Ordinis asservato', *AFP*, v (1935), 5–123, nos. 84–94, 96, 97. The first surviving copies for the Franciscans date from 1235 (*BF*, i (Gre.IX) no. 190), 1240 (*ibid.*, no. 309) and 1245 (Delorme, no. I, 6)

crusaders against Frederick II, to confirm Willibrand's mission.[190]

It seems that this time Willibrand's appointment was respected by his superiors, despite the fact that they could have replaced him with some other friar. Both mendicant orders, in fact, had recently been granted a papal privilege which allowed them to substitute different friars for those appointed by the papacy as crusade preachers or inquisitors.[191] But there is no evidence as to whether, or how frequently, the privilege was ever enforced; it certainly was not in Willibrand's case. Just before Willibrand's return from Lyons, the Franciscans in Frisia were involved in a major scandal. Another Franciscan named Renold, who had also been appointed to preach the cross by the pope, apparently died on his way to Frisia, whereupon a fellow friar used the powers conferred on Renold by the pope to collect money donations and testamentary bequests in aid of the crusade with the intention of enriching himself personally. This continued for some time before people became aware of the fraud and the Franciscan superiors captured and imprisoned him. Against the background of this incident, it must have seemed wise not to risk another scandal in the case of Willibrand. Although Willibrand repeated his earlier success when he returned to Frisia to preach the cross to the Holy Land, Innocent IV's strategy ultimately failed. The time to prepare for the general passage of 1248 seems to have been too short and many Frisian crusaders commuted their vows when the campaign in Germany got under way and served in the army that besieged Aachen between April and October 1248.[192] In fact, Innocent IV had already changed his mind immediately after the anti-Hohenstaufen campaign had begun and had allowed his legate in Germany, Cardinal Peter of St George, to commute the vows of Frisian Holy Land crusaders.[193] And still, the pope did not neglect the Holy Land crusade all together and urged the Dominican prior of the Province of *Teutonia*, Brother Hydus, as late as June 1248 to

---

[190] Menko, 'Chronicon', *MGHS*, xxiii, 523–61, here 539–40. Two undated papal bulls concerning Willibrand's preaching of the Holy Land crusade have survived. See P. Sambin, *Problemi Politici Attraverso Lettere Inediti di Innocenzo IV* (Istituto Veneto Scienze Lettere ed Arti. Memorie classe di Scienze Morali e Letterare 31, fasc. 3; Venice 1955), nos. 52, 53.

[191] *BP*, i (Inn.IV) no. 46 (= *Inn.IV R*, nos. 449, 452) [1244] for the Dominicans. *BF*, i (Inn.IV) no. 123 (= *Inn.IV R*, no. 1963) [1246] for the Franciscans; see also Planzer, 'Codice', nos. 98, 98a; Scheeben, 'Bullario', nos. 106, 107.

[192] Menko, 'Chronicon', 540.   [193] *Inn.IV R*, no. 3779.

compel crusaders from Frisia, Holland and Zeeland to join the general passage to the Levant in 1249.[194]

Recruitment for Louis IX's crusade was equally difficult in Languedoc. Louis IX had gone to considerable lengths to make Count Raymond VII of Toulouse and other noblemen from south-western France join the crusade as a sign of peace, penitence and reconciliation after the rebellion of 1242–4.[195] But enthusiasm for the king's crusade was guarded in these parts and only small contingents of crusaders were said to have come from there. Feelings towards the French crown were most certainly still marred by the memory of the Albigensian crusade and the king's recent military campaign against the rebels in Languedoc.[196] In order to facilitate recruitment, Innocent IV appointed the Franciscan Hugh of Turenne as crusade preacher in the lands of Raymond of Toulouse in December 1247. Hugh was to call upon fellow Franciscans as his helpers, with whom he was also to collect money for Raymond's crusade.[197] Like the majority of personally appointed mendicant crusade preachers, he, too, was of local, southern French origin. But there is little more information about the rest of his life, save that, later, in 1270, he was guardian of the Franciscan convent at Limoges.[198] In the late 1260s another Franciscan crusade preacher was given a similar role to that of Hugh of Turenne during the preparation for Alfonse of Poitiers's crusade in the late 1260s.[199] The papacy's choice of Franciscans as crusade preachers in south-western France may have been determined by the fact that their order was relatively well regarded, even by former heretics. In his deposition in front of the inquisition, the alleged heretic Peter Garcia pointed out that he considered the Franciscans the only acceptable order of the Church, even though they were preaching the cross. He also quoted an example of a certain unnamed friar who had given the cross to as many as 700 people at Auvillars.[200] It is not known whether the

---

[194] *BP*, i (Inn.IV R) no. 199 (= *Inn.IV R*, no. 3967).

[195] C. de Vic and J. Vaisette, *Histoire Générale de Languedoc*, 16 vols (Toulouse 1872–1905), vi, 786–9; W.C. Jordan, *Louis IX and the Challenge of the Crusade. A Study in Rulership* (Princeton 1979), 16–22, 67–8.

[196] J. Richard, *Saint Louis. Roi d'une France féodale, soutien de la Terre Sainte* (Paris 1983), 96–108.

[197] *BF*, i (Inn.IV) no. 275 (= *Inn.IV R*, no. 3869); *APP*, i, nos. 616, 617, 623, 624, 627; Delorme, no. III, 3; Delorme, 'Trois Bulles', 291–3

[198] Delorme, 'Trois Bulles', 291; see also below, 143–5.   [199] See below, 81.

[200] W.F. Wakefield, *Heresy, Crusade and Inquisition* (London 1974), 246

Franciscan gave the cross to repentant heretics or to orthodox Christians or to both. Neither is it certain whether these crusaders were actually intending to go on crusade or redeemed their vows for money. But the example illustrates the persuasive power of a Franciscan preacher of the cross in an area where recruitment was potentially difficult.

There is evidence that the inquisition provided quite a few crusaders in the 1230s and 1240s during a time when both Dominican and Franciscan friars were involved in the inquisition in Languedoc.[201] In southern France they initially recruited crusaders to the Holy Land.[202] Generally these crusaders were not allowed to join crusading armies lest they corrupted the other participants.[203] But in the early 1240s the inquisition in southern France was primarily recruiting crusaders to the Latin Empire. The surviving penitential register of Peter of Seila, the Dominican inquisitor at Toulouse, for the period between May 1241 and April 1242, reveals that many heretics chose, or were compelled, to do penance as crusaders in the Latin Empire.[204] Within less than one year, Peter recruited ninety-five crusaders, all of them male, who were told to spend between one and eight years in the East.[205] Nothing is known of the circumstances in which these penances were imposed; nor are there any other inquisitorial records to establish how many former heretics became crusaders elsewhere or at other times.[206] But if Peter of Seila's activities are in any way representative, it is obvious that the inquisition provided a good number of crusaders. Since no other crusade appeared as penance in Peter of Seila's register, it seems likely that the pope had given orders that repentant heretics be sent to crusade to the Latin Empire rather than anywhere else. Not all heretics would have been people used to, or suitable for, the battlefield – the Seila register for

---

201 Wakefield, *Heresy*, 168–91; L. Kolmer, *Ad Capiendas Vulpes: Die Ketzerbekämpfung in Südfrankreich in der ersten Hälfte des 13. Jahrhunderts und die Ausbildung des Inquisitionsverfahrens* (Pariser Historische Studien 19; Bonn 1982), 127–45

202 *Gre.IX R*, nos. 3188, 3201, 4295, 4775, 4776; *BF*, ii (Urb.IV) no. 108. There is one piece of evidence which shows that the Dominican inquisition in Germany also sentenced repentent heretics to crusading to the Holy Land around this time, see *Gre.IX R*, no. 2133.   203 *Gre.IX R*, nos. 4145, 4146.

204 P. Segl, '"Stabit Constantinopoli". Inquisition und päpstliche Orientpolitik unter Gregor IX.', *Deutsches Archiv für die Erforschung des Mittelalters*, xxxii (1976), 209–20; Kolmer, *Ad Capiendas Vulpes*, 150–62.

205 Segl, '"Stabit Constantinopoli"', 212–14.

206 In the mid 1230s, the Dominican inquisitor in northern France, Robert 'le Bougre', was reported to have sentenced heretics to exile rather than crusading in Constantinople. See Philippe Mouskes, *Chronique*, ii, 612.

instance mentioned a *ioculator*. It would, however, have been possible to allocate them as individuals or in small groups to do garrison duty. This would have met the needs of the defence of the Latin Empire in the 1240s, when no major crusading armies were in the field. It also would have helped to avert fears that the presence of former heretics might subvert Catholic Christians.

The task of recruiting crusaders from amongst repentant heretics for Louis IX's first crusade seems to have been particularly difficult. In 1247 and 1248 the French king himself tried to oblige former heretics in Narbonne to fulfil vows they had taken long ago by going on crusade in 1246; but most of them chose exile instead of crusading.[207] At the same time, the archbishop of Auch was ordered by Innocent IV to make repentant heretics in Count Raymond of Toulouse's lands take the cross to the Holy Land; the same directive has survived for the bishop of Albi concerning Philip of Montfort's territories.[208] There is certainly no evidence that heretics did join Louis's army to the same extent as they went crusading to the Holy Land and the Latin Empire in the 1230s and early 1240s.[209] Some heretics' aversion to crusading was, however, not specifically with regard to Louis's crusade. One forceful statement was recorded in Peter Garcia's deposition in the court of the inquisition at Toulouse in 1247, where he denounced any type of crusade, against Muslims, against the emperor or against heretics.[210]

Propaganda by preaching did not stop with the departure of Louis's royal army in August 1248. Only part of the army sailed with the king at this early stage, with smaller contingents following later in the year and throughout 1249 and 1250. The last major force under Alfonse of Poitiers probably left France in summer 1249 and arrived in Egypt in October 1249.[211] On the eve of its departure, in February 1249, the pope issued a new bull, *Planxit hactenus non*.[212] The bull was sent to the archbishops of Rheims, Bourges, Sens, Rouen and Narbonne and to the Franciscans and

[207] R. Emery, *Heresy and Inquisition in Narbonne* (Studies in History, Economics and Public Law 480; New York 1941), 88.   [208] *Inn.IV R*, nos. 3508, 3677, 3866–8.

[209] The former alleged heretic Oliver of Termes, however, went on crusade in 1250 with four knights and twenty arbalesters. See B.Z. Kedar, 'The Passenger List of a Crusader Ship, 1250: towards the History of the Popular Element of the Seventh Crusade', *Studi Medievali (third series)*, xiii (1972), 267–79, here 276–8.

[210] Wakefield, *Heresy*, 246.

[211] J.R. Strayer, 'The Crusades of Louis IX', *A History of the Crusades*, ii, 487–518, here 493–7.

[212] *Regestum Visitationum Archiepiscopi Rothomagensis*, ed. T. Bonin (Rouen 1852), 737–40.

Dominicans of the Provinces of *Francia* (northern France). The pope forbade any other crusade to be preached at the same time, expecting crusaders to join the general passage of March 1250.[213] In May the crusade preachers' powers were further enhanced by allowing them to grant to crusaders and those who gave money to the French king the right to visit churches and receive the sacraments in places under interdict.[214] Two northern French bishops, those of Evreux and Senlis, were sent to the County of Toulouse and the March of Provence to force crusaders who had not yet fulfilled their obligations to join the next general passage or to redeem their vows.[215] The same directive was given to the German friars regarding crusaders from Frisia and Norway.[216]

The mendicants were also involved in various attempts to supply Louis IX with further crusading aid during his stay in the Holy Land, in the hope that the king of France's crusade could be turned into a success. A renewed propaganda effort was made in England after Henry III had taken the cross in March 1250.[217] A new crusading bull, *Filiorum dextera pia*, was sent to the Dominicans and Franciscans of the English provinces, the archbishops of York and Canterbury and to the bishops of Chichester, St David's and Exeter.[218] In June the mandate also reached the secular clergy and the mendicants in Ireland, accompanied by a letter from King Henry.[219] In France, *Planxit hactenus non* was used once again in 1253, when Alfonse of Poitiers was preparing to go back to the Holy Land to assist his brother. It was sent to the friars in the Provinces of *Francia*, and this time the pope demanded that the cross be preached in the Kingdoms of France and Navarre, in Brittany, Burgundy, and in the south-western French territories which were now under the overlordship of Alfonse of Poitiers.[220] A papal letter to the bishop of Avignon from the previous year suggests that the secular clergy was also involved in the preaching of the cross at the time.[221] But even though Alfonse of Poitiers did not return to the Holy Land, the propaganda efforts continued for

[213] *Regestum Visitationum*, 740–1.   [214] *Layettes*, iii, no. 3869 (= *APP*, i, no. 667).
[215] *Inn.IV R*, no. 4926.
[216] *ES*, iii, no. 20 (= *Inn.IV R*, no. 4927).   [217] Lloyd, *English Society*, 58–9, 211–13.
[218] *Foedera, Conventiones, Litterae et Cuiuscunque Generis Acta Publica inter Reges Angliae et Alios Quosvis Imperatores, Reges, Pontifices, Principes vel Communitates*, ed. T. Rymer *et al.*, 4 vols. (London 1816–69), i, 272–3
[219] *Calendar of Documents Relating to Ireland preserved in Her Majesty's Public Record Office London*, ed. H.S. Sweetman and G.F. Handcock, 5 vols. (London 1875–1886), i, no. 3067
[220] *Inn.IV R*, no. 6469 (= *APP*, i, no. 714).   [221] *Inn.IV R*, no. 5556.

some time and in 1255 the new Pope Alexander IV reconfirmed the preaching of the cross with the French mendicants.[222] It is, however, doubtful whether these latter propaganda campaigns obtained much response, given the fact that the preaching of the cross had depleted much of France of her crusading resources for the support of the Holy Land and the Latin Empire during the previous ten years.

Whereas the propaganda for the Holy Land crusade in the late 1240s and early 1250s was concentrated on France and the British Isles, Germany was expected mainly to supply the crusades against the Hohenstaufen and in the Baltic. But the success of the preaching in north-west Germany and in the borderlands with France before the siege of Aachen was not repeated elsewhere in Germany. Until William's coronation in 1249 and Frederick's death the following year, broadcasting anti-Hohenstaufen propaganda, especially in southern Germany, was a risky and dangerous business. Several friars were known to have been harassed or even killed in the process of promoting the papal cause and some convents were burnt down.[223] Despite the fact that the Dominican general chapters in 1246, 1247, and 1248 ordered all friars to support the cause of the church actively,[224] one Swabian Dominican, Brother Arnold, openly defied his superiors by writing a tract, *De correctione ecclesiae epistola*, in which he praised Frederick II and condemned the pope as Anti-Christ.[225] But it seemed that, generally speaking, the friars tried to carry out the papal assignments as best as they could, in strict accordance with their orders' precept of obedience towards the Roman Church.[226] The Franciscan chronicler Jordan of Giano made it clear that he believed that the friars of his order were fighting and suffering for the right cause.[227] Their zeal for the Church in another context of the same crusade was recorded by Matthew Paris, who described how Frederick II ordered that all Franciscan friars and other *religiosi* in Cardinal Rainer of St Mary's army, who went between the lines to hear the confessions and administer indulgences to the dying, should be killed.[228] Despite

[222] *APP*, i, no. 786.   [223] Freed, *Friars*, 159–60.

[224] 'Acta Capitulorum Generalium Ordinis Praedicatorum', *MOPH*, iii, 37, 39, 42.

[225] *Fratris Arnoldi Ordinis Praedicatorum de correctione ecclesiae epistola et anonymi de Innocentio IV. P.M. Antichristo libellus*, ed. E. Winkelmann (Berlin 1865), 9–19.

[226] Matthew Paris, *Chronica Majora*, v, 259–61.

[227] Jordan of Giano, *Chronica*, ed. H. Boehmer (Collection d'études et de documents sur l'histoire religieuse et littéraire du moyen âge 6; Paris 1908), 60–1.

[228] Matthew Paris, *Chronica Majora*, v, 66.

the difficult conditions, the Franciscans seem to have been successful in broadcasting anti-Hohenstaufen propaganda.

Three months after William of Holland's coronation, in January 1249, Innocent IV exhorted the friars in Germany, Holland, and Flanders, together with Bishop Henry of Courland and the abbot of Egmont, to continue preaching the cross as before, despite the attacks on mendicant crusade propagandists.[229] Later the pope even threatened the German Franciscans with excommunication if they refused to carry out his orders.[230] But Innocent IV soon realized that public preaching of the cross was not profitable in these circumstances. Shortly before Frederick II's death, he changed his strategy and mainly relied on individual propagandists to promote the crusade by diplomatic missions to potential supporters of the anti-Hohenstaufen cause. Prominent among them were three mendicant friars, the Dominicans William Maaseik and Henry of Montfort and the Franciscan John of Diest.[231] John of Diest and William Maaseik were both chaplains of William of Holland.[232] In addition, John may have been a relative of the Brabantine nobleman Arnold of Diest, who was a follower of William of Holland.[233] William of Maaseik, too, seems to have moved in the same social circle, since he appeared as one of the testamentary executors of Godfrey of Bredal, Arnold of Diest's uncle.[234] John of Diest first appeared in papal service as early as March 1249, when he was given powers by the pope to excommunicate anyone who refused to do homage to the new King William.[235] A first commission to William of Maaseik to preach the cross against Conrad in the Kingdom of Germany has survived from November 1250.[236] After the sudden death of Frederick II, this commission was re-confirmed to both William and John of Diest in February 1251, with powers to appoint other preachers as assistants.[237] The indulgence and privileges were the same as for the Holy Land crusade, the attendance of sermons was rewarded with forty days' indulgence, and the preachers were given the right

---

[229] *ES*, ii, no. 630 (= *Inn.IV R*, no. 4265).   [230] *ES*, ii, no. 720 (= *Inn.IV R*, no. 4509).
[231] A fourth Dominican friar, Leo of *Broma*, was involved in crusade propaganda in Germany at the time. But too little is known about his activities to assess the exact role he played. See *BP*, i (Inn.IV) no. 214.
[232] *BP*, i (Inn.IV) no. 213; *ES*, iii, no. 54 (= *Inn.IV R*, nos. 5031, 5032); see also W. Lampen, 'Joannes van Diest, O.F.M., Hofkapelaan van Graaf Willem II en eerste Nederlandsche Bisschop uit de Minderbroedersorde', *Bijdragen voor de Geschiedenis van het Bisdom van Haarlem*, xliv (1926), 299–312.   [233] Freed, *Friars*, 133, n. 94.
[234] *Inn.IV R*, no. 4549.   [235] *ES*, i, no. 669 (= *Inn.IV R*, no. 4397).
[236] *BP*, i (Inn.IV) no. 213.   [237] *ES*, iii, no. 48 (= *Inn.IV R*, no. 5036).

to impose ecclesiastical censures against those who impeded the preaching. John of Diest may already have been given similar orders at some earlier stage and seems to have used these powers somewhat lavishly. He was reminded to adhere strictly to the papal orders concerning the procedures against supporters of the Hohenstaufen. At the same time, however, his commission to preach the cross was extended to the German-speaking parts of Flanders.[238] Little is known about how these papal commissions were executed, but it seems that, at least in William of Holland's homeland along the border between the French kingdom and the Empire, William and John were initially supported by other preachers. Matthew Paris confirmed that the cross was being widely preached in these areas in 1251.[239]

In other parts of the Empire crusading propaganda appears to have become more and more difficult. It seems that the recruitment of crusaders was now mainly done by diplomatic negotiation rather than by any form of public preaching. In early 1253 Innocent IV addressed an urgent appeal to the two royal chaplains, ordering them not to relent in their efforts and to seek the assistance of other reliable preachers of the cross from among the secular and regular clergy.[240] John of Diest had meanwhile been appointed bishop of Sambia in Courland and was later transferred to the see of Lübeck. Despite this John was still operating as a crusade propagandist for William of Holland and was repeatedly issued with new papal commissions to conform with his new positions.[241] In order to facilitate the negotiations with individual nobles, additional powers were given to John of Diest and other crusade preachers appointed by him. They now also had the right to allow secular lords who were usurping clerical tenths to keep them during their life time and to absolve them for the sins involved in this practice if they took the cross.[242] In addition, they were granted powers to allow church burials for those who had died in tournaments if financial subsidies were paid to William of Holland, presumably by the family of the dead persons.[243] On special papal orders, John also granted dispensations from uncanonical marriage to several

---

[238] *ES*, iii, no. 54 (= *Inn.IV R*, nos. 5031, 5032).
[239] Matthew Paris, *Chronica Majora*, v, 260–1.
[240] *ES*, iii, nos. 187, 188 (= *Inn.IV R*, nos. 6304, 6305, 6322).
[241] *ES*, iii, nos. 259, 274 (= *Inn.IV R*, nos. 7312, 7428). John, in fact, never went to Courland and did not take up his new office at Lübeck until after William of Holland's death in 1256. See Thomson, *Friars*, 52–7.
[242] *ES*, iii, no. 265 (= *Inn.IV R*, no. 7329)   [243] *ES*, iii, no. 260 (= *Inn.IV R*, no. 7457).

German noble couples, a practice which during this time was widely used by Innocent IV to attract and reward followers of William of Holland.[244]

Much of the papal propaganda at the beginning of the 1250s was directed at the southern German nobility. Judging from the geographical distribution of the marriage dispensations granted by John of Diest in 1253 and 1254, he operated mainly in south-western Germany. As to William of Maaseik's whereabouts and activities the sources yield no information. To south-eastern Germany Innocent IV sent another prominent friar with similar assignments, the Dominican Henry, who was a papal penitentiary and came from the family of the Swabian counts of Montfort.[245] In the early months of 1251, Henry served as a member of two papal missions to the dukes of Saxony and Bavaria in order to win them over to the side of William of Holland. Together with James Pontaléon, then papal chaplain and archdeacon of Liège (the later Pope Urban IV), Henry was sent to Duke Otto II of Bavaria and to other noblemen in south-eastern Germany. If their mission proved successful, they were to organize the public preaching of the cross in those parts of Germany with the help of other secular and regular clergy, especially the Dominicans.[246] But it seems that Henry of Montfort and James Pontaléon were not very successful. Duke Otto II was relentless, even after another appeal by the famous Franciscan preacher Berthold of Regensburg shortly before Otto's death in November 1253.[247] Because of this, Henry and James were re-directed to preach the cross in Swabia, from where Count Ulrich of Würtemberg had signalled his willingness to the pope to support William of Holland.[248] What their new mission achieved is not known in detail, but together with John of Diest's activities in 1253–4, it may very well have contributed to the eventual success in winning over much of south-western Germany to the anti-Hohenstaufen party.[249] Like John of Diest, Henry of Montfort was given a bishopric as a reward for his services to the papacy. In

[244] H. Kroppmann, *Ehedispensübung und Stauferkampf unter Innozenz IV. Ein Beitrag zur Geschichte des päpstlichen Ehedispensrechtes* (Abhandlungen zur mittleren und neueren Geschichte 79; Berlin 1937), 46–88 *passim*. This must be read in connection with F. Baethgen's review in: *Zeitschrift der Savigny Stiftung für Rechtsgeschichte*, lix (*Kanonische Abteilung*, xxviii) (1939), 511–14.   [245] Freed, *Friars*, 154, 226.

[246] *ES*, iii, nos. 59, 69, 78 (= *Inn.IV R*, nos. 5291–3, 5302, 5316).

[247] Hermann of Altaich, 'Annales', *MGHS*, xvii, 381–416, here 396.

[248] *ES*, iii, no. 101 (= *Inn.IV R*, no. 5335).

[249] Hintze, *Königtum*, 80–4; Freed, *Friars*, 154.

1252 he became bishop of Chur and no longer had direct involvement in the pope's service.[250] But by then the focus of the papal campaign against the Hohenstaufen was already shifting across the Alps to Italy.

Despite the fact that a good deal of information has survived for the preaching and organization of the Italian crusades,[251] relatively little is known about the mendicants' involvement. In the late 1250s the friars do not seem to have been ordered to preach the cross against Ezzelino da Romano and his followers expressly.[252] But they may have supplied crusading support for the war against Ezzelino as part of their inquisitorial activities. The conflicts between the papacy and the Hohenstaufen and their Italian supporters were primarily responsible for creating conditions in which the fear arose that heresy in Italy might spread at a threatening pace.[253] The Dominicans, and to a lesser extent also the Franciscans, were supporting the armed struggle against heretics in Italy. The friars were actively involved with the anti-heretical confraternities which came into existence in many northern Italian towns in the 1230s and 1240s. Members of these confraternities enjoyed a crusader-like status since they were granted a plenary indulgence if they died fighting heresy.[254] But the recruitment by preaching was not instituted until the 1250s. In 1251 Innocent IV instructed the Dominican inquisitors Peter ('the Martyr') of Verona and Vivian of Bergamo to preach against heresy in Lombardy, especially at Cremona, and warn the heretics of the possibility of a crusade being preached against them.[255] After the assassination of Peter of Verona in April 1252, however, the pope decided to have the cross preached generally and publicly in the fashion of the crusades against the Albigensians and the German and Hungarian heretics. The earliest surviving commission dates from April 1253 and was addressed to the Dominicans of the Province of Rome, who were ordered to preach the cross in the Patrimony of St Peter and in Tuscany.[256] It was not until March

---

[250] Freed, *Friars*, 131.   [251] Housley, *Italian Crusades*, 111–44.

[252] One reference only mentions the Dominicans in Lombardy and France who were ordered by the pope in 1259 to compel crusaders who had taken the cross against Ezzelino da Romano to join the papal army. See *APP*, i, no. 1004.

[253] Housley, 'Politics', 197–206; Housley, *Italian Crusades*, 53–62. For the Franciscans' involvement in the inquisition, see also M. D'Alatri, 'I francescani e l'eresia', *Espansione del Francescanesimo tra Occidente e Oriente nel secolo XIII. Atti del VI Convegno Internazionale, Assisi 12–14 Ottobre 1978*, ed. Società Internazionale di Studi Francescani (Assisi 1979), 241–70.   [254] Housley, 'Politics', 195–9.

[255] *BP*, i (Inn.IV) no. 227 (= *Inn.IV R*, no. 5345).   [256] *BP*, i (Inn.IV) no. 298.

1254 that all Dominican and Franciscan inquisitors and crusade preachers in Italy were instructed to take on the task of preaching the crusade against heretics.[257] Throughout the following summer the commission was confirmed and specified several times.[258] By July, at the latest, all prelates of the church in Italy had been given the same powers,[259] and in the following year, after Innocent IV's sudden death, his commissions were reconfirmed by Pope Alexander IV.[260] The fact that Ezzelino da Romano, who himself was excommunicated as a heretic in 1256, was said to have killed as many as sixty Franciscans in the mid 1250s, may suggest that the friars did in fact actively support the propaganda against him as part of their inquisitorial activities.[261] The sources do not, however, contain sufficient evidence to establish the size or impact of the support which the inquisition was giving to the Italian crusades in the 1250s and thereafter.

Another crusading theatre requiring renewed help during the mid 1240s was the Baltic. After an ill-fated campaign by the Teutonic Knights and by German and Scandinavian forces against the Russians of Novgorod at the beginning of the 1240s, the Teutonic Knights set about consolidating their power in Prussia and Livonia.[262] Prussia, however, turned out to be tough ground for the Teutonic Order in the following decade, mainly because the Polish nobility had started to compete with the Teutonic Knights for the subjugation of non-Christian lands. In 1242 Duke Swantopelk of Gdansk rallied the Prussians and staged the first major revolt against the rule of the Teutonic Order in Prussia, which lasted until 1246.[263] The situation for the Teutonic Order, in fact, became worse because of a major attack by the Samogitians under the Lithuanian leader Mindaugas in 1244–5.[264] As a result, shortly after his election as pope, Innocent IV issued a new bull, *Qui iustis causis*, which was sent to the Dominicans in northern Germany, Bohemia, Poland, Pomerania, and Scandinavia and which in essence reconfirmed the crusading politics for the Baltic

---

[257] *BF*, i (Inn.IV) no. 532.
[258] *BP*, i (Inn.IV) nos. 334 (= *Inn.IV R*, no. 7792), 335 (= *BF*, i (Inn.IV) no. 560; *Inn.IV R*, no. 7796), 337 (= *Inn.IV R*, no. 7794); *BF*, i (Inn.IV) no. 575.
[259] *BP*, i (Inn.IV) no. 341.
[260] *BF*, ii (Ale.IV) no. 42; *BP*, i (Ale.IV) no. 40; *BF*, ii (Ale.IV) no. 91 (= BSA, viii, 607, no. 99).
[261] 'Cronica Minor Minoritae Erphordensis', *MGHSS*, xlii, 486–671, here 664.
[262] Urban, *Baltic Crusade*, 162–70; Christiansen, *Northern Crusades*, 108, 127–30.
[263] Christiansen, *Northern Crusades*, 101–2.   [264] Urban, *Baltic Crusade*, 181–3.

developed by Gregory IX.[265] However, when the preaching of Louis IX's crusade started in summer 1245, the pope announced that the preaching for the Holy Land crusade was not to supersede that for the Baltic.[266] In an attempt to counteract the negative impact the preaching of the cross to the Holy Land might have had, Innocent IV allowed the Teutonic Knights themselves to receive crusaders who had not been recruited by public preaching in the mid 1240s.[267] By 1250 the Teutonic Knights had regained control of Prussia. The treaty of Christburg of 1249 put the quarrels between the order and the native Prussians to rest. The following year also brought the settlement of the disputes between the Knights and the new archbishop of Prussia, Albert Surbeer. Around the same time the Lithuanian leader Mindaugas converted to Christianity and was awarded a kingship by the pope.[268] This event marked the beginning of the conquest of Courland, Samogitia, and Semgallia in order to consolidate and secure Livonia and Prussia by establishing a land bridge between the two territories. As soon as the last elements of Louis IX's crusade to the Holy Land had left for the East, Innocent IV again stepped up the propaganda for the Baltic crusade. In 1251 he instructed the Dominican crusade preachers to collect alms, vow redemptions and other goods for the purchase of arms and horses for the Teutonic Knights in Livonia.[269] Shortly thereafter the Dominicans in Bohemia, and probably also elsewhere, were reminded to continue the recruitment of crusaders for Prussia.[270]

The recruitment of crusaders for the Latin Empire, too, continued throughout the 1240s and 1250s. But the death of John Asen in 1241 and the Mongol invasions of the Balkans and Asia Minor meant that the outside threats to the Latin Empire were receding in the early 1240s. Following a truce between Baldwin II and Vatatzes, new talks were begun about church union between the Byzantine emperor and Pope Innocent IV. During the 1240s and 1250s Constantinople was, in fact, relatively secure from any major attack from outside.[271] In accordance with the reduced need for

---

[265] *PUB*, i, 1, no. 146 (= *Inn.IV R*, nos. 162–3), 151. Around this time a Dominican called Henry was made legate 'pro negotio crucis' for the departing papal legate, Cardinal William of Sabina, until the arrival of the new papal legate, Abbot Opizo of Menzano. See *PUB*, i, 1, nos. 164, 165, 170 (= *Inn.IV R*, nos. 1029, 1032, 1567).

[266] *PUB*, i, 1, no. 169.   [267] *PUB*, i, 1, nos. 167, 168.

[268] Urban, *Baltic Crusade*, 184–6.   [269] *BP*, i, no. 218 (= *Inn.IV R*, no. 5134).

[270] *PUB*, i, 1, no. 255.

[271] K.M. Setton, *The Papacy and the Levant (1204–1571)*, 4 vols. (Memoirs of the American Philosophical Society 114; Philadelphia 1976–1984), i, 68–84; Wolff, 'Latin Empire', 222–9

crusading support in the Latin Empire, the propaganda was kept on a low flame. The papacy was obviously cautious not to divert resources from the crusade to the Holy Land and the anti-Hohenstaufen crusade, whose needs of men and money were much greater and more urgent during these two decades. With the exception of the patriarch of Constantinople, who was given permission to recruit crusaders in Venice and the Latin Empire in the mid 1250s, there is no indication that the secular clergy became involved in the preaching of the cross during that time.[272] Crusading propaganda seems to have been strictly reserved for the mendicant friars. In 1245–6, the Franciscans and Dominicans in the Provinces of *Provincia* (southern France) and England are known to have received orders from the pope to preach the cross.[273] Northern France and Germany were excluded presumably because Louis IX's crusade and the anti-Hohenstaufen campaign were given precedence in those areas.

During Innocent IV's pontificate the demands on the papacy for crusading support were as great and as varied as during Gregory IX's. The organization of the associated propaganda campaigns was even more complicated, however. While Louis IX's crusade to the Holy Land was being preached throughout Europe, the Baltic crusade and the campaigns against Frederick II and his successors in Germany were making heavy demands on the resources of the Empire. Nevertheless, Innocent IV managed to supply all crusades with the necessary aid by planning the propaganda very carefully and by trying to reduce the competition for the crusading resources in certain areas to a minimum. Like his predecessor, he chose the mendicant friars as his main instrument for implementing and sustaining his strategies.

THE LATER THIRTEENTH CENTURY

The 1260s saw a new flurry of attempts by successive popes to raise a large-scale expedition to the Holy Land. This resulted in a few minor expeditions[274] and ultimately in Louis IX's second crusade

---

[272] *Inn.IV R*, nos. 6829, 6845.

[273] Delorme, 'Bulle d'Innocent IV en faveur de l'empire latin', 309–10; Matthew Paris, *Chronica Majora*, iv, 564–6.

[274] R. Röhricht, *Geschichte des Königreichs Jerusalem (1100– 1291)* (Innsbruck 1898), 922–40; J. Richard, *Le Royaume Latin de Jerusalem* (Paris 1953), 311; R. Bleck, 'Ein oberrheinischer Palästina-Kreuzzug 1267', *Basler Zeitschrift für Geschichte und Altertumskunde*, lxxxvii (1987), 5–28.

of 1269–70. Almost continuously papal letters poured out of Italy demanding the preaching of the cross. The records are patchy, especially during the latter years of the decade when the papal throne was vacant for almost three years between the pontificates of Clement IV and Gregory X. But there is ample evidence to suggest that during the 1260s the preaching of the cross to the Holy Land was given more attention by the papacy than ever before.

During spring and early summer 1262 Urban IV, formerly patriarch of Jerusalem and pope since late August 1261, called for a new crusade to the Holy Land to be preached universally.[275] The earliest extant papal letters documenting the new campaign date from mid April when Urban instructed the Dominicans in France, Germany, and Lombardy to preach the cross.[276] Over the following three months numerous papal letters were sent to the mendicants of various areas all over Europe. These letters either recommissioned the preaching or specified points about the indulgences or the privileges and about the collection of money which went hand in hand with the preaching.[277] It was in the context of this propaganda drive that Albert the Great preached the cross to the Holy Land in Germany from early 1263 onwards. Albert was a former Dominican who was now exempted from the precepts of poverty and obedience of his former order and lived at the Curia as a private scholar and adviser to the papacy.[278] To support Albert, Pope Urban IV commissioned the famous Franciscan preacher, Berthold of Regensburg, to preach the cross in Germany, Bohemia, and in other German-speaking areas.[279] After Urban IV's death, the new Pope Clement IV re-confirmed the propaganda campaign to all mendicant and non-mendicant crusade preachers in May 1265.[280] This was quickly followed in August by a new crusading bull, *Expansis in cruce*, in reaction to news from the Holy Land of renewed Muslim attacks by Baibars earlier in the year. The bull is known to have been sent to the Franciscans and the

---

[275] Cramer, *Albert der Grosse*, 48–59.   [276] *APP*, ii, nos. 1119, 1120.

[277] *BF*, ii (Urb.IV) no. 30; *BP*, i (Urb.IV) no. 9–11, 18–20; *APP*, ii, nos. 1127–31, 1133–40, 1144; BSA (x), 185, no. 170; *Urb.IV R*, nos. 2906, 2909, 2912; Delorme, nos. V, 1–10; *Regesta Pontificum*, no. 18335; AFB, no. 81; Sevesi, no. XI–XVIII; *Doat*, ff. 44v–55r; Verci, ii, doc. nos. CXVI–CXX; *Diplomatarium Suecarum*, ed. J.G. Liljegren, 2 vols. (Holm 1829, 1837), no. 481; *La Documentacion Pontifica de Urbano IV (1261–4)*, ed. I.R.R. De Lama (Monumenta Hispaniae Vaticana. Seccion Registros 6; Rome 1981), nos. 41–43. For the collection of money see below, 126.

[278] *Urb.IV RCam*, nos. 310–32; Cramer, *Albert der Grosse*, passim.

[279] *Urb.IV R*, no. 326.   [280] *APP*, ii, nos. 1301–2 (= *Cle.IV R*, no. 1628).

Dominicans in France, Germany, and Scandinavia.[281] The *Annales Basileenses* confirm that the Basel Franciscans, in particular one Brother Achilles, were preaching the cross in 1266 with great success.[282] Mendicant friars may also have been among the members of a papal legation through northern France and Flanders in summer of the previous year,[283] whereas English chroniclers confirmed that the friars were also preaching in Britain.[284] Thus, the propaganda machinery was already in full swing when Louis IX took the cross in March 1267.

Preaching the cross in the south-west of France was still difficult, judging by the continued efforts to force crusaders who had taken the cross in the 1240s to fulfil their vows.[285] As during the preparations for Louis IX's first crusade, again a local Franciscan was appointed personally as crusade preacher by the pope. Brother William of Monteills must have been made 'praedicator crucis Jerosolimitane in partibus Tholosanis' during Clement IV's lifetime, since in December 1268 Alfonse of Poitiers recommended him to his seneschal as advisor concerning the financial privileges of crusaders.[286] Additional recruiting efforts were, however, not only made in south-western France and but also in the Iberian Peninsula, where selected Dominican and Franciscan houses were ordered to recruit crusaders in Navarre for King Thibald II's army and in Portugal for the Portuguese king's army respectively, since both of them had planned to join Louis IX's crusade.[287] There was, of course, a danger of depriving the Spanish crusades of their indigenous resources by intensifying the preaching of the cross in the lands of the Spanish and Portuguese Holy Land crusaders. But

[281] *BF*, iii (Cle.IV) no. 28; *BP*, i (Cle.IV) no. 36; *Corpus der Altdeutschen Originalurkunden bis zum Jahr 1300*, ed. F. Wilhelm *et al.*, 4 vols. (Lahr 1932–63), i, no. 93; see also *Cle.IV R*, no. 827.   [282] 'Annales Basileenses', *MGHS*, xvii, 193–202, here 193.

[283] 'Compte d'une mission de prédication pour secours à la Terre Sainte (1265)', ed. Borelli de Serres, *Mémoires de la Société de l'histoire de Paris et de l'Ile de France*, xxx (1903), 243–80. Seven 'fratres' are mentioned in the account, but none of them can definitely be identified as members of the Dominican or Franciscan orders, despite Borelli de Serres assertion to the contrary (p. 245).

[284] Thomas Wykes, 'Chronicon', *Annales Monastici*, ed. H.R. Luard, 4 vols. (Rolls Series 36; London 1864–9), iv, 6–352, here 217–18; Lloyd, *English Society*, 53–4.

[285] *Correspondance Administrative d'Alfonse de Poitiers*, ed. A. Molinier, 2 vols. (Collection des documents inédits sur l'histoire de France; Paris 1894, 1900), ii, no. 1408.

[286] *Correspondence*, i, no. 640. Other than this, nothing is known about either William's preaching or other aspects of his life and career.

[287] 'Bulles originales du XIIIe siècle conservées dans les Archives de Navarre', ed. L. Cardier, *Mélanges d'Archéologie et d'Histoire*, vii (1887), 33, 34, nos. 366, 367; *BF*, iii (Cle.IV) nos. 178–182 (= *Cle.IV R*, nos. 656–9, 661).

overall this does not seem to have caused any serious problems, also because Clement IV tried to re-establish a balance by boosting the propaganda for the Spanish crusades during this time.

As a rule the Spanish crusades did not require much additional propaganda. The Reconquista was closely bound up with the expansive tendencies and the frontier mentality in Spanish society and the crusades in the Spanish peninsula were part of the slow, continual process of pushing forward the Christian frontier against the Spanish Muslims. The military campaigns were mainly attempts to colonize and defend occupied territories, with the major forces consisting of feudal armies and urban militias. There is no evidence that there was ever a lack of enthusiasm for these crusades. Where there was willingness to fight, either to defend or expand home ground, there was not much need for propaganda. For the whole of the thirteenth century, the Spanish mendicants were never known to have been drafted into preaching the cross for a campaign on mainland Spain. It seems that the local secular clergy was well accustomed to dealing with the technicalities of crusading, such as administering, commuting, and redeeming vows, as part of everyday business.[288] Several of the Spanish campaigns in the thirteenth century were, however, aimed at the conquest of overseas territories. These crusades required a much greater degree of organization, more finance to pay for naval support, and, therefore, also a greater propaganda effort to lure potential crusaders away from the cheaper option of fighting on the Spanish mainland. In these exceptional cases the friars were regularly used as propagandists by the papacy.

Raymond of Penyaforte's role as crusade preacher in 1229 for King James of Aragon's conquest of Majorca has already been described.[289] In connection with this crusade, the Dominicans in the archbishopric of Embrun were ordered to promote immigration to the island by offering plenary indulgences to new settlers.[290] Later, in the 1250s, 1260s, and 1270s, King Alfonso X of Castile-Leon made several attempts to attack Muslim bases in northern Africa.[291] During these decades the papacy intermit-

---

[288] The most comprehensive study of the crusading element of the Reconquista remains that by Goñi-Gaztambide (*Historia, passim*).

[289] See above, 33. Raymond was later directed to supervise the establishment of a bishopric on Majorca, see *Gre.IX R*, nos. 3775–7.   [290] *Gre.IX R*, no. 524.

[291] Goñi-Gaztambide, *Historia*, 187–96; C.J. Bishko, 'The Spanish and Portuguese Reconquest 1095–1492', *A History of the Crusades*, iii, 396–456, here 433–5.

tently called upon the friars to back Alfonsos's campaigns by preaching the cross. In 1253 the friars in the Kingdoms of Navarre and Castile-Leon were ordered to do so by Innocent IV.[292] A few years later, the bishop of Ceuta in Morocco, the former Franciscan Lope, was preaching the cross for Alfonso's crusade throughout the Spanish peninsula and in Gascony.[293] And in 1265, during the preparations for Louis IX's second crusade, the Franciscan João Martins, who had been involved in the collection of crusade taxes in the Archdiocese of Braga in the mid 1240s,[294] was commissioned to preach the cross together with the archbishop of Seville against 'the Muslims of Africa and the king of Granada'; they were told to preach throughout the Spanish peninsula as well as in the Archdioceses of Genoa and Pisa.[295] Their preaching thus seems to have been specifically directed towards obtaining naval support from the two major Italian ports in the western Mediterranean at a time when these resources might well otherwise have gone wholesale to support Louis IX.

In a similar fashion, ten years later, the crusade against the north African Muslims was still operating. In April 1275 Pope Innocent V granted special powers to Archbishop Raymund of Seville to draw on the resources of the mendicant orders for the preaching of a crusade against the Muslims in Africa.[296] The archbishop was commissioned as 'crucis negotii executor' in the Kingdom of Castile-Leon with express powers to depute work to other ecclesiastical prelates and also the provincial heads of the Franciscan and Dominican orders. The surviving evidence makes it clear that the archbishop in July of that same year commissioned the Franciscans in the Province of St James to execute the said tasks without delay and with care.[297] Generally speaking, however, the evidence for use of friars as crusade preachers in the context of the Reconquista is patchy and there may well have been a greater volume of propaganda activity by mendicants than the sources reveal. But from the surviving documents it is clear that the papacy intensified

---

[292] *BF*, i (Inn.IV) nos. 456–7 (= *Inn.IV R*, nos. 6212, 6213).

[293] *Ale.IV R*, no. 483. For Lope, see Thomson, *Friars*, 28–34.

[294] See below, 130–1.   [295] *BF*, iii (Cle.IV) no. 20 (= *Cle.IV R*, no. 89).

[296] A. Lopez: 'Cruzada contra los Sarracenos en el Reino de Castilla predicada por los Franciscanos de la Provincia de Santiago', *Archivo Ibero-Americano*, ix (1918), 321–7. See also Goñi Gaztambide, *Historia*, 201–2. Both authors mistakenly thought that the crusade in question was against Muslims in the Iberian peninsula, but the papal bull clearly says 'contra Saracenos Africe'.

[297] Lopez, 'Cruzada', 322–7; see also below, 103.

the recruitment of crusaders by commissioning the friars to preach for crusades which were aimed at Muslim territories beyond the Spanish peninsula and which were in danger of not obtaining enough support because of other crusades taking place elsewhere in the Mediterranean at the same time.

To avoid similar a situation as during Louis IX's first crusade, when the propaganda initially did not manage to attract a sufficient number of crusaders, the Curia was very cautious about allowing other crusades to be preached universally during the preparations for Louis IX's second crusade. Thus Urban IV's reaction to the news that Michael VIII Palaeologus was planning a new attempt to oust the Latins from Constantinople was guarded. Despite the fact that the very existence of the Latin Empire was at risk, the preaching of the cross to the Latin Empire was restricted to the mendicant friars.[298] Urban also reinstated the crusading taxes of the First Council of Lyons, certainly in France and Spain, and probably elsewhere, in order to support the Latin Empire financially.[299] But even though the cross was preached and money collected, there was no time to get a crusade under way and the Greeks conquered Constantinople by August of the following year.[300] The West was probably surprised at the quick downfall of the Latin Empire, since in 1260 Baldwin II and Michael VIII had signed a one-year truce. Urban IV might otherwise have tried to organize some kind of quick relief force in the way that Gregory IX had done in the late 1230s.

The Latin establishments in the East were not only threatened by the conquest of Constantinople. At the beginning of the 1260s the second invasion of the Mongols also threatened the Holy Land. After the Mongols' sudden withdrawal from Central Europe in 1241, the threat of a renewed attack had remained all along, causing the new pope Innocent IV in 1243 to reconfirm the powers to preach the cross against them in Germany.[301] But until the late 1250s nothing happened. When a new Mongol onslaught on north-eastern Europe was looming in 1258, Alexander IV promptly authorized the friars in Germany, Bohemia, Moravia, and Poland to preach the cross against them.[302] Again the friars

---

[298] *APP*, ii, no. 1126; *BP*, i (Urb.IV) nos. 12, 13; *BF*, ii (Urb.IV) no. 33 (= *Urb.IV R*, no. 131); see also Goñi-Gaztambide, *Historia*, 207–8.

[299] *Urb.IV R*, nos. 133–7; *Urb.IV RCam.*, nos. 460–2; see also Lunt, *Financial Relations*, 228–9. [300] Setton, *Papacy*, i, 85–94; Wolff, 'Latin Empire', 228–32.

[301] *Inn.IV R*, no. 30. [302] *PUB*, i, 2, no. 59.

seem to have preached successfully in those areas during the following three years, for several times the pope reminded the friars of these areas not to neglect the preaching for the Baltic crusade in favour of the one against the Mongols.[303] But once more the Mongol attack did not take place. Instead, the Mongols were advancing in the south threatening to attack the Latin establishments in the Holy Land.[304] An entry in Archbishop Eudes of Rouen's register of visitations makes it clear that in 1260 Alexander IV called upon the secular clergy generally to preach the cross.[305] Other evidence confirms that a major propaganda effort was undertaken around this time. One of Eudes of Châteauroux's sermons for the recruitment of crusaders to the Holy Land seems to go back to around the year 1260 since it deals with the Mongol threat to the Holy Land.[306] Eudes, in fact, tried to involve the friars, for one of his sermons to an audience of Dominican friars on St Dominic's day (4 August) includes an appeal to assist his efforts by preaching the cross for the defence of the Holy Land against the Mongols.[307] Evidence from the Diocese of Marseille proves that the friars were also directly called upon by the pope to preach the cross; in August 1260 the bishop of Marseille endorsed a papal letter of May to the friars of that same town for the preaching of the cross in Marseille and the County of Provence.[308] Since the cross is also known to have been preached by Archbishop Frederick of Pisa around this time,[309] Alexander IV may have been trying to concentrate propaganda in and around the southern French and Italian ports in order to raise a quick relief force of crusaders by drawing on the naval capacities of these cities. This was a frequent recruitment strategy, which Innocent IV, Clement IV, and Nicholas IV also employed in other crusading contexts.[310]

The mid 1260s also witnessed a renewed military effort against the Hohenstaufen in Italy. After Urban IV had managed to gain the French royal family's support for his fight against Manfred in southern Italy, the crusading propaganda for the support of Charles of Anjou's campaign reached its peak in 1264–5. Because at the time the cross to the Holy Land was being preached throughout

---

[303] *PUB*, i, 2, nos. 61, 114, 131.
[304] P. Jackson, 'The crisis in the Holy Land in 1260', *English Historical Review*, xcv (1980), 481–513.   [305] *Regestum Visitationum*, 398.   [306] See below, 171, no. 8.
[307] Eudes of Châteauroux, 'Sermones sex de sancto Dominico', ed. A. Walz, *Analecta Sacri Ordinis Fratrum Paedicatorum*, xxxiii (1925), 174–233, here 189–94. The sermon otherwise does not deal with the crusade.   [308] Delorme, no. IV.
[309] See below, 172, no. 21.   [310] See above, 79, 83 and below, 94.

Europe, the recruitment for the Italian crusade was limited to northern Italy and France and most of the preaching was undertaken by especially appointed papal legates.[311] Three of the legates involved in the propaganda for the crusade against Manfred are known to have been given powers to call upon local mendicant friars to preach the cross: Cardinal Simon of Sta. Cecilia, legate in France in 1264 and 1265,[312] Cardinal Simon of St Martin, legate in northern Italy in 1264,[313] Geoffrey of Belmont, papal chaplain and legate in northern Italy in 1265.[314] But it is not clear whether, or to what extent, they actually made use of these powers. In order to boost the propaganda against Manfred within and around the Papal State, the pope called upon the mendicant friars directly. A papal bull of July 1264 ordered the Franciscans in the Diocese of Foligno and in the Franciscan Provinces of Rome and St Francis (= Umbria) to preach the cross, together with eighteen Italian bishops.[315] Another commission, this time to both mendicant orders in the March of Ancona, has survived from July 1265 and in late autumn of that year, the same letter was also sent to the Dominicans and Franciscans in the Kingdom of France, as well as to the archbishops of Bourges, Narbonne, and Rouen.[316] The 1265 letters might well be the confirmation by the new pope Clement IV of earlier commissions which have not survived. Likewise only one extant commission mentions the mendicants' preaching the cross against Conradin; six months after the preaching campaign had started, the Franciscan guardian of Perugia was advised to preach the cross in April 1268.[317] The first evidence for the friars' involvement in the preaching campaign against Peter of Aragon also stems from one and a half years after the preaching had begun. This might be due to the fact that before April 1284 crusade preaching in general seems to have been conducted on a low scale.[318] But after the attempted translation of the Kingdom of Aragon to Charles of Valois, the propaganda was intended to be resumed. Pope Martin IV ordered the Franciscans and Dominicans in Sardinia and Corsica and in the Kingdom of France to preach the

---

311 Housley, *Italian Crusades*, 17–19.
312 *BF*, ii (Urb.IV) nos. 138, 139 (= *Urb.IV R*, nos. 829, 833); *Cle.IV R*, no. 1432.
313 *Urb.IV R*, no. 634.   314 *BP*, i (Cle.IV) no. 28 (= *Cle.IV R*, no. 165).
315 *BF*, ii (Urb.IV) R, no. 163 (= *Urb.IV R*, no. 870).
316 *BP*, i (Cle.IV) no. 31 (= *ES*, iii, no. 645; *Cle.IV R*, no. 240), *BF*, iii (*Cle.IV R*) no. 23 (= *Cle.IV R*, no. 1751).
317 *BF*, iii (Cle.IV) no. 162; Housley, *Italian Crusades*, 19.
318 Housley, *Italian Crusades*, 20–1.

cross in June 1284.[319] In addition, the papal legate Cardinal
Bernard of Oporto commissioned the Franciscans in Tuscany
and Bologna in October 1285 to preach against Peter of Aragon
on the basis of the same papal bull.[320] But the cross does not seem
to have been preached because of the sudden deaths of King
Charles and Pope Martin IV.[321] Following the recruitment strategies developed by Innocent IV for gathering support in southern Germany in the 1250s, Clement IV and Martin IV seemed to
have relied on special envoys to spread propaganda for the
crusade in Italy. These envoys were now mainly chosen from
amongst the cardinals, which may account for the fact that the
mendicants' involvement was much less prominent than at other
times.[322]

In the Baltic, too, things changed after the early 1250s. The
Teutonic Knights' predominant position in the Baltic was challenged seriously for the first time between 1247 and 1254 when
Prince Daniel of Galicia and several Polish noblemen fought a
campaign against the Jatwingians and Lithuanians.[323] In connection with this, Innocent IV had as early as 1247 authorized the
bishop of Cracow to grant indulgences 'iuxta quantitatem subsidii'
to those who fought against non-Christians with the duke of
Cracow and Sandomir.[324] Shaken by the Prussian rising under
Duke Swantopelk, the Teutonic Order may initially have acknowledged the legitimate interest of the Polish nobility in coloniz-
ing and christianizing parts of Prussia and Lithuania.[325] But when
Innocent IV renewed grants of newly colonized territory to a
number of Polish noblemen in 1253, this was likely to cause friction

---

[319] *Mar.IV R*, no. 591. In connection with this it has been said that some Dominican friars
were attacked by people from Lille while preaching the cross at an abbey near that
town. See C.V. Langlois, *Le Règne de Philippe III le Hardi* (Paris 1887), 152; Housley,
Italian Crusades, 186. This is, however, not borne out by the source which referred to
'graves et enormes excessus in predicatores assumentes crucem', without saying that
these preachers were Dominican friars. See *Lois et Coutumes de la Ville de Lille*, ed. Brun-
Lavin and Rosin (Lille and Paris 1842), 308–9.   [320] AFB, no. 324.

[321] Salimbene de Adam, 'Cronica', 564.

[322] It is interesting that in the 1280s the papacy no longer fell back on the services of the
Franciscans for conducting secret diplomacy in the *Regno* in the way that Gregory IX
and Innocent IV had done. For the mid 1280s there is evidence that Pope Honorius IV
relied on Dominican friars as secret agents in the *Regno*, at least in some cases. See
Bartholomew of Neocastro, 'Historia Sicula', *RISNS*, xiii(3), 78–94.

[323] Christiansen, *Northern Crusades*, 102–3, 134–5.

[324] *Vetera Monumenta Poloniae et Lithuaniae gentiumque finitimarum Historiam illustrantia*, ed.
A. Theiner, 4 vols. (Rome 1860–4), i, no. 88 (= *Inn.IV R*, no. 2387).

[325] *Vetera Monumenta Poloniae*, i, no. 92 (= *Inn.IV R*, no. 4079).

with the Teutonic Knights.[326] The papal legate to north eastern Europe, the abbot of Menzano, was, therefore, given express orders to proceed with ecclesiastical censures against any one who molested the Polish dukes.[327] Evidence from a letter of January 1257 to the Dominicans of Elblag (Elbing) and Chelmno (Culm) and to the Franciscans of Torun (Thorn) suggests that some Teutonic Knights had, in fact, incurred excommunication in connection with this. No details as to the exact circumstances of the excommunication were provided, but the friars were told to make sure that the legate's sentence was observed.[328]

Pope Alexander IV finally conceded full crusading status to the Lithuanian wars of the Polish nobility. The Franciscan provincial minister of Austria, Bartholomew of Bohemia, the Dominicans at Kulmbach, and the bishop of Wroclaw (Breslau) were instructed to approach Duke Casimir of Cujavia as a possible leader of the campaign. The duke accepted after repeated requests by Bartholomew and the bishop of Gnesen.[329] The task of preaching the cross was given to Bartholomew of Bohemia, and he was told to recruit crusaders himself and to commission other Franciscan preachers to do the same in Poland, Bohemia, Moravia, and Austria in 1255.[330] Bartholomew was also empowered to proceed with ecclesiastical censure against anyone who might help the non-Christians and to absolve those excommunicated if they went on crusade.[331] While Bartholomew and the other Franciscans were preaching the cross to Lithuania, the Dominicans were still recruiting crusaders for the Teutonic Knights in Prussia and Livonia. In March 1256 Alexander IV had re-issued *Qui iustis causis* of 1243 to the Dominicans in northern Germany, Scandinavia, Bohemia, Poland, and Austria.[232] Considering that this meant that crusade preachers were competing for the resources of the same areas of Poland and Bohemia for two separate crusades, it is not surprising that problems arose. What exactly happened is not clear, since the

---

[326] *Vetera Monumenta Poloniae*, i, no. 109 (= *Inn.IV R*, nos. 6592, 6593, 6601).

[327] *Vetera Monumenta Poloniae*, i, no. 108 (= *Inn.IV R*, no. 6553).

[328] *Vetera Monumenta Poloniae*, i, no. 141 (= *Ale.IV R*, no. 1576).

[329] *Ale.IV R*, no. 1578; see also *PUB*, i, 1, no. 329 (= *Ale.IV R*, no. 1429).

[330] *PUB*, i, 1, no. 322 (= *Ale.IV R*, nos. 704–7). A papal safe-conduct for Bartholomew to the secular clergy of these countries mentions that he was accompanied by four 'personae' on horseback. See *Ale.IV R*, no. 1914.

[331] *BF*, ii (Ale.IV) no. 95 (= *Ale.IV R*, no. 1915); *Ale.IV R*, no. 1916.

[332] *PUB*, i, 1, no. 326 (= *BP*, i (Ale.IV) nos. 65–82; *Ale.IV R*, no. 1448). Christiansen (*Northern Crusade*, 130) seems to link this re-issue to the Russian campaign of Dietrich of Kiwel, but the text of the bull does not bear this out.

only evidence for the quarrels between Bartholomew and his fellow Franciscans and the Dominican crusade preachers are the papal directives aimed at ending them. It could be that there was a problem over the commutation of crusading vows from one to the other crusade. Thus, the Franciscan crusade preachers, after complaining to the pope, were given the right to proceed against any crusaders who had their vows commuted without a papal mandate.[333] In order to solve the problem, Alexander IV decided to make out separate recruitment areas for the two crusading ventures. In August 1257, Bartholomew and the Franciscans were restricted to the areas of Lethowia and Gotzewia in central Poland; the bishop of Wroclaw (Breslau) was notified of the new arrangement and he published the papal letter in November.[334] Meanwhile, the Dominican crusade preachers were told to respect the new regulations and to refrain from further interference with the crusade preaching for the Polish crusade.[335] In addition, the bishop of Olomouc (Olmütz) was instructed to make sure that no further disturbances occurred in Bohemia.[336] How serious the disagreements between the Franciscan and Dominican crusade preachers had been is difficult to say, but they certainly were fought out with determination. Bartholomew of Bohemia seems to have proceeded with excommunication and other ecclesiastical censures, probably against rival Dominican crusade preachers. He was warned by the pope no longer to use these weapons outside his newly assigned area of recruitment, whereas the Dominicans were allowed to absolve preachers who had been put under sentence of excommunication. Bartholomew's fervour for the Lithuanian crusade may be explained in part by a certain amount of personal ambition, since the pope had promised to install him as bishop of Lithuania if the crusade were successful.[337]

It was probably to compensate for any loss of crusading resources for Prussia and Livonia, resulting from the Polish campaign, that Alexander IV extended the preaching of the cross in support of the Teutonic Knights beyond the Dominican friars for the first time since 1230. When *Qui iustis causis* was re-issued to the Dominicans in March 1256, it was also sent to the bishops of Chelmno (Culm) and Courland.[338] Heidenreich of Chelmno

---

[333] *PUB*, i, 2, no. 12 (= *Ale.IV R*, no. 1955). [334] *PUB*, i, 2, nos. 28, 36.
[335] *PUB*, i, 2, nos. 21, 23, 30; accompanying this was yet another re-issue of *Qui iustis causis*.
[336] *PUB*, i, 2, no. 29.
[337] *PUB*, i, 2, no. 4. The bishopric was, however, not established.
[338] *PUB*, i, 1, no.3 26 (= *Ale.IV R*, nos. 1448, 1449, *BF*, ii (Ale.IV) no. 231).

(Culm) was a former Dominican and Henry of Courland a former Franciscan, who both owed their bishoprics to papal appointments.[339] The commissions of Heidenreich and Henry extended only to the Archdioceses of Mainz and Cologne, where they were expected to appoint suitable assistants from among the secular or regular clergy. The period of preaching of the Baltic crusade by Dominicans alone had definitely come to an end by 1260. The situation of the Teutonic Order was at the time threatened by forces within and outside their Baltic lands and increased military support was badly needed. In the mid 1250s, the Teutonic Knights had managed to crush a series of minor revolts in Courland and Samogitia, which had been triggered by the Order's increasingly aggressive policies towards the natives. Although the Knights concluded a two-year truce in 1257 with King Mindaugas's support, it was already becoming clear that Mindaugas was reverting to the non-Christian camp; despite his conversion to Christianity, the Knights had not allowed him to assume a leading role in the affairs of the eastern Baltic. Mindaugas, in turn, became the driving force behind a major revolt against the Teutonic Order by both non-Christian and renegade Christian Lithuanians and Prussians. The insurrection lasted throughout most of the first half of the 1260s and inflicted on the Order the most serious military defeats since it had established itself in the Baltic lands.[340] The papacy was well aware of the Teutonic Order's precarious situation. In February 1260 Alexander IV allowed the clerical brothers of the Teutonic Knights in Prussia and Livonia to preach the cross themselves. They were advised to take counsel from the crusade preachers of the two mendicant orders and the bishops of Chelmno (Culm) and Courland as to the way in which they ought to proceed in this matter.[341] This implied that Franciscans were preaching alongside the Dominicans before February 1260 and probably referred to Bartholomew of Bohemia's activities in Poland and Bohemia in the late 1250s. In June 1260, however, the pope also sent a copy of *Qui iustis causis* to the Franciscans in the Archdiocese

---

[339] Heidenreich was prior of Leipzig before 1238, and provincial prior of Poland in 1238–1240, before becoming bishop of Chelmno in 1245. See T. Kaeppeli, 'Heidenricus von Kulm (t.1263). Der Verfasser eines Traktates *De Amore S. Trinitatis*', *AFP*, xxx (1960), 196–205, here 196–7. For Henry of Courland, see W.R Thomson, *Friars in the Cathedral. The First Franciscan Bishops 1226–61* (Pontifical Institute of Mediaeval Studies. Studies and Texts 33; Toronto 1975), 45–50. For Henry see also above, 65.

[340] Urban, *Baltic Crusade*, 197–226; Urban, *Prussian Crusade*, 242– 85.

[341] *PUB*, i, 2, nos. 94, 95 (= *Ale.IV R*, nos. 3068, 3069).

of Magdeburg.[342] Another papal letter to the Franciscans of
Bohemia, Moravia, Poland, and Pomerania survived from January
of the following year.[343] An almost contemporary letter to the
secular clergy who were preaching the cross against the Mongols –
and to the king of Bohemia and the margrave of Brandenburg who
had agreed to lead that crusade – confirms that the re-commission
of *Qui iustis causis* to both mendicant orders was a recent measure.[334] This letter pointed out that the calamities in Prussia and
Livonia had caused the Teutonic Knights to request the pope to
order both mendicant orders and 'certain bishops' to preach the
cross. It also mentioned that, despite the propaganda drive for the
crusade against the Mongols, those who recruited for the Teutonic
Knights were not to be hindered from doing so.

In 1261 another forceful supporter of the northern crusades,
James Pontaléon, was elected pope Urban IV. While James was still
archdeacon of Liège he had been papal legate in the Baltic between
1247 and 1249, and he was thus intimately familiar with the
conditions in Prussia and a good judge in matters concerning the
Teutonic Order.[345] Urban IV probably had little doubt about the
seriousness of the situation in the Baltic in the early 1260s.
Immediately after his accession to the papal throne, he issued a new
crusading bull for the Baltic, *Gementibus olim dilectis*, to all who
were preaching the cross already. The crusade now also encom-
passed the Teutonic Knights' wars in Courland, which had become
a new battleground in the early 1260s.[346] Between 1261 and 1262
the quarrels between Danes and Germans over Holstein flared up
again and once more affected the recruitment of crusaders for the
Baltic. It was also during this time that King Mindaugas finally
broke with the Baltic Christians.[347] Probably as a result of this,
Urban IV reminded the mendicant crusade preachers of the
urgency of the situation several times in 1262.[348] But when the
preaching for a new crusade to the Holy Land got under way all
over Europe at around the same time, crusading resources were
again in danger of being diverted from the Baltic. In May 1263
Urban, therefore, wrote to all preachers of the cross, saying that the

[342] *Codex Diplomaticus Prussicus, Urkundensammlung zur älteren Geschichte Preussens aus dem königlichen Archiv zu Königsberg nebst Regesten*, ed. J. Voigt *et al.*, 6 vols. (Königsberg 1836–61), i, no. 128.   [343] *PUB*, i, 2, no. 127.
[344] *PUB*, i, 2, nos. 110–13. The cross against the Mongols was being preached in Germany, Bohemia, Moravia, and Poland. See above, 84–5.
[345] Christiansen, *Northern Crusades*, 125.   [346] *PUB*, i, 2, nos. 141–43; see also no. 147.
[347] Urban, *Baltic Crusade*, 211–16.   [348] *PUB*, i, 2, nos. 158, 169.

propaganda for the Holy Land was not to supersede the recruitment of crusaders to the Baltic; to stress this point, *Gementibus olim
dilectis* was now also issued to the Cistercians and Premonstratensians.[349]

After Urban IV's death, the new pope Clement IV reconfirmed
his predecessors' crusading bulls for the Baltic.[350] He also issued
personal appointments as crusade preachers to another Baltic
bishop and former Franciscan, Albert of Marienwerder, and Henry
de Spinis, a clerical brother of the Teutonic Order.[351] During the
1260s the crusading support for the Teutonic Knights was thus
massively increased. The papacy was in no way willing to let this
outpost of Christianity slip from the Order's control. Clement IV,
however, seems to be the last pope to have actively supported the
Teutonic Knights in the Baltic with major crusading aid. Large
contingents of crusaders from Germany and Bohemia arrived in
the mid and late 1260s, and with their help the Teutonic Order
managed to fend off the Lithuanian threat and regain their
predominant position in the eastern Baltic.[352] Although it took
almost thirty years thereafter to consolidate the territorial gains in
Courland and Semgallia against the Lithuanians, no major initiative to renew or continue crusading propaganda for the Baltic
came forward from the Roman Curia during the remainder of the
thirteenth century. This did not mean that the Teutonic Knights no
longer drew on crusading support, but it seems that they took over
the propaganda themselves. As early as 1265 the crusade preachers
of the Teutonic Order had also been authorized to collect vow
redemptions.[353] There is evidence that, in 1266, Clement IV
confirmed the personal commission of a cleric of the order,
Brother Conrad, as crusade preacher and that Conrad was still
recruiting in 1278.[354] At other times, the grand masters of the
order themselves went into Germany to gather crusaders.[355] By
the 1290s, the practice of enlisting penitent crusaders into the
service of the Teutonic Knights had become part of the Order's

---

[349] *PUB*, i, 2, nos. 199, 205.
[350] *PUB*, i, 2, nos. 234, 235 (= *Cle.IV R*, nos. 1545, 1579), 238, 243, 244.
[351] *PUB*, i, 2, nos. 236, 237 (= *Cle.IV R*, no. 1629).
[352] Urban, *Baltic Crusade*, 217–20; Urban, *Prussian Crusade*, 269–85.
[353] *PUB*, i, 2, no. 242. Later in the year the archbishop of Riga was expressly told to stop
collecting vow redemptions because it was considered to be to the detriment of the
Teutonic Order. See also no.248 (= *Cle.IV R*, nos. 1898, 1899).
[354] *PUB*, i, 2, nos. 252, 365.   [355] Urban, *Prussian Crusade*, 308–9.

constitution.[356] With the Baltic territories now safe and secure under Christian rule, the increasing influx of German settlers was adding to the defensive potential of the Baltic lands. On the whole, it seems that the Baltic crusade had gained so great a momentum that there was little need to continue the recruitment of crusaders by public preaching. The Curia seems to have been content with leaving things to be managed by the Teutonic Knights themselves.[357]

During Louis IX's second crusade of 1269–70 one of its participants, the archdeacon of Liège, Tedaldo Visconti, was elected Pope Gregory X. His pontificate saw the greatest effort to launch a crusade for the liberation of the Holy Land since the Fourth Lateran Council. The *Constitutiones pro zelo fidei* promulgated at the Second Council of Lyons in May 1274, outlined Gregory's far-reaching programme.[358] The preaching of the cross was commissioned in the autumn of that same year. The bull *Si mentes fidelium* was sent to all bishops of Christendom and to all Franciscan and Dominican provinces. The painstaking accuracy with which the papal registers list all archbishops and the heads of thirty-two Franciscan and eleven Dominican provinces illustrates the sense of thoroughness and determination with which the new pope went about the business of the cross.[359] But Gregory X's death in January 1276 left the ambitious crusade without a *spiritus rector* and the project was doomed to failure. But the hope of launching another large-scale crusade to the Holy Land was kept alive throughout the 1270s and 1280s. During this period the preaching of the cross by friars continued, presumably based on the decrees of the Second Council of Lyons.[360] But substantial aid did not materialize until it was too late and Acre fell in 1291. In a last attempt to raise a relief army, Pope Nicholas IV in January 1290

[356] Christiansen, *Northern Crusades*, 152–3.

[357] Urban, *Baltic Crusade*, 229–52; Urban, *Prussian Crusade*, 287–377; Christiansen, *Northern Crusades*, 103, 139–40.

[358] *Conciliorum Oecumenicorum Decreta*, 309–14; V. Laurent, 'La croisade et la question d'Orient sous le pontificat de Grégoire X', *Revue historique du Sud-Est européen*, xxii (1945), 105–37; L. Gatto, *Il pontificato di Gregorio X* (Istituto Storico Italiano per il Medio Evo. Studi Storici 28–30; Rome 1959), 63–106. P.A. Throop, *Criticism of the Crusade. A Study of Public Opinion and Crusade Propaganda* (Amsterdam 1940), *passim*.

[359] *Gre.X R*, no. 569; *BF*, iii (Gre.X) no. 59 (= AFB, nos. 153, 154); *BP*, i (Gre.X) no. 32; *Diplomatarium Suecarum*, i, no. 584.

[360] 'Annales Basileenses', 198, 200; *Acta Capitulorum Provincialium Fratrum Praedicatorum*, ed C. Douais (Toulouse 1894), 199, 291.

wrote to all crusade preachers in order to make them aware of the seriousness of the situation.[361] The appeal by the pope, who had himself been a Franciscan, was directed especially to the mendicants. For the first time he also approached the master general of the as yet small order of the Augustinian Hermits, ordering him to instruct his friars to join in the preaching of the cross.[362]

The papal registers recorded the dispatch of the January appeal to the two Italian Dominican Provinces of Lombardy and Rome.[363] But copies also survive addressed to several Italian provinces of the Franciscans.[364] The pope seems to have regarded Italy as the most promising ground for the fast recruitment of a relief force, organized with the help of the Italian maritime cities. In fact, a number of Italian crusaders left in early summer 1290 accompanying the Venetian fleet.[365] There is also evidence for a Franciscan crusade preacher operating in Marseille, which suggests that there was a similar attempt to enlist naval help from the French maritime cities.[366] These efforts appear to have been successful indeed; in August 1290 Nicholas IV even had to instruct the Franciscans and Dominicans in the March of Ancona to prevent crusaders in Fabriano (Umbria) from leaving individually, and to ensure that they waited until he announced a date for the departure of an army.[367] In March 1291 the English and Irish mendicants were re-commissioned to preach the cross by Nicholas IV after King Edward I had agreed to lead a general passage in the summer of 1293.[368] In August the date for the new crusade was announced throughout Europe and the clergy generally was reminded to preach the cross.[369] The pope again addressed the master-general of the Augustinian Hermits ordering him to dispatch thirty friars to preach the cross in Sicily, France, Hungary, Bohemia, and Poland.[370] He gave especial orders to the Dominicans in the Provinces of *Francia* and *Lombardia* to supply as many as forty

[361] *Nic.IV R*, no. 2268.
[362] *Nic.IV R*, no. 2267.
[363] *Nic.IV R*, nos. 2265, 2266.
[364] Verci, iii, doc. no. CCCXVI (= *Nic.IV R*, no. 7529); AFB, no. 436 (= BSA, x, 194, no. 230); BSA, xi, 207, no. 377 (= *BF*, iv (Nic.IV) nos. 200–1; Nic.IV R, no. 7530).
[365] Röhricht, *Geschichte*, 1004–5; Riley-Smith, *Crusades*, 206.
[366] 'Documents inédits concernant l'orient Latin et les croisades (XIIe–XIVe siècle)', ed. C. Kohler, *Revue de l'Orient Latin*, vii (1899), 1–37, here 33–4.
[367] *BF*, iv (Nic.IV) no. 300 (= *Nic.IV R*, no. 3078).
[368] *Nic.IV R*, nos. 6690–2. The same letter went to the secular clergy of England, Scotland, and Ireland. See also nos. 6684–9; Lloyd, *English Society*, 232–9.
[369] *Nic.IV R*, nos. 6800–5.   [370] *APP*, ii, no. 1897 (= *Nic.IV R*, no. 6805).

crusade preachers each.[371] Extant letters to the Italian Franciscans show that the pope also increased their contingents of preachers to seven in each province.[372] As could be expected, the English clergy, owing to the projected royal crusade, responded vigorously to the papal appeals.[373] On the feast of the Exaltation of the Cross on 14 September 1291, for instance, Archbishop Romeyn of York organized crusade preaching rallies throughout his archdiocese. He dispatched three masters of theology from his secular clergy to Beverly, Ripon, and Southwell, while he himself preached in York Minster. The bulk of the preachers, however, were taken from the friars of seven Franciscan and six Dominican houses. Romeyn asked them to dispatch a total number of thirty-five friars to preach the cross in places where major congregations might be expected.[374]

This last example once again indicates that by the end of the thirteenth century mendicant crusade preachers far outnumbered those of the secular clergy. It also shows that, by then, the mendicant orders had become a channel of communication which allowed the papacy to broadcast crusade propaganda covering a given area remarkably thoroughly and, if necessary, at short notice. By the 1290s the number of mendicant houses had risen sharply all over Europe.[375] This allowed the popes of the second half of the thirteenth century to follow Gregory IX's and Innocent IV's propaganda strategies closely and allowed them to organize localized recruitment campaigns as far away as Poland and in as isolated places as Sardinia and Corsica. There is no evidence that crusade propaganda decreased in volume during the second half of the thirteenth century or that it lost its intensity. Even the quick succession of popes seems to have caused little or no discontinuity with regard to the propagation of the crusades.

---

371 *BP*, ii (Nic.IV) no. 28 (= *Nic.IV R*, no. 7622); *Nic.IV R*, no. 7377. Another letter survived to the Scandinavian Dominicans without asking for a specific number of preachers. See *Diplomatarium Danicum*, ed. A. Afzelius *et al.* [in progress] (Copenhagen 1938), ii, 4, no. 16. Lloyd (*English Society*, 54) seems to be mistaken by saying that the figure was fifty rather than forty.

372 *BF*, iv (Nic.IV) no. 516 to the Provinces of St Francis (Umbria) and Austria; AFB, no. 511 to the Province of Bologna. *Nic.IV R*, nos. 6803, 6804 to the Province of March of Ancona and to all other provinces.

373 Lloyd, *English Society*, 42–4.

374 *The Register of John le Romeyn. Lord Archbishop of York 1286–1296*, ed. W. Brown, 2 vols. (Surtees Society 123, 128; Durham 1913, 1916), i, 113; Lloyd, *English Society*, 55–6. See also below, 106.

375 In Germany alone there were well over 200 Franciscan and Dominican houses by then. See Freed, *Friars*, 182–223.

Chapter 4

THE ORGANIZATION OF THE PREACHING OF THE CROSS IN THE PROVINCES OF THE MENDICANT ORDERS

When it came to marking out the areas in which the cross was to be preached, the terminology of the Curia was variable and not always very exact. As a rule, recruitment areas were determined by the groups of potential crusaders which had been singled out for a specific crusading campaign. These areas were mostly defined in political terms, whereas the Curia's usual way of thinking about European geography principally seems to have been in terms of dioceses and archdioceses, which rarely matched political boundaries. For example, when in 1240 the pope commissioned the Dominicans in the Province of *Francia* to remind *crucesignati* of their duty to leave for the east or redeem their vows, the areas of recruitment were specified as the Kingdom of France and the Archdioceses of Vienne, Besançon and the Dioceses of Toul, Verdun, Metz, Liège, and Cambrai.[1] Similarly, when in 1262 both mendicant orders in *Francia* were told to preach the cross to the Holy Land their area was described as the Kingdom of France together with the Archdioceses and Dioceses of Lyons, Vienne, Besançon, Tarantaise, Embrun, Aix, Cambrai, Toul, Verdun, Liège, and Metz.[2] Here, the aim must have been to include the French-speaking regions along the border of Germany. The borderlands between the French kingdom and the Empire were, in fact, often divided in this way. When the Dominicans of Louvain and Antwerp collected money for William of Holland's anti-Hohenstaufen crusade in 1248, they were told to do so in the whole of Germany, in the Archdiocese of Cologne and the imperial parts of the Dioceses of Cambrai and Tournai.[3] By the same token, in 1251 John of Diest, who was already preaching the cross in the German parts of the Empire, was told to include the German-

[1] *BP*, i (Gre.IX) no. 202 (= *Gre.IX R*, no. 5302).
[2] *Urb.IV R*, no. 2909 (= *APP*, ii, no. 1139).
[3] *ES*, ii, no. 589 (= *Inn.IV R*, no. 4166).

speaking parts of Flanders.[4] In a similar case Berthold of Regensburg was ordered in 1263 to support Albert the Great's recruitment efforts, his assigned area consisting of Germany, Bohemia, and other German-speaking areas.[5] Linguistic boundaries were thus often used to define the recruitment areas of individual preachers who would most certainly have preached in their mother tongue.

The majority of papal letters were addressed to the provinces of the mendicant orders, and only in exceptional cases to individual convents. Sometimes, however, the Curia sent the orders to the friars in a geographical or political area which might comprise several provinces or parts of provinces. But the provinces of the Franciscans and Dominicans did not follow the limits of ecclesiastical provinces either. Throughout the thirteenth century their boundaries were still fluid, owing to the continual growth of the mendicant orders.[6] Letters were, for example, addressed to the Dominicans and the Franciscans in the Kingdom of France, which included the Provinces of *Francia* (northern France) and *Provincia* (southern France). Similarly, a papal letter to the Franciscans in the Kingdom of *Alemania* would have concerned the three Provinces of Strasbourg, Cologne, and Saxony and probably part of the Province of Austria. The Kingdom of Bohemia, on the other hand, was part of the Dominican Province of Poland in the thirteenth century.[7] Seldom were the instructions by the Curia as accurate as Innocent IV's commission for the preaching of the cross to the Baltic of September 1243 to the Dominicans of Germany, Poland, and Scandinavia; in an unparalleled way the papal registers assigned separate recruitment areas to many individual Dominican houses.[8]

---

[4] *ES*, iii, no. 54 (= *Inn.IV R*, nos. 5031, 5032).   [5] *Urb.IV RCam.*, no. 326.

[6] A prime example of this process of the ongoing redefinition of provincial borders has been described by Freed, *Friars*, 69–77.   [7] Freed, *Friars*, 14–15, 56.

[8] *PUB*, i, 1, no. 146 (= *Inn.IV R*, nos. 162–3). The assignments were the following: The Dominicans (OP) of *Alemania* in the Archdioceses of Bremen and Magdeburg and the Dioceses of Regensburg, Passau, Halberstadt, Hildesheim, and Verden; OP Poland: Kgd. Bohemia, Poland, Pomerania; OP *Dacia*: Kgds. Denmark, Sweden, Norway; OP Magdeburg: Diocs. and towns Magdeburg, Brandenburg; Diocs. Havelberg, Halberstadt, Verden; OP Hildesheim: Dioc. and town Hildesheim; OP Bremen: Diocs. and towns Bremen, Verden; OP Vienna: Dioc. and town Passau; OP Halberstadt: Dioc. and town Halberstadt; OP Leipzig: Diocs. and towns Merseburg, Naumburg; Diocs. Magdeburg, Halberstadt, Minden; OP Hamburg: Diocs. Bremen, Ratzeburg, Verden; OP Lübeck: Diocs. and towns Lübeck, Ratzeburg, Schwerin; Dioc. Verden; OP Regensburg: Dioc. and town Regensburg; OP Olomouc (Olmütz) and Brno (Brünn): Dioc. and town Olomouc; OP Prague: Dioc. and town Prague; OP Freiberg: Dioc. and town Minden; Dioc. Naumburg; OP Cracow: Dioc. and town Cracow; OP Wroclaw (Breslau): Dioc. and town Wroclaw; OP Visby: Gotland.

At times the friars of one particular house or area were ordered to go beyond their immediate neighbourhood or province and preach elsewhere. In 1239 the Dominican prior of Paris was told to preach, and make other friars preach, the cross in the whole of the Kingdom of France, presumably because the Parisian convent had a great number of well-trained preachers.[9] In June 1248 the heads of the mendicants of *Alemania* were ordered to compel crusaders in Frisia, Holland, and Zeeland to join the general passage to the Holy Land the following spring.[10] The same was expected of them in 1250 with regard to crusaders in Frisia and Norway.[11] And to quote a final example, in May 1260 the friars of the two mendicant houses in Marseille were commissioned to preach the cross to the Holy Land in the town of Marseille and in the whole of the County of Provence.[12] It seems that the Curia was generally keen to make sure that areas where there were few or no mendicant houses were also covered by the friars. Sometimes these areas were huge and remote, thus requiring preachers to travel far.

In cases where the papal commission either addressed the friars of an area comprising several provinces or where it specified the preaching in areas which cut across the provincial boundaries, the provincial priors (of the Dominicans) or the provincial ministers (of the Franciscans) were presumably expected to organize the distribution of the duties amongst themselves. But there is no evidence as to how this would have happened. The failure to organize themselves properly could at times lead to friction, as became obvious in the propaganda for the Baltic crusade in Poland and Bohemia in the mid 1250s. But what happened then was exacerbated by the political circumstances.[13] Only one papal letter of 1291 to the Franciscans in Umbria actually warns crusade preachers not to recruit from places where other preachers were already doing so.[14] But this may have been aimed at making the propaganda more broadly based rather than at preventing competition. Generally speaking, it seems that with regard to the preaching of the cross the superiors of both orders managed to organize their friars in such a way as to avoid rivalries. Or at least, there is no evidence that this was not the case.

The only indications as to the number of crusade preachers envisaged by the pope stem from the 1230s and the 1290s. When

---

[9] *BP*, i (Gre.IX) no. 188.   [10] *BP*, i (Inn.IV) no. 199 (= *Inn.IV R*, no. 3967).
[11] *Inn.IV R*, no. 4927.   [12] Delorme, no. IV.   [13] See above, 88–9.
[14] *BF*, iv (Nic.IV) no. 516.

the mendicants were first called upon to preach the cross to the Holy Land in 1234 and 1235, Gregory IX specifically asked for two preachers from each province.[15] Reflecting the growth of the mendicant orders throughout the remainder of the thirteenth century, the number of crusade preachers also increased. In January 1290, Nicholas IV at first called for six Franciscan crusade preachers in each Italian province,[16] raising this number to seven in the following year.[17] The pope, on the other hand, asked the Dominicans to provide as many as forty preachers in the Provinces of *Francia* and Lombardy, presumably because the continental provinces of the Dominicans were fewer and bigger.[18] In Britain, however, where the two mendicant orders' provincial boundaries matched each other, the numbers seem to have been roughly the same. There is evidence that around the same time the Franciscan minister of the Province of *Anglia* had commissioned at least thirty-five friars.[19] In general, however, the papacy did not ask for specific numbers of preachers and presumably left it to the heads of the mendicant provinces to determine how many friars were to be employed in promoting the business of the cross. There is only one piece of evidence for the number of crusade preachers being limited. In the acts of the Dominican provincial chapter of *Provincia* in 1285, it was decreed that no more than three suitable friars in each convent, to be selected by the prior and two experienced friars, were to preach the cross. The wording of the decree suggests that the number had been exceeded and that a quota of three crusade preachers per convent had been set some time before. But when and how such a level would have been determined is not clear.[20]

There is some evidence that, at times, the general chapters were monitoring the preaching of the cross. At the Dominican general chapters of 1266 and 1269 the friars were reminded to be 'diligenter in executione' when preaching the cross; the latter general chapter was also used to let all Dominican crusade preachers know that King Louis IX would be leaving from Aigues Mortes in the first

[15] *BF*, i (Gre.IX) no. 146 (= AFB, no. 4); *Pontifica Hibernica*, ii no. 214; *BP*, i (Gre.IX) no. 112.
[16] Verci, iii, doc. no. CCCXVI (= *Nic.IV R*, no. 7529); *BF*, iv (Nic.IV) nos. 200, 201 (= *Nic.IV R*, no. 7530).   [17] *BF*, iv (Nic.IV) no. 516; AFB, no. 511.
[18] *BP*, ii (Nic.IV) no. 28 (= *Nic.IV R*, no. 7622); *Nic.IV R*, no. 7377.
[19] *The Rolls and Registers of Bishop Oliver Sutton 1280–1299*, ed. R.M.T. Hill, 8 vols. (Hereford 1948–86), iii, 195.   [20] *Acta Capitulorum Provincialium*, 291.

week of May the following year.[21] But it seems that most of the actual organization of the preaching of the cross was done by the heads of the provinces. Thus, in the Dominican Province of *Dacia* (Scandinavia), the preaching campaign for the general passage of 1293 was announced by the provincial prior at the chapter of Lund in 1292 to Brother Israel, lector at Sigunta, and probably also to the heads of other Dominican houses of his province.[22] The Dominican chapter of *Provincia* in 1263 exhorted their crusade preachers to proceed with care ('in predicatione crucis circumspecte se habeant'), while that of 1268 decreed that crusade preachers ought to use modest seals and that they should return them to their priors once their commission was ended.[23] By the same token the 1272 chapter told preachers to return their seals at the end of a preaching tour until they obtained a new commission.[24] In 1277 the Dominican prior of *Teutonia* even forbade the election of one crusade preacher, Brother Eberhard, to a priorate, because he did not want him to stop preaching the cross.[25] These examples suggest that the heads of the mendicant provinces monitored and supervised the preaching campaigns, but the lack of evidence makes it impossible to know how exactly this was done.

There is also relatively little evidence for the way in which a papal commission for the preaching of the cross was dealt with once it had reached the head of a province or an individual convent of one of the mendicant orders. The process of appointing friars as crusade preachers and of copying and distributing the papal bulls necessary for the preaching was not uniform, but seems to have varied from area to area, according to the needs of a specific crusade. When Leo of Perego, the Franciscan provincial minister of Lombardy, received orders to preach the cross in 1234, he sent a copy of *Pium et sanctum*, which commissioned the preaching, to the convent at Verona together with a copy of *Rahel suum videns*, the bull on which the preaching was based.[26] Another piece of evidence shows that, when the Franciscan provincial minister of Bologna, Brother Adam, was advised to preach the cross in a letter of 5 January 1290, he initially passed on the order orally to Brother Petrizolo of Aposa on 25 April. It was not until 14 June that Adam

---

[21] 'Acta Capitulorum Generalium', 134, 149.
[22] *Diplomatarium Danicum*, ii, 4, no. 86.
[23] *Acta Capitulorum Provincialium*, 99, 132. For the use of these seals see below, 106.
[24] *Acta Capitulorum Provincialium*, 167–8.
[25] *Ungedruckte Dominikanerbriefe des 13. Jahrhunderts*, ed. H. Finke (Paderborn 1891), no. 82.
[26] *BF*, i (Gre.IX) no. 146 and notes.

sent him a letter formally confirming his appointment as crusade preacher in the province, while asking him to concentrate his efforts on the Custody of Bologna. Enclosed was a copy of the crusading bull of January.[27] There also is evidence for another of Adam's commissions, that of Brother Iohanninus on 29 September 1291.[28] This time the accompanying crusading bull was *Illuminet super vos* issued on 1 August 1291. Three more copies of the same bull have survived in the Bolognese archives and were probably used by other friars.[29] It thus seems that the heads of the mendicant provinces usually commissioned crusade preachers by giving them a copy of the papal bull.

An enlightening document has survived from the Dominican Province of Provence.[30] It was written in December 1247 and consists of six papal bulls copied on to one long piece of parchment. In a passage at the beginning, the provincial prior, Ponce of Lesparre, addressed a certain Friar John whom he called 'balistarius Dei', a word play on his second name of Balistar. John Balistar was one of the first friars at the Dominican house of Périgeux, which was founded in 1241, and was mentioned by a number of Dominican chroniclers, notably for his penitential preaching.[31] In the introduction to the six bulls, the provincial prior reminded John that their province and other Dominican friars elsewhere had been ordered by papal mandate to preach the cross to the Holy Land and for the defence of the Latin Empire and to publicise the deposition of Emperor Frederick II. He went on to explain that, as provincial prior, he had been ordered to chose suitable friars to execute the task in strict accordance with the papal orders. Ponce then formally commissioned John, repeating that this was done on the authority of the pope and of his legate in the Kingdom of France.[32]

After the preamble, there follow the six papal bulls, one after another, in the following order:

(i) dated 21 December 1246, addressed to the Dominican prior of Provence, stating that crusaders to the Latin Empire were to

---

[27] AFB, nos. 436, 457.   [28] AFB, no. 512.   [29] AFB, no. 511.

[30] Ms. Limoges, Archives de la Haute Vienne, *H 9640*, which is partly edited by Delorme ('Bulle d'Innocent IV en faveur de l'empire latin', 307–10).

[31] [C.] Douais, 'Les frères Prêcheurs de Limoges (1220–1693)', *Bulletin de la Société Archéologique et Historique du Limousin*, xl (1892/1893), 270–363, here 314. John also wrote sermons, some of which have survived. See J.B. Schneyer, *Repertorium der Lateinischen Sermones des Mittelalters für die Zeit von 1150–1350* [in progress] (Munich 1969), iii, 337–49; T. Kaeppeli, *Scriptores Ordinis Praedicatorum* [in progress] (Rome 1970), ii, 383.

[32] The papal legate was Eudes of Châteauroux. See above, 62.

enjoy the same indulgences as those to the Holy Land and granting a plenary indulgence to the provincial prior and to those friars who preached the cross;

(ii) dated 29 September 1245, to the Dominicans in *Francia*, repeating the bull *Inter cetera desiderabilia* for the preaching of the cross to the Latin Empire;[33]

(iii) dated 29 September 1246, to the master-general and all provincial priors of the Dominican order, concerning the collection of testaments 'in pios usos' and of usurious interest that could not be returned to the debtors; the friars were advised to avoid scandal, not to use force when collecting but to rely on preaching and exhortation only;[34]

(iv) dated 13 Febuary 1246, to the Dominican provincial prior of Provence, authorizing the absolution of anyone excommunicated for fraud in return for the taking of the cross to the Latin Empire, provided satisfaction has been done to the damaged party;[35]

(v) dated 18 January 1247, to the master-general and all provincial priors of the Dominican order, allowing crusade preachers to celebrate mass once a month in areas under interdict;[36]

(vi) dated 20 March 1247, to the same, stating that forty days' indulgence might be granted for the attendance of crusade sermons on feastdays and other days and a plenary indulgence awarded to those preachers of the cross who suffered any offence, such as bans, detention, imprisonment, flogging, or other physical maltreatment while carrying out their duties.

The six bulls are followed by a confirmation clause guaranteeing that the cited documents were attested and confirmed by seal by the provincial prior at Limoges on 14 December 1247. The document must have been meant for John Balistar to carry along on his propaganda tour of the province to preach the cross for the defence of the Latin Empire. A similar document was prepared for the preaching of the cross to the Holy Land in south-west Germany in 1265.[37] It has survived in the archives at Freiburg i.Br. and consists of a single piece of parchment with a copy of Clement IV's bull *Expansis in cruce* on one side. The bull is addressed to the Dominican provincial prior and the Franciscan provincial ministers in the Kingdom of Germany. On the other side is written a

---

[33] See above, 79.   [34] See below, 125.   [35] See below, 125.
[36] See below, 107.
[37] *Corpus der Altdeutschen Originalurkunden*, 133–43, no. 93, and *(Regesten)*, 11.

Middle-High German translation of the same bull, followed by a Latin copy of the crusading indulgences and privileges of the Fourth Lateran Council (*Ad liberandam*). The document bears the seal of the Dominican prior of the German province. Although the document is not addressed to anyone in particular it was certainly meant to be given to a Dominican crusade preacher, helping him to read out the papal bull in the vernacular, as Pope Clement IV had ordered it; at the same time it supplied him with a copy of the relevant indulgences and privileges for consultation.

Other surviving documents illustrate the appointment of mendicant crusade preachers by papal legates. In 1248 a written order to preach against Frederick II and Conrad was given by Cardinal Peter of St George in Velabro to Ulrich, the Franciscan guardian of the Custody of Lake Constance. Ulrich, in turn, sent a copy of the order to one Brother H. ordering him to preach the cross.[38] Albert the Great, when preaching the cross in Germany in the mid 1260s, was known to have used form letters to appoint individual subdelegates, among whom was the Franciscan Berthold of Regensburg.[39] One such form letter has survived in the Würzburg archives. It consists of the crusading bull *De summis dominus* with an introductory clause, in which Albert appointed the subdelegate, and a confirmation clause at the end, which formally authorized the subdelegate to preach the cross and use the powers to confer indulgences and absolve from excommunication granted in the bull. The surviving copy, however, does not seem to have been used since the space reserved for the subdelegate's name is blank.[40] It seems that this procedure was fairly standard. When Pope Innocent V granted special powers to Archbishop Raymund of Seville to draw on the resources of the mendicant orders, a document was drawn up consisting of a copy of the papal bull of 9 April 1275 with a preamble in which the archbishop addressed the ministers, custodians, guardians, and all preachers of the Franciscans in the Province of St James and a confirmation clause ordering the friars to execute the said tasks without delay and with care. It was issued at Burgos on 8 July. This document was subsequently confirmed by *inspeximus* by the bishop of Leon on 27 August 1275.[41] A similar document has survived in the Franciscan archives

---

[38] X. Bernet, 'Beiträge zur Geschichte der Kreuzzüge gegen die Mongolen im 13. Jahrhundert', *Geschichtsfreund*, i (1843), 351–64, 376–8, here 376–8 (= *Archiv der Oberdeutschen Minoritenprovinz*, 84).   [39] See above, 80.

[40] Cramer, *Albert der Grosse*, 33–6, 75–8, and Abb. 4.   [41] Lopez, 'Cruzada', 322–7.

at Bologna which the papal legate Cardinal Bernard of Oporto used to commission Franciscans in the 1280s. In it the cardinal ordered the Franciscan ministers in Tuscany and Bologna to preach the cross against the Aragonese on the basis of the papal crusading bull of 4 June 1284, a copy of which was inserted in the commission. The document is dated 29 October 1285.[42]

Local bishops in general seem to have played an important role in confirming papal commissions to friars preaching the crusade in their own dioceses. This was a measure to assure people that the commission was genuine and a way of showing people that the local bishop approved of the friar's mission, which would have added to the crusade preacher's authority and safety.[43] Thus in August 1243 Bishop Henry of Constance issued a safe conduct for Franciscan crusade preachers against the Mongols throughout his diocese.[44] A similar letter was issued by Archbishop Giffard of York in 1276, in which he confirmed that the Franciscans had been commissioned to preach the cross and exhorted the clergy and laity throughout the Archdiocese of York to attend their sermons and treat them with respect.[45] Simpler versions of this type of letter were episcopal endorsements confirming the authenticity of papal letters. Thus, for example, the bishop of Wloclawek (Leslau) confirmed Bartholomew of Bohemia's revised commission of August 1257.[46] And in 1260 the bishop of Marseille endorsed the papal letters to the friars of his city for the preaching of the cross in Marseille and the County of Provence.[47] A further example of this kind of episcopal endorsement comes from the Diocese of Lincoln, where Bishop Sutton confirmed the commission of Brother Walter *de Langele*, who was preaching in the Archdeaconries of Oxford and Buckinghamshire; Walter was one of the thirty-five crusade preachers appointed by the Franciscan provincial minister of England for the 1290–3 preaching campaign.[48] Two entire

---

[42] AFB, no. 324.

[43] Only one example of the confirmation of a papal commission by a public notary has survived. It concerned the powers for conducting the inquisition and the preaching of the cross given to the Franciscans of Bologna. The papal letter of 23 March 1254 was confirmed *in dorso* in the following way: '1256 die xxiii augusti, Faventie in Episcopatu . . . ego Bencevenne f. Bonutii q. Zucoli fornari civis Fav. not. suprascriptum *exemplum* ex originali suo integro et incorrupto . . . fideliter sumpsi et exemplavi.' See AFB, no. 45 (= *BF*, i (Inn.IV) no. 532).

[44] Bernet, 'Beiträge', 355–6 (= *Archiv der Oberdeutschen Minoritenprovinz*, 83).

[45] *Historical Papers and Letters from the Northern Registers*, ed. J. Raine (Rolls Series 61; London 1873), no. XXXIII. [46] *Codex Diplomaticus Prussicus*, i, no. 112.

[47] Delorme, no. IV. [48] *Rolls and Registers*, iii, 195.

series of crusading commissions with additional endorsements by a local bishop have survived for the mendicant Provinces of *Provincia* from the beginning of the 1260s. Eleven letters issued by the Curia between May and July 1262 to the Franciscans of the Province of Aquitaine were given confirmation clauses by the bishop of Toulouse in February 1263.[49] Ten letters to the Dominicans of Provence that were issued during June 1262 were additionally confirmed as being authentic and valid by the bishop of Maguelonne.[50] The upsurge in the survival of episcopal endorsements of papal commissions at the beginning of the 1260s was probably due to Pope Urban IV's attempts to encourage the local clergy and the friars to collaborate. In December 1261 he wrote to the archbishops and bishops of the areas of north-eastern Europe where the Dominicans were preaching the cross for the Baltic crusade, ordering them to support the friars' efforts in whichever way they saw fit.[51] A similar letter was sent to the archbishop of Trondheim and his suffragans in October 1263 with regard to the Dominicans' crusade preaching to the Holy Land.[52] Documents such as these were important because the presentation of a copy of the papal bull issued for the specific crusade was the normal way of proving authority to preach the cross and to grant indulgences. The issue of the crusade preacher's authority was indeed crucial. In 1224, for example, Frederick II complained to Pope Honorius III that some crusade preachers were rejected and ridiculed by their audiences because they seemed unworthy people ('infime persone') and because they did not have the usual credentials for conferring indulgences.[53] In the light of the appearance of false crusade preachers during the 1220s, it seems likely that Frederick was referring to people's guarded response to those preachers who could not prove papal authority conclusively.[54] Writing about the preaching of the papal legate for Lombardy at Venice in 1258, Salimbene confirmed that the status and authority of a preacher was vital if he was to persuade people to take the cross.[55] Apart

---

[49] Delorme, nos. V, 1–11. [50] *Doat*, ff. 44r–55r. [51] *PUB*, i, 2, no. 142.
[52] *Urb.IV R*, no. 436.
[53] *Historia Diplomatica*, ii, 412. It seems to be this piece of evidence which Riley-Smith (*Crusades*, 150) had in mind when suggesting that Frederick II was referring to the first mendicant friars preaching the cross. Frederick did, however, not talk about friars, but simply about 'predicatores'. There is no reason to believe that the papacy should generally have employed the friars as crusade preachers at this early date. It is also inconceivable that, had this be the case, the friars would not have been given sufficient proof of authority. [54] See below, 138. [55] Salimbene de Adam, 'Cronica', 366.

from papal bulls, crusade preachers also had their own seals which were instruments and also visible signs of their authority.[56] Not much is known about these seals, but it must be assumed that they were used for various purposes, such as the sealing of money bags, the commissioning of subdelegates, and the confirmation of accounts and of agreements between crusader and preacher concerning vow redemptions.

Judging from the evidence for the preaching tours of Baldwin of Canterbury in the 1180s, and of Albert the Great and a papal legation in northern France in the 1260s, which are the only ones well documented over a longer period of time, crusade preachers moved quickly from place to place sometimes on a daily basis.[57] As a rule preachers chose locations for their sermons which were likely to attract large audiences, that is towns or rural centres like big villages, castles, and monasteries.[58] When the archbishop of York organized his preaching rally in September 1291, he indicated some of the towns in which preaching was to take place, but in other cases he told the friars to chose 'places where they believed that many people would be likely to attend'.[59] But the preference of towns and large villages does not mean that the rural population in more remote areas were necessarily neglected. In his *De Eruditione Praedicatorum*, the Dominican master general Humbert of Romans reminded preachers not only to preach in 'urbes' and 'villae magnae', but also in 'loca minus populosa'.[60] Preachers normally announced the places and times for their sermons in advance.[61]

---

[56] *Acta Capitulorum Provincialium*, 132, 167–8. See also the surviving seal of Albert the Great (Cramer, *Albert der Grosse*, Abb. 2).

[57] Gerald of Wales, *Opera*, ed. J.S. Brewer *et al.*, 8 vols. (Rolls Series 21; London 1861–91), vi, 3–152; Cramer, *Albert der Grosse*, 26–32; 'Compte d'une mission', 262–80.

[58] Matthew Paris, *Chronica Majora*, iii, 287.

[59] *Register of John le Romeyn*, i, 113; *Historical Papers and Letters*, no. LVII. The allocations were as follows: Franciscans (OM) of Nottingham: one friar in Nottingham, Newark, Bingham. OM Doncaster: Doncaster, Blyth, East Redford. OM York: Howden, Selby, Pocklington. OM Beverly: Driffield, Malton, South Cave. OM Scarborough: Bridlington, Whitby. OM Richmond: Richmond 'et alium ubi major creditur esse congregatio populi in Coupland'. OM Preston: Preston and 'in loco ubi creditur esse major concursus populi'. Dominicans (OP) of York: Otley, Skipton, Leeds. OP Beverly: 'Preston vel Hedon', 'Ravenshere', Wyke (or Wykeham). OP Scarborough: Scarborough, Pickering. OP Yarm: Northallerton, Yarm, Thirsk. OP Lancaster: Lancaster, 'ubi est major congregatio in Kendal', 'ubi est major congregatio in Lonsdale'. OP Pontefract: Pontefract, Rotherham, Wakefield. See also above, 95.

[60] Humbert of Romans, *Opera de vita regulari*, ed. J.J. Berthier, 2 vols. (Turin 1956), ii, 428–9.

[61] Caesar of Heisterbach, *Dialogus miraculorum*, ed. J. Strange, 2 vols. (Cologne 1851), i, 136, 182, ii, 333–4; Gerard of Fracheto, 'Vitae', 229; 'Gesta Episcoporum Traiectensium', *MGHS*, xxiii, 400–26, here 421, 423; 'Emonis Chronicon', 515; Matthew Paris, *Chronica Majora*, v, 73.

This was obviously aimed at giving people enough time to assemble at the places where they preached; if necessary, it also allowed time to erect platforms for the preaching outdoors.[62] In this respect the preaching of the cross probably differed little from other preaching activities of the friars.[63] In order to attract audiences crusade preachers were given the right to grant lesser indulgences for attendance at crusade sermons. This practice had been established by Innocent III who conceded an indulgence of twenty days, which was increased to one hundred as the century progressed.[64] In addition, papal bulls from the end of Innocent IV's pontificate onwards granted crusade preachers powers to convoke parish priests and their parishioners for the preaching of the cross, if necessary by threatening ecclesiastical censure.[65] At the same time crusading bulls conceded the right to preach and celebrate mass in places under interdict, thus allowing crusade propaganda to be spread everywhere.[66]

Crusade preachers also tried to make use of events where people had come together for other reasons. Thus in 1236 a Dominican crusade preacher delivered a sermon before King Henry III and an assembly of English noblemen in Winchester.[67] John of Wildeshausen and William of Cordelle were both reported to have preached at tournaments.[68] These latter events provided propagandists with an audience of many knights and potential crusaders. Moreover, preachers could take advantage of the church ban on tournaments by employing their powers to absolve the participants in return for taking a crusade vow.[69] Other events likely to favour the recruitment of crusaders were church feasts with a particular significance for the business of the cross. Oliver of Cologne, for example, chose the feastday of local Frisian saints and

---

62 'Compte d'une mission', 244, 251, 269. Salimbene de Adam ('Cronica', 560) reported, although not in connection with the preaching of the cross, that Berthold of Regensburg's platforms had a wind indicator on top so that people could stand downwind.

63 D.L. d'Avray, *The Preaching of the Friars. Sermons diffused from Paris before 1300* (Oxford 1985), 39–41.

64 Brundage, *Canon Law*, 154; Purcell, *Papal Crusading Policy*, 62–4.

65 *Inn.IV R*, no. 6469; *ES*, iii, no. 259 (= *Inn.IV R*, no. 7312); *BF*, ii (Urb.IV) nos. 30, 33; *PUB*, i, 2, no. 200; *BF*, iii (Cle.IV) no. 23 (= *Cle.IV R*, no. 1751); *Corpus der altdeutschen Originalurkunden*, no. 93; *BP*, i (Cle.IV) no. 31 (= *Cle.IV R*, no. 240); *AFB*, no. 420.

66 E.g., Ms. Limoges, Archives de la Haute Vienne, *H 9640*; *BF*, iii (Gre.X) no. 59 (= *Gre.X R*, no. 569); *BF*, iv (Nic.IV) nos. 200, 201 (= *Nic.IV R*, no. 7530); *BF*, iv (Nic.IV) no. 516. See also Purcell, *Papal Crusading Policy*, 176–7.

67 Nicholas Trevet, *Annales sex Regum Angliae, 1135–1307*, ed. T. Hog (London 1845), 221.

68 Gerard of Fracheto, 'Vitae', 229; *AF*, i, 416.

69 Purcell, *Papal Crusading Policy*, 29, 79, 178.

martyrs to preach the cross for the Fifth Crusade.[70] Likewise the exposition of relics in processions could serve as a context for crusade recruitment. In 1240 Gregory IX preached the cross in Rome while carrying the heads of SS Peter and Paul through the streets of the city,[71] and in 1267 Archbishop Eudes Rigauld of Rouen preached the cross on the occasion of the translation of the relics of St Mary Magdalen which his cathedral church had been given by Louis IX.[72] There is, however, no direct evidence for friars having preached the cross during such occasions.

Owing to the devotional character of crusading, the feastdays of the Invention of the Cross (3 May) and of the Exaltation of the Cross (14 September) were of prime importance in recruitment programmes. In 1275, for example, the Dominican prior of Basel made the former feast the beginning of a preaching campaign.[73] In 1291 Archbishop John of York chose the latter date for a crusade preaching rally throughout his diocese.[74] Equally, if not more, important seems to have been Lent and especially the week before Easter. Christ's act of redemption, which was the foundation for the spiritual rewards pertaining to crusading indulgences, was the liturgical theme of Easter week. Lent, therefore, was a time of heightened awareness of the necessity to do penance to which thirteenth-century preaching in general referred increasingly.[75] On a more practical level, Lent was a convenient time to remind new and old recruits to the Holy Land crusade of the imminent spring and summer passages to the East by the French and Italian merchant fleets.[76] Back in 1188, Emperor Frederick I's *Curia Dei*, as well as Baldwin of Canterbury's tour of Wales took place in Lent.[77] In Lent 1252, King Henry III called upon the friars to

---

[70] J.J. Moolenbroek, 'Signs in the Heavens in Groningen and Friesland in 1214: Oliver of Cologne and Crusading Propaganda', *Journal of Medieval History*, xiii (1987), 251–72, here 258.

[71] 'Annales Placentini Gibellini', *MGHS*, xvii, 457–581, here 483; *Historia Diplomatica*, v, 776–9.   [72] *Regestum Visitationum*, 597.   [73] 'Annales Basileenses', 198.

[74] See above, 95, 106.

[75] R. Rusconi, 'De la prédication à la confession: Transmission et contrôle de modèles de comportement au xiiie siècle', *Faire Croire. Modalités de la diffusion et de la réception des messages religieux du xiie au xve siècle* (Collection de l'École Française de Rome 51; Rome 1981), 67–85, esp. 68.

[76] The French and Italian merchant fleets usually left in late March/early April and late July/early August. See J.H. Pryor, *Geography, technology, and war. Studies in the maritime history of the Mediterranean, 649–1571* (Cambridge 1988), 3–4, 117.

[77] 'Historia peregrinorum', *MGHS rg*, v, 116–72, here 125; Gerald of Wales, *Opera*, vi, 3–152.

support the preaching of the cross in the city of London,[78] and in
1292 a special recruitment effort was made by the Franciscan prior
of England by commissioning thirty-five friars to preach the cross
to the Holy Land in his province during that same season.[79]
Preaching to an audience at such and other occasions allowed
crusade preachers to bring communal pressure on the members of
an audience. In one of his crusade sermons James of Vitry explained
that often people took the cross after a sermon despite the fact that
they had never intended to do so because they saw others taking the
vow.[80] The Franciscan Gilbert of Tournai also commented on the
theme of communal pressure. While confirming that the example
of others played an important role, he added that the scenario of a
crusade sermon also allowed people who had sinned 'in public' to
confess their guilt 'in public'. Communal pressure could thus be
brought against those members of a local society who were known
to lead morally objectionable lives or had caused disruption to
public law and order. As Gilbert put it, those who had at some time
given a bad example to the community, now had the chance to
redeem themselves by setting a good one.[81] In some instances
crusade preachers were even known to have pre-arranged with
certain people to take the cross at an appropriate moment of the
sermon in order to excite others to do the same, although this did
not always work.[82] By the same token, Humbert of Romans
suggested that crusade preachers took the cross themselves as a way
of giving an example and making their messages more credible.[83]

The evidence for the organization of crusader recruitment in the
provinces of the mendicant orders is sparse. But what we know
about it suggests that great care was generally taken to spread the
propaganda as efficiently as possible. The hierarchical organization
of the two orders, spanning the whole of Europe, made it relatively
easy for the popes to pass orders down the internal administrative
lines by contacting the heads of the orders' provinces. They, in

---

[78] *Close Roll of the Reign of Henry III Preserved in the Public Record Office, 1226–72*, 14 vols.
(London 1902–38), vii [1251–3], 201–2; Matthew Paris, *Chronica Majora*, v, 281–2.
[79] See above, 99.
[80] *Analecta Novissima*, ed. J.P. Pitra, 2 vols. ([Paris] 1885, 1888), ii, 428.
[81] Gilbert of Tournai, *Sermones ad omnes status de novo correcti et emendati* (Lyon [1510]), ff.
135rb–135va. Humbert of Romans in essence reiterated these thoughts of Gilbert's in his
De predicatione S. Crucis. See Humbert of Romans, *De predicatione Sancte crucis*
([Nürnberg 1495]), ch. 7.
[82] Matthew Paris, *Chronica Majora*, v, 281–2; Gerald of Wales, *Opera*, i, 73–4.
[83] Humbert of Romans, *De predicatione S. crucis*, ch. 28.

turn, commissioned friars to preach the cross throughout their provinces by copying and distributing papal letters. The Curia did not generally need to contact the friars in particular areas unless there was a specific reason to do so, as, for example, when there was a special need to attract naval support from certain maritime cities for the organization of overseas expeditions. The evidence also illustrates the close cooperation between the friars and the local secular clergy. They not only assisted the friars' activities by endorsing and confirming papal comissions but also drew on the friars to support their own efforts in promoting the crusades.

Chapter 5

FRIARS, CRUSADE SERMONS, AND PREACHING AIDS

Despite the fact that there is ample evidence to illustrate that the friars preached the cross, it has not been recorded what they actually said in their sermons. Medieval chroniclers rarely wrote about the preaching in detail, that is the contents of crusade sermons, their audiences and context. This is not to say that there is no information at all, but it exclusively relates to the preaching of prominent secular clerics. From the late twelfth and the early thirteenth century, there are the sermons of Bishop Henry of Strasbourg and Martin of Pairis, preached at Strasbourg in 1188 and Basel in 1201 respectively, which the chroniclers claimed to report more or less *verbatim*.[1] Then there are the descriptions of Baldwin of Canterbury's tour of Wales in 1188,[2] of Eustace of Flay's preaching in England in 1200–1,[3] and of the activities of Oliver of Cologne in Frisia prior to the Fifth Crusade.[4] All of these contain more or less detailed information about the actual crusade sermons. In addition, there are snippets of information about Pope Innocent III's preaching in Italy in 1216.[5] For later in the thirteenth century, when the friars were preaching the crusade, the only substantial surviving evidence also concerns the preaching of two secular crusade preachers, both papal legates in northern Italy, who preached the cross against the Romano brothers in the later 1250s.[6]

There are, of course, a number of preaching aids from the thirteenth century, notably model sermons and *exempla*, which were concerned with the preaching of the cross.[7] Crusade model

---

[1] 'Historia peregrinorum', 122–4; Günther of Pairis, 'Historia captae a Latinis Constantinopoleos', *PL*, ccxii, cols. 226–56, here cols. 227–8.

[2] Lloyd, *English Society*, 60–5; Tyerman, *England*, 60–70, 156–63 *passim*.

[3] Roger of Howden, *Chronica*, ed. W. Stubbs, 4 vols. (Rolls Series 51; London 1868–71), iv, 123–4, 165–72.   [4] Van Moolenbroek, 'Signs', *passim*.

[5] M. Maccarrone, *Studi su Innocenzo III* (Italia Sacra. Studi e Documenti di Storia Ecclesiastica 17; Rome and Padova 1972), 8–9.

[6] Salimbene de Adam, 'Cronica', 365–6, 394–5; Housley, *Italian Crusades*, 167–9.

[7] See below Appendix 2.

sermons first appeared in sermon collections at the beginning of the thirteenth century. This coincided with a general revival of pastoral theology and popular preaching promoted in particular at Paris University at the turn of the twelfth and thirteenth centuries.[8] It may be that Pope Innocent III encouraged the production of crusade sermons amongst former fellow students at Paris University, whom he sometimes also employed as preachers of the cross;[9] all authors of surviving thirteenth-century crusade sermons had at one time been students at Paris. And since Paris University remained the foremost European centre of sermon production and diffusion,[10] its importance for the writing of crusade sermons during the remainder of the thirteenth century comes as no surprise. It has repeatedly been said that only very few crusade sermons have survived and historians have been puzzled for some time over this alleged dearth of material.[11] This is mainly due to the fact that, as has already been said, the narrative sources of the period were unlikely to report this kind of activity in detail. But despite this, at least twenty-one complete sermons written for the preaching of the cross have survived from the thirteenth century.[12]

By the late twelfth century the theme of crusading had already appeared in a *sermo de cruce domini* by Alain of Lille which was meant for preaching on the feastdays of the Invention (3 May) and the Exaltation of the Cross (14 September).[13] The connection between these *de cruce* sermons and crusade sermons is made clear in an incomplete, anonymous sermon collection of the late thirteenth century now at Oxford. There, a fragment of a crusade recruitment sermon is followed by a *de cruce* sermon, both being attributed to the English Franciscan John Russel. Although the *de cruce* sermon has no direct reference to the crusade, it seems that it was meant to provide material for a *distinctio* on 'signum crucis' which was indicated in the crusade sermon fragment in schematised form only.[14] Similarly, one of Eudes Châteauroux's sermons for the Invention of the Cross is not marked as a crusade sermon, but includes passages concerned with the recruitment of cru-

---

[8] D'Avray, *Preaching*, 13–28.   [9] Cole, *Preaching*, 109–10, 139–40.

[10] D'Avray, *Preaching*, 132–63.

[11] See, for example, J.B. Schneyer, *Geschichte der Katholischen Predigt* (Freiburg i.Br. 1969), 172–3; Powell, *Anatomy*, 51; Cole, *Preaching*, xii.   [12] See below, 171–2.

[13] Alain of Lille, *Textes inédits avec une introduction sur sa vie et ses oeuvres*, ed. M.-T. d'Alverny (Études de Philosophie Médiévale 52; Paris 1965), 279–83.

[14] B. Smalley, 'John Russel, O.F.M.', *Recherches de Théologie Ancienne et Médiévale*, xxiii (1956), 277–320, here 280–1; see below, 172, no. 22.

saders.[15] The connection between the preaching of the cross and preaching on the feastdays of the cross is obvious. Sermons for the feastdays of the cross usually concentrate on the properties and the symbolism of the cross and the devotion on the crucified Christ. In such sermons the theme of crusading is often used as a metaphor for the journey to the heavenly Jerusalem.[16] Model sermons for the feastdays of the cross might thus have provided crusade preachers with themes or illustrative material for crusade recruitment sermons.

Sermons for Lent sometimes also featured the theme of crusading. Here the primary common ground was that of penitence. St Bonaventure, for example, used the crusading theme in such a way in one of his sermons for the Easter week.[17] The general penitential thrust of the whole of Lent, and especially the week leading up to Easter, could be expected to favour the promotion of crusading as the highest form of penitential exercise known to thirteenth-century laymen. A good example of such a sermon is the sermon for the Fourth Sunday in Lent (*Laetare Jerusalem*) by the Dominican William Peyraut. It was widely circulated, and crops up in various versions, each time with the act of crusading and the figure of the crusader being used as an outstanding example of a life of penance.[18] Here, too, crusade preachers might have been able to find material for their sermons, even though the main subject of

---

[15] Ms. Pisa, Biblioteca Cateriniana del Seminario, 21, ff. 60r–61v (*sermo in exaltatione crucis*). The same can be said for a second sermon for the same feastday of this collection (ff. 61v–63v), although the dual purpose character is less obvious.

[16] See, for example, a sermon for the feastday of the Invention of the Cross by the mid thirteenth century Franciscan Nicholas of Biard in: Ms. Paris, Bibliothèque Nationale, lat. 18081, ff. 143r–144r; Schneyer, *Repertorium*, iv, 243, no. 175.

[17] St Bonaventure, *Opera Omnia*, ed. A.C. Peltier, 15 vols. (Paris 1864–71), xiii, 235–7 (*sermo iii Dominica in octava paschae*).

[18] Ms. Basel, Universitätsbibliothek, *B.V.7*, ff. 38v–39v; and William Peyraut, *Sermones dominicales ex epistolas et evangelys atque de sanctis secundum ecclesie ordinem* (Tübingen 1499), no. 39; Schneyer, *Repertorium*, ii, 546, no. 167, 552, no. 260. The sermon was very popular and appears in many later compilations: e.g., Aldobrandinus Toscanella (Schneyer, *Repertorium*, i, 255, no. 412.); Antonio Arazo de Parma (Schneyer, *Repertorium*, i, 310, no. 269.); Henricus de Friemar (Schneyer, *Repertorium*, ii, 643, no. 53.); James of Lausanne (Schneyer, *Repertorium*, iii, 66, no. 152); Martinus Strebus (de Truppau) (Schneyer, *Repertorium*, iv, 129, no. 69.); Thesaurus Novus (Schneyer, *Repertorium*, v, 552, no. 385.); anon. Vatican lat. 1255 (Schneyer, *Repertorium*, vi, 617, no. 58.); anon. Assisi 432 (Schneyer, *Repertorium*, vii, 127, no. 220); anon. Avignon 295 (Schneyer, *Repertorium*, viii, 59, no. 46); Cole (*Preaching*, 232–4) edited a version of this sermon found in an Oxford manuscript (Schneyer, *Repertorium*, ix, 62, no. 78). According to the rubric to this sermon, it was preached in the extant form at the nunnery of Elstow on Sunday *Laetare* (26 March) 1283 and certainly not as a crusade recruitment sermon.

these model sermons was the inducement to the spiritual journey to the heavenly Jerusalem and not the recruitment of crusaders.

Apart from model sermons there are two known crusade preaching tracts of the thirteenth century. The longer one of these is Humbert of Romans' preaching handbook *De predicatione S. crucis*, written around 1266–8.[19] In it Humbert collected materials for the preaching of the cross to the Holy Land, probably with the intention that it might be carried by crusade preachers on their recruitment tours. The wealth of material, presented in this small, portable handbook, would have facilitated the task of preaching a great number of sermons to different types of audiences during these tours. A handbook like the *De predicatione* thus made it no longer necessary for preachers to carry a large number of books during preaching tours or to prepare a huge number of sermons prior to embarking on such a tour. Still, it is difficult to say how widely known or how popular Humbert's *De predicatione* was among thirteenth-century crusade preachers. Although it has survived in numerous manuscripts, none can be dated safely to before 1300.[20] The only comparable thirteenth-century handbook for the preaching of the cross is the shorter and less systematically arranged *Ordinacio de Predicacione S. Crucis in Anglia*, which was also written for the preaching of the cross to the Holy Land. There is no certainty about its author or its date. It was probably written for an Anglo-Norman audience sometime after 1216 and has survived in two thirteenth-century manuscripts only.[21]

In *De predicatione S. crucis* Humbert of Romans advocated succinct sermons with simple argumentative structures, whilst condemning overly long and complicated sermons. He also suggested that in certain cases preachers ought to abandon formal sermons and try to persuade individuals or small groups in 'colloquia familiaria'.[22] When commenting on Philip of Raven-

---

[19] Humbert of Romans, *De predicatione Sancte crucis* ([Nürnberg 1495]). For a short description and further secondary material, see E.T. Brett, *Humbert of Romans. His Life and Views of Thirteenth-Century Society* (Studies and Texts 67; Toronto 1984), 167–75; Cole, *Preaching*, 202–17. [20] Kaeppeli, *Scriptores*, ii, 288–9; Cole, *Preaching*, 202–3.

[21] 'Ordinacio de Predicacione S. Crucis in Anglia', *Quinti Belli Sacri Scriptores Minores*, ed. R. Röhricht (Publications de la Société de l'Orient Latin. Série historique 2; Geneva 1879), 2–26. For the date and provenance, see Röhricht's introduction (p. vii–x). The *Ordinacio* again and again is referred to as having been written by Philip of Oxford around 1216, most recently by Powell (*Anatomy*, 51–2). This must stop. Philip's authorship is but a most tenuous piece of conjecture and the date 1216 is a *terminus post quem* not *ad quem*. See also Cole, *Preaching*, 110–1.

[22] Humbert of Romans, *De predicatione*, chs. 1, 28.

na's crusade sermon at Ferrara, Salimbene confirmed that this type
of sermon had above all to be short in order to be effective.[23]
Humbert of Romans also suggested that preachers divided their
sermons up into relatively short passages and that after each
division they addressed the audience with a formal 'invitatio' to
take the cross.[24] Throughout the first part of his treatise, usually at
the end of each chapter, Humbert inserted various of these
formulaic 'invitationes', which were marked out in the margin so
that they could be found more easily during a sermon.[25] Humbert
of Romans further advised preachers to compose their own
sermons according to the requirements of each specific occasion
and audience. In chapters 2–26 of his treatise, Humbert set out
twenty-five different themes considered suitable for crusade
sermons. A preacher was expected to make his own selection of the
topics he wanted to address. In this case, the handbook provided
him with ready-made arguments and phrases which he only had to
string together in some kind of conclusive arrangement. To those
preachers who were well capable of writing their own sermons,
Humbert suggested they use the handbook as a source of information and inspiration. In the opening chapter he pointed them to
the raw material ('materia rudi') presented in the second section of
the tract, comprising chapters 26–46. Humbert listed 138 passages
from the bible upon which a crusade sermon might be preached.[26]
This was followed by two chapters about the character, qualities
and the general background knowledge required of crusade
preachers. Apart from impeccable character and excellent skills as a
preacher, Humbert expected a sound knowledge of the crusading
indulgences and privileges, of those parts of the scriptures which
relate to the Holy Land in particular, of world geography, of the
origins and the doctrine of the Muslim religion, and of the past
history of Muslim aggression against Christians. Humbert advised
preachers to inform themselves elsewhere about these matters and
suggested several theological and historical works.[27] In the final
section of *De predicatione* Humbert provided preachers with a

---

23 Salimbene de Adam, 'Cronica', 394–5.
24 It seems to have been this technique which Gerald of Wales used during one of his
  recruitment sermons in Wales in 1188. See Gerald of Wales, *Opera*, i, 74–6.
25 Humbert of Romans, *De predicatione*, ch. 1.
26 Humbert of Romans, *De predicatione*, ch. 27.
27 Humbert of Romans, *De predicatione*, chs. 28 ('De necessariis predicatoribus crucis'), 29
  ('De sex generibus scientie que sunt necessaria eisdem').

number of *exempla* from various historical writings, which he considered suitable for the preaching of the cross.[28]

Model crusade sermons and crusade preaching tracts are not, however, conclusive evidence for establishing what mendicant, or other, crusade preachers actually said when they preached the cross. Model sermons were sources to be quarried by individual preachers; the choices made by individual mendicant friars when selecting material from such preaching aids are unknown and there is no way of knowing their preferences. Looking at chronicle reports of crusade sermons by secular clerics and the reaction of the audiences, it seems that, generally speaking, there were two main ways in which crusade preachers could proceed. The first was to concentrate on the penitential and devotional aspects of crusading by stressing their audience's duty towards God, themselves, and their fellow Christians, and by praising the spiritual rewards that could be gained. The preachers did this mainly by pointing out people's moral deficiencies and sins, as well as their neglect of duty in defending Christianity and the Roman Church against their enemies. The aim behind this was to create feelings of contrition, shame, and compassion. Chroniclers described audiences successfully addressed in this way as overcome with emotion and tears. This had already happened when Pope Urban II first preached the cross at Clermont in 1095.[29] Likewise the assembly of noblemen whom Bishop Henry of Strasbourg addressed in 1188 were said to have been excited by 'devotion' and to have shed tears of 'piety' and 'compassion'.[30] Similarly, Martin of Pairis, preaching at Basel in 1201, moved his audience to tears.[31] The sermons of Baldwin of Canterbury and of Innocent III seem to have had similar effects.[32] The other way of making people take the cross was by exciting their anger, rage, and aggression towards the enemy of the faith against whom the crusade was preached. When the papal legate for Lombardy preached the cross against Alberigo da Romano at Venice in 1258, he chose to provoke the Venetians by demonstrating Alberigo's wickedness. Before his sermon he paraded in front of the audience a number of women who had been captured and raped by Alberigo. The people were appalled by the sight of the half-naked, ravaged women, vociferously condemned Alberigo

---

[28] Humbert of Romans, *De predicatione*, chs. 30–43.
[29] Baldric of Bourgueil, 'Historia Jerosolimitana', *RHC oc.*, iv, 1–111, here 15.
[30] 'Historia Peregrinorum', 124.   [31] Günther of Pairis, 'Historia', col. 228.
[32] Gerald of Wales, *Opera*, i, 74–6; Maccarrone, *Studi*, 8.

and his family and demanded their deaths. The legate skilfully played on the mood of the audience by whipping up emotions during his sermon. At the end, when they were full of anger and rage, he called upon people to take the cross, which many of them did.[33] In a similar way, Philip of Ravenna, when preaching the cross at Ferrara two years earlier, branded Ezzelino da Romano a 'limb of the Devil' and a 'son of iniquity' for having maltreated orphans, waifs, widows, and other people, thus exciting feelings of disgust and revenge in his audience.[34] In general terms, the main idea behind a crusade sermon seems to have been to create an interior and external *Feindbild*, that is an image of the enemy within and without. The aim was to make an audience respond to these *Feindbilder* by assuming the cross. The spiritual reward in the form of the indulgence offered to *crucesignati* was believed to relieve people from the consequences of their interior enemy, that is their sinfulness. The participation in, or support of, the holy war was a means of combatting the external enemy, that is the enemy of Christianity or of the Roman Church.

Before embarking on the actual sermon, however, a preacher had to explain to his audiences the specific circumstances of a crusade, such as the state of the Holy Land or the Latin Empire, or the danger facing the Christian communities in the Baltic. Model sermons were obviously unable to provide the kind of information which was pertinent to the promotion of a particular crusade. This information would normally have been taken from the specific crusade bulls, since the preambles of most crusade bulls provided a set of arguments and reasons for each crusade. The preambles varied in length and content, but they probably were the primary points of reference for most crusade propagandists' arguments. As early as 1213 Innocent III instructed crusade preachers to use the material of the crusading bull *Quia maior* as the basis for their preaching.[35] At times, popes even demanded of crusade preachers that they read out crusade bulls *verbatim*.[36] For the more immediate news about the Holy Land or other crusading theatres, preachers

---

[33] Salimbene de Adam, 'Cronica', 365–6.   [34] Salimbene de Adam, 'Cronica', 394–5.
[35] Innocent III, 'Opera Omnia', iii, cols. 817–22.
[36] E.g., *Regestum Visitationum*, 737–40; see also above, 102–3. Some sections of the so-called *Romersdorfer Briefbuch*, which mainly consists of letters concerning the crusade, may have served as reference material for crusade propagandists. If this is correct, it would confirm that crusade bulls, even outdated ones, were used as preaching aids. See F. Kempf, 'Das Romersdorfer Briefbuch des 13. Jahrhunderts', *Mitteilungen des Österreichischen Instituts für Geschichtsforschung. Ergänzungsband*, xii (1933), 502–71, here 561–2.

could also rely on letters and on information passed on by word of mouth from returning crusaders and other travellers.[37] Generally speaking, mendicant friars were in a good position to obtain this kind of news. Matthew Paris quoted several examples of friars sending letters concerning the crusade to England and France.[38] In addition, the regular meetings of the general chapters, which brought together the heads of provinces from all over Europe, certainly provided a valuable opportunity to exchange this kind of information.[39] Preachers also had to reserve some time for the re-affirmation and explanation of the crusading indulgences and privileges. As a rule, however, preaching aids did not discuss the indulgences and privileges to any great extent, although most model sermons mentioned them in passing. In his *De predicatione S. crucis* Humbert of Romans demanded that crusade preachers know about them, but the treatise did not itself contain detailed information.[40] Again, the terms of the indulgence and privileges were usually provided in the crusade bulls. In the 1260s popes in addition issued crusade preachers with a copy of Innocent III's *Ad liberandam* in which both were defined in an exemplary manner.[41] If indulgences were mentioned in preaching aids, their theological and doctrinal aspects were rarely touched on. Instead the enormity of the plenary indulgence, for example, was explained in more or less striking images. Some described it as a 'key to paradise',[42] and one particularly vivid *exemplum* suggested that as people in Flanders pole vaulted across the small canals, so the indulgence allowed crusaders to 'pole vault' across purgatory.[43]

Preaching aids sometimes also touched on certain features of the indulgence which were not explicitly mentioned by the papal bulls and thus could be suspected of falling outside papal approval. To support their own views, authors normally quoted miracles and visions suggesting divine approval instead. An open question, even amongst theologians and canon lawyers of the thirteenth century, was whether a crusader could earn an indulgence for his or her dead parents. Raymond of Penyafort considered this possible, but it

---

[37] Lloyd, *English Society*, 34–41 and appendix 3.

[38] Matthew Paris, *Chronica Majora*, iv, 344–5, 433–4, 488–9, v, 72, 305–6, vi, 80–3.

[39] For a general discussion of the transmission of news of this kind and of the mendicants' role, see B.J. Cook, 'The Transmission of Knowledge about the Holy Land through Europe 1271–1314', 2 vols. (unpublished Ph.D. thesis; Manchester University 1985).

[40] Humbert of Romans, *De predicatione*, ch. 29.   [41] See below, 158.

[42] *Analecta Novissima*, ii, 423 (James of Vitry); Gilbert of Tournai, *Sermones*, f. 137va.

[43] See below, 173, no. 21.

was denied by others including Hugh of St Cher and Hostiensis.[44] Some model sermons, however, suggest that in practice Raymond's stance was acceptable. James of Vitry and Eudes of Châteauroux each presented this possibility almost as a matter of course.[45] There is also a thirteenth-century *exemplum* illustrating this particular point. It concerned a crusader of the Albigensian crusade who had finished his forty-day period of service required for a full indulgence. He was, however, persuaded by the papal legate to stay for another forty days so as to earn an indulgence for his dead father. The crusader agreed to this and was said later to have had a vision of his father confirming that he had, in fact, benefited from his son's additional crusade.[46] Another issue was that of crusading against one's wife's express wish. Again, thirteenth-century canon lawyers were not altogether sure whether Innocent III's ruling that a crusader could take a crusading vow without his wife's consent should be universally applicable.[47] Crusade sermons, like many other literary genres, portrayed the crusader's wife first and foremost as an impediment to crusading. Potential crusaders were advised not to listen to wives who tried to discourage them. The benefits of a crusade for the good of an individual's soul and for the protection of the whole of Christian society were seen as a justification for temporarily abandoning one's family.[48] In an attempt to make this practice more acceptable, James of Vitry, writing in the first half of the thirteenth century, already claimed that the wife and children of a crusader were entitled to full participation in the plenary indulgence.[49] But it was not until late in Innocent IV's pontificate that the papacy actively supported this view.[50] Lastly, there was the question of allowing the dying and the sick to take the cross and redeem their vows by paying money out of their testaments, an arrangement which became increasingly common.[51] There was no conclusive canon law ruling whether this should be permitted. Before vow redemptions were common, people had left legacies for the

[44] B. Poschmann, *Penance and the Anointing of the Sick*, trans. and revised by F. Courtney (Freiburg i.Br. and London 1964), 227–8.

[45] Analecta Novissima, ii, 333 (Eudes of Châteauroux), 426 (James of Vitry).

[46] See below, 172, no. 16.

[47] J.A. Brundage, 'The Crusader's Wife: a Canonistic Quandry', *Studia Gratiana*, xii (1967), 425–41.

[48] E.g., *Analecta Novissima*, ii, 311 (Eudes of Châteauroux), 429 (James of Vitry); Ms. Pisa, Biblioteca Cateriniana del Seminario, 21, f. 79vb (Eudes of Châteauroux); Gilbert of Tournai, *Sermones*, f. 135va.   [49] *Analecta Novissima*, ii, 426.

[50] Brundage, *Canon Law*, 154.   [51] See below, 125–6.

business of the cross without gaining a plenary indulgence. The sudden change was bound to make people suspicious. Three surviving thirteenth-century *exempla* were constructed to address this issue. Two of them concerned dying people who took the cross and redeemed it, and after their death appeared to close relatives in visions confirming their salvation and direct ascent to heaven.[52] The third one told the story of a seriously ill person whose confessor had suggested that he take the cross. The sick man initially had doubts about the benefits of this, but eventually donated all his possessions for a vow redemption after having had a vision of his own soul in heaven.[53]

At times, however, totally different techniques of persuasion were employed which lay outside the kind of orthodox preaching suggested by preaching aids. Miracles and visions were said to have happened during the propaganda campaigns of Eustace of Flay and Fulk of Neuilly before the Fourth Crusade.[54] The most striking example is that of Oliver of Cologne in Frisia in 1214. Several times Oliver's preaching was said to have evoked visions of the crucified Christ in the sky which caused a multitude of people to take the cross. The event was subsequently broadcast widely in France in the hope that it might attract crusaders there. It also was incorporated into various *exempla* collections and chronicles, and a few years later, similar visions were, in fact, reported in connection with the preaching of the cross near Cologne and in Bedfordshire in England.[55] Only a few incidents of this kind were said to have occurred during sermons of the friars. In the mid 1270s the preaching of an unnamed Franciscan crusade preacher in south west Germany was said to have created similar visions to those of Oliver of Cologne. During his sermons two white circles appeared around the sun, which cut into each other so as to create the signs of two crosses. There is, however, no information as to the context or the effect of his sermons.[56] Similarly, an English Franciscan, Roger of Lewes, was said to have acquired miraculous powers while preaching the cross in 1235. During one of his sermons he healed a

[52] See below, 173, nos. 29, 32.
[53] See below, 173, no. 31.
[54] Roger of Howden, *Chronica*, iv, 123–4, 165–72; A. Charasson, *Un curé plébeien au xiie siècle. Foulque curé de Neuilly-sur-Marne 1191–1202. Prédicateur de la IVe croisade, d'après ses contemporains et chroniques du temps* (Paris 1905), 86–7, 144–6.
[55] Van Moolenbroek, 'Signs', *passim*; see also below, 172, nos. 3, 9–14.
[56] 'Annales Basileenses', 200.

paralysed woman.[57] But the power to inspire visions and miracles was by no means a common gift among crusade preachers.

The difficulties crusade preachers may at times have experienced are well illustrated by two *exempla* from a manuscript collection now at Bern, which was probably compiled by a Dominican.[58] The first one tells the story of a papal legate and his companions ('socii et religiosi') who spent a long time preaching the cross to the people of a village, but without success. In the end they asked for a local cleric who could preach in order to help them out. They were referred to a priest who was described as unlearned ('sacerdos simplicissimus scripture et literature') and who normally preached about saints' legends. This priest was reluctant to address the people in the presence of the legate, but was finally forced to do so. He managed to make almost everybody take the cross by preaching without any reference to scriptural authorities ('sine aliqua auctoritate scripture') and by making his point through a simple, but suitable illustrative story ('simplicitate boni exempli ostencio'). First of all the priest asked the members of the audience to stand up if they belonged to his village. This was an attempt to overcome the awe and intimidation caused by the presence of the pompous papal legation, by appealing to their sense of local pride. He went on to ask them which they considered the more laborious work, threshing the grain or winnowing it. They all responded that it was threshing, because it took just one person to winnow the grain which ten others had threshed. The priest then explained to the villagers that this was what was happening now. The legate and his clerics had 'threshed them with the word of God all day long' and it was now his task to do 'the winnowing'. He then preached a short sermon, staying within the metaphor with which he had started. He reminded people of the opportunity to be absolved from their sins which Christ had offered them through his passion on the cross, his death and the shedding of his blood. He said that they had the choice of either taking the cross and thus becoming the grains which were brought to the barn of paradise ('paradysi horreum'), or of becoming the husks which were burnt in the everlasting fire of hell ('ignis eternus'). At the end of the sermon almost everybody was said to have taken the cross, convinced by a combination of the straightforward argument, the metaphor from their own rural

[57] Matthew Paris, *Chronica Majora*, iii, 312–13.   [58] See below, 173, n. 28.

environment and a sense of local pride and loyalty to their local priest in the presence of the papal legate who had been shamed by his performance.[59]

In the second *exemplum* a friar came to preach the cross in a certain town. He knew that the people there had all promised each other not to take the cross. So at the beginning of his sermon he asked them all to make the sign of the cross so that the devil would stay away from them. After they had done so, he continued by saying that he found himself in the midst of perjurers who had given their word not to be signed with the cross, but had all just done it. This amused the audience so much that they honoured his cunning and all took the cross.[60] Both these *exempla* may be invented or grossly exaggerated, but they were certainly meant to teach preachers of the cross a lesson: to make people take the cross was not simply a matter of choosing obvious and accepted arguments. To preach the cross successfully required skill and circumspection to devise the right kind of sermon for each individual occasion.

[59] See below, 173, no. 38.   [60] See below, 173, no. 40.

Chapter 6

THE FRIARS AND THE FINANCING OF THE CRUSADES

Throughout the thirteenth century the task of preaching the cross included the collection of financial subsidies in aid of the crusades. After Innocent III's *Quia major* the redemption of crusade vows for money and the collection of voluntary donations, normally referred to as *subsidia* or *obventiones*, in return for partial indulgences were regular features of all thirteenth-century crusading bulls.[1] As the century progressed, other means of raising money for the crusade became important, too. Preachers were also made responsible for the collection of testamentary legacies, referred to as *legata* or *deputata*, and the seizure of unlawfully acquired money. The borderline between subsidies and vow redemptions was often fluid. If people were willing to pay enough money, they probably took the cross and redeemed it afterwards for a plenary indulgence.[2] Any payment of money in aid of the crusade in return for an indulgence had to be handled by crusade preachers or papal collectors because all crusading indulgences could only be granted by those who were authorized by the pope. The mendicant friars certainly collected subsidies for the crusade from the very beginning of their appointment as crusade preachers. The earliest letters of 1234 which commissioned the friars to preach the cross to the Holy Land stipulated that they should also collect donations. These were to be deposited in churches or other religious establishments, and the pope informed about the amount, the provenance and the whereabouts of the money at the end of each year.[3] In connection with the publication of the bull *Rahel suum videns*, Matthew Paris remarked that crusade preachers everywhere, but in particular those of the Franciscan and Dominican orders, gave the cross to an infinite number of people, many of whom redeemed their vows

[1] Lunt, *Financial Relations*, 420–4, 428–32.
[2] See below, 135–60.
[3] BF, i (Gre.IX) no. 146 (= AFB, no. 4); *Pontifica Hibernica*, ii no. 214; BP, i (Gre.IX) no. 112.

almost immediately.[4] Matthew repeatedly stressed the mendicants' success in preaching the cross and raising money for the crusade by way of vow redemptions in England throughout the 1230s and 1240s.[5] Orders concerning the collection of subsidies and vow redemptions were repeated regularly whenever the friars were commissioned to preach the cross throughout the remainder of the century. There is next to no information about how exactly such payments were made, nor is there sufficient evidence to say how much money was forthcoming generally or by whom it was most commonly paid. Nevertheless, occasional references to such payments prove that the friars were regularly engaged in these financial dealings.

In connection with the Holy Land crusade of 1239–41 Gregory IX introduced the practice of forcing all *crucesignati* to redeem their vows if they failed to leave with the crusading army. Such an order was sent to the papal legate in England once the crusade of Richard of Cornwall was under way.[6] William of Cordelle, the Franciscan collector in France for Thibald of Champagne's crusade, was also sent back to France in order to collect outstanding vow redemptions after returning from the crusade in which he himself had taken part.[7] The policy of enforcing outstanding vow redemptions seems to have been successful, since money is known to have been collected by the friars not only in France and England but also in other parts of Europe.[8] In a similar fashion, there seems to have been a renewed attempt to collect vow redemptions for the defence of the Latin Empire, after the first contingent of crusaders had left France in summer 1238. Pope Gregory IX reminded the Dominicans of northern France to make sure that crusaders who had not yet gone, including those who had commuted their vows from the Holy Land to the Latin Empire, should prepare themselves for the next passage, or else redeem their vows.[9] One year after the remainder of the army had left with Baldwin II, the pope reiterated these orders.[10] Again the friars can be shown to have been involved in the collection of these moneys in France and England.[11]

---

[4] Matthew Paris, *Chronica Majora*, iii, 287–8; see also below, 139.
[5] Matthew Paris, *Chronica Majora*, iii, 312, 373–4, iv, 9, 133–4, v, 67, 73–4, 194–5.
[6] Matthew Paris, *Chronica Majora*, iv, 6–7.
[7] *Gre.IX R*, no. 5352; see also above, 34, 39–41 and below, 139–40.
[8] *Gre.IX R*, no. 6003; *Diplomatarium Suecarum*, i, no. 308.
[9] *Gre.IX R*, nos. 4621, 4622.   [10] *BP*, i (Gre.IX) no. 202 (= *Gre.IX R*, no. 5302).
[11] *BF*, i (Gre.IX) no. 320 (= *Gre.IX R*, no. 5312); *BF*, i (Inn.IV) no. 8 (= *Inn.IV R*, nos. 122, 123).

Gregory IX's successor, Innocent IV, expanded the scope of this kind of collection in aid of the crusades. In September and October 1245 he issued an appeal to the mendicants in Provence to seek out and collect for the subsidy of the Latin Empire any money that had been acquired by usury, theft, or by any other unlawful means.[12] This was to include testamentary legacies which comprised the proceeds of usurious practices or other illegally acquired money and which had been left for the settlement of outstanding debts, but had not been claimed by anyone after three years.[13] The same applied to testaments that had been made out for pious purposes in general, but had not yet been disposed of.[14] These papal orders have also survived for the Franciscans in the Province of Lombardy,[15] and Matthew Paris reported them being sent to both mendicant orders in England.[16] The task of collecting illegally acquired money may not have been easy. The friars were given the power to proceed with ecclesiastical censures if necessary, and the superiors of the two orders were allowed to absolve friars who were excommunicated for alleged frauds.[17] The seizure of bequests for pious purposes, in particular, was likely to be opposed by the heirs of such testaments. The problems, in fact, seem to have been more serious than the Curia had thought. In September 1246 Innocent IV had to order the friars to restrain their zeal in seeking out testaments and usuries. He wrote to all Dominican provincial priors, ordering them to change their strategy. Force and coercion were no longer to be used, and the friars were to rely on persuasion by preaching instead, accepting only voluntary donations.[18] This was in practice a recall of the original assignments. There must also have been many problems in establishing whether money had been acquired unlawfully or what form of money lending was obviously usurious. The latter also included the investigation of Jewish money lenders, which required the collaboration of secular authorities since the jurisdiction over the Jews generally was regarded as being a royal prerogative. In the late 1230s, Gregory IX had already encouraged Louis IX of France and Thibald of

---

[12] Delorme, nos. I, 4–5.   [13] Delorme, nos. I, 2–3.
[14] Delorme, no. I, 1.   [15] Sevesi, nos. I, II, IV, V.
[16] Matthew Paris, *Chronica Majora*, iv, 564–6; Lunt, *Financial Relations*, 435–6; Lloyd, *English Society*, 17–18.
[17] Sevesi, nos. VI; Delorme, no. I, 1; Ms. Limoges, Archives de la Haute Vienne, *H 9640*; Matthew Paris, *Chronica Majora*, iv, 565–6.
[18] Ms. Limoges, Archives de la Haute Vienne, *H 9640*; see also Planzer, 'Codice', no. 102; Scheeben, 'Bullario', no. 96.

Champagne to pay as subsidy to the Latin Empire money bor-
rowed from Jews if the money was known to have been acquired
by usury and if the original debtors could not be found.[19] By
assigning the task of collecting this kind of money to the friars,
Innocent IV seemed to be infringing a royal prerogative and it is
not surprising that the only evidence that the matter was pursued
with some success comes from the French kingdom during the mid
1240s when the proceeds of such seizures were assigned to the king
anyway. Louis IX appointed a number of friars as *enquêteurs*, who
amongst other tasks were ordered to inquire into unjustified
usury.[20] But the king was careful to control the seizure of such
money. Only sums under 100 shillings could be handled by the
enquêteurs by way of mandate; higher sums were subject to
decisions of the royal courts or officials.[21] But even if the collection
of illegally and usuriously acquired money proved almost impossible, the collection of testamentary legacies in support of the
crusades alongside redemptions and donations remained a regular
feature of the friars' activities as promotors of the crusade.
Alexander IV recommissioned the collection of testaments to the
friars at Marseille in 1260,[22] and his successor Urban IV in May
1262 wrote to the Dominicans in Poland, France, and Scandinavia,
and probably elsewhere, asking them to keep collecting money for
the support of the Holy Land.[23] He also reminded the friars of both
mendicant orders to continue seizing unspecified testaments and to
collect other donations in most parts of Europe.[24] There is
evidence to show that these orders were in fact carried out.[25]

Apart from commissions to the mendicants *en bloc* the papacy
repeatedly used friars as special envoys in connection with the
collection of vow redemptions, testamentary legacies, and other
donations for the crusade. In France a prominent role in this was
given to the Franciscan William of Cordelle in connection with the
crusades to the Holy Land and the Latin Empire during the later
1230s.[26] During his mission in France, William of Cordelle was

---

[19] *Gre.IX R*, nos. 3899, 4601; R. Chazan, *Medieval Jewery in Northern France. A Political and
Social History* (John Hopkins University Studies in Historical and Political Science [91st
series] 2; Baltimore and London 1973), 110–13. [20] Jordan, *Louis IX*, 53–64, 184–5.

[21] Chazan, *Medieval Jewery*, 118–21. [22] Delorme, no. IV.

[23] *Diplomatarium Suecarum*, i, no. 481; *APP*, ii, nos. 1128, 1129.

[24] *APP*, ii, nos. 1130 (= *Layettes*, iv, no. 4760), 1138, 1140; *BP*, i (Urb.IV) nos. 14, 16, 19–21;
Doat, ff. 47v–48v, 52r–53r, 53r–54r, 54r–54v; Delorme, nos. V, 2, 4, 9, 10; Sevesi, no. XI;
Verci, ii, doc. nos. 117, 118.

[25] *Urb.IV R*, no. 125; *BF*, iii (Cle.IV) no. 18 (= *Cle.IV R*, no. 741).

[26] See above, 39–41 and below, 139–40.

assisted by a certain *magister* Paul and by another Franciscan, called Geoffrey, who later on became involved in the collection of money in England for the defence of the Latin Empire.[27] Another Franciscan, Brother Peter *de Philistiim*, collected vow redemptions for Humbert of Beaujeu during this time, together with the abbot of Belleville.[28] In addition, the Dominican William of Oléron, who had been appointed as crusade preacher in connection with the attempt to make Peter of Brittany commute his Holy Land vow to a crusade for the defence of the Latin Empire in 1237–38, was also told to collect vow redemptions, *legata* and *deputata* in Brittany and the Dioceses of Poitiers and Angers for Peter of Brittany and other prospective crusaders.[29] Like William of Cordelle, William of Oléron was collaborating with local bishops for the collection of crusading funds.[30] Later other mendicant friars were given similar assignments, although none of them can be shown to have taken such a prominent position as William of Cordelle. John of Limoges, also a Franciscan papal penitentiary, was operating in western France in the late 1240s. He was first mentioned as collector of vow redemptions and testamentary legacies in 1247 and is known to have worked in close cooperation with the archbishop of Rouen.[31] Other evidence comes from the British Isles. John *de Canter*, also a Franciscan, had been similarly commissioned in 1255. John was based at the convent at Worcester and collaborated with the archdeacon of Middlesex. Their commission may have been shortlived and was probably meant to cover only a few months until the arrival in England of the new papal collector, Rostand, who was in charge of all aspects of papal finance in England including the crusading tenth during the later 1250s.[32] In 1258, on King Henry III's request, Pope Alexander IV appointed another Franciscan, Mansuetus, to deal with the collection of redemption money in particular, probably because Rostand was pre-occupied with the collecting of taxes.[33] Once again, however, no details have been recorded about either John *de*

---

[27] Paul was rewarded for his services as William's *clericus* by a papal appointment to a benefice in the archbishopric of Sens. See *Gre.IX R*, no. 3908. Geoffrey was referred to as one time *socius* of William in 1243. See *BF*, i (Inn.IV) no. 8 (= *Inn.IV R*, no. 123).

[28] *BF*, i (Gre.IX) no. 281 (= *Gre.IX R*, no. 4627).

[29] *Gre.IX R*, nos. 3945, 4025, 4026, 4266; see also above, 42.   [30] *Gre.IX R*, no. 4265.

[31] *Inn.IV R*, no. 3059; *Regestum Visitationum*, 736. John of Limoges appears as papal penitentiary in 1251. See *Inn.IV R*, no. 4999.

[32] *Foedera*, i, 325; Lunt, *Financial Relations*, 269–86, 442–5.

[33] Matthew Paris, *Chronica Majora*, v, 679–80.

Canter's or Mansuetus's mission. Equally little is known about the activities of the Dominican Gerald who was collecting donations for the Holy Land in the Kingdom of Portugal together the bishop of Evora.[34] Slightly more information has survived for the Dominican, Ivo of Ayr, who during the late 1250s or early 1260s was commissioned to collect money in Scotland for the subsidy of the Holy Land. In January 1262 Pope Urban IV wrote to the prior and chapter of the Premonstratensians at Whithorn about money which Ivo had collected and stored at their priory. The money was to be sent to the London Templars from where it would be given to Florentine merchants.[35] In September of the same year the pope again ordered them to hand over the money, supposed to be at least 36 pounds sterling, this time to the papal chaplain, Master Leonard, or to his deputy.[36] What exactly was the reason for the delay in paying is unclear, but in 1266 the money had still not reached the Curia.[37]

Papal commissions purely concerned with the collection of money do not, however, seem to have been popular with some friars. Towards the end of Innocent IV's reign, the mendicant orders, therefore, obtained papal privileges giving them the right to refuse commissions which required them to collect money. The earliest papal privilege of this type dates from 1253. In it the pope granted the friars the right to refuse commissions involving the collection of money unless the privilege was suspended by papal authority for special assignments.[38] In 1262 Urban IV, however, repeatedly made clear *vis-à-vis* both the Franciscans and the Dominicans that the indult was not meant to apply to the collection of money which was given to crusade preachers while they were preaching the cross, that is vow redemptions, legacies, and donations.[39] The reason for seeking exemption from money collections appears to have been based on the friars' experiences as papal tax collectors in the 1240s. The papacy initially seems to have accepted the friars' reservations about tax collecting. Having to deal with business of a purely financial nature might easily run counter to the friars' sentiments, given their dedication to the ideal of absolute poverty. In 1238 Pope Gregory IX had ordered the

[34] *Nic.III R*, nos. 480, 481.   [35] *Urb.IV RCam.*, no. 133.
[36] *Urb.IV RCam.*, no. 141.   [37] *Cle.IV R*, no. 762; Macquarrie, *Scotland*, 55.
[38] *BF*, i (Inn.IV) no. 494.
[39] *Diplomatarium Suecarum*, i, no. 481; *BP*, i (Urb.IV) nos. 19, 21; Delorme, no. V, 10; *APP*, ii, no. 1132; *BSA*, x, 186, no. 174; Sevesi, nos. XI, XIII; Verci, ii doc. no. CXIX.

Dominicans in France and England to admonish clerics and laymen to pay the thirtieth and other subsidies for the Holy Land. But they were given no powers to collect, or enforce collections, and it must be assumed that the papacy expected the friars to approach the local clergy by preaching, personal admonitions, or other forms of persuasion.[40] An exception, however, was made for areas where there was a lack of an established local clergy. In southern Greece, for example, the pope imposed taxes on the income of both Latin and Greek clerics in 1241 and 1244. Both times the money was to be collected by local clerics with the help of the Dominicans, who were by then well established in those parts.[41]

It was the financial burdens of the conflict with Frederick II which led the papacy to the first systematic attempt to involve the friars in the collection of taxes on clerical income. Indications of this came as early as 1239 when, according to Matthew Paris, the Franciscans and the Dominicans were for the first time collecting money for the papal war against Frederick.[42] Little is known about the nature and extent of the subsidy of 1239, but it seems to have been levied in England and France and probably comprised the payment of a fifth of the annual income of foreigners' benefices and a voluntary subsidy from the native clergy.[43] It seems to be these collections that Louis IX referred to in a complaint to the pope at Lyons in 1245, in which he specifically condemned the Franciscans for collecting a subsidy for the Apostolic See from the French clergy.[44] Nevertheless, after the excommunication of Frederick II at the First Council of Lyons in 1245, the collection of subsidies was stepped up and mendicant friars remained involved. Franciscans and Dominicans were said to have transported money from England to Henry Raspe in 1246.[45] Around the same time Innocent IV made an attempt to confiscate the legacies of intestate clerics in England, which the mendicant friars were also ordered to collect; but royal resistance rendered the collection impossible.[46]

In May 1247 Innocent IV issued new requests for a subsidy from

---

[40] *Gre.IX R*, nos. 4619–22.
[41] *Gre.IX R*, no. 6035; *Inn.IV R*, no. 707. See also A. Gottlob, *Die Kreuzzugssteuern des 13. Jahrhundert. Ihre rechtliche Grundlage, politische Geschichte und technische Verwaltung* (Heiligenstadt 1892), 62–8, and above, 42–3.
[42] Matthew Paris, *Chronica Majora*, iii, 627.
[43] Lunt, *Financial Relations*, 197–205.
[44] Matthew Paris, *Chronica Majora*, vi, 99–112, esp.106.
[45] Matthew Paris, *Chronica Majora*, iv, 551.
[46] Matthew Paris, *Chronica Majora*, iv, 552–3, 604–5; Lunt, *Financial Relations*, 508–9.

the clergy of England, Scotland, Ireland, Germany, France, Gascony, Burgundy, Provence, and the Spanish peninsula to support the military efforts of the Roman Church against Frederick II.[47] According to Matthew Paris, the pope again sent Franciscan and Dominican friars to all French bishops asking them for voluntary subsidies.[48] One Brother Blancus, a Franciscan, is known to have been assigned to collect the subsidy in the town and Diocese of Avignon.[49] In Poland, too, the subsidy seems to have been collected since there is evidence showing that the Dominican Brother Godfrey, a papal chaplain, was collecting it.[50] But because of King Louis IX's disapproval – probably with a view to the financing of his own crusade to the Holy Land – little was collected, at least in France.[51] Other evidence, however, shows that elsewhere the collection of the subsidy was already well under way by 1247. For England, Innocent IV had already chosen as special envoy John the Englishman, the Franciscan provincial minister of Provence, by late 1246. John was accompanied by a fellow Franciscan named Alexander.[52] During their stay in England they can be shown to have been in contact with other Franciscans.[53] John's mission was successful in as much that he managed to overcome resistance against payment of the subsidy, which was the second in only two years, by King Henry III and large sections of the English clergy. John seems to have been particularly good at combining his qualities as a Franciscan friar with the powers of a papal representative. He apparently talked Henry III into supporting the levy of a subsidy by adopting a humble air and by drawing on the art of verbal persuasion, whereas he was firm and strict when dealing with local clergy and, insisting on his authority as papal representative, did not shun the use of ecclesiastical censure.[54] In the Spanish peninsula the resistance of the local clergy even led to the replacement of the Franciscan collectors. The Franciscan João Martins, guardian of Lisbon, was collecting the subsidy in the Archdiocese of Braga with little success, when in January 1247 the

---

[47] *Inn.IV R*, nos. 2997, 3025.   [48] Matthew Paris, *Chronica Majora*, iv, 601.

[49] *Inn.IV R*, no. 3026.

[50] *Inn.IV R*, no. 3957; 'Annales Capituli Cracoviensis', *MGHS*, xix, 582–608, here 599; see also Gottlob, *Kreuzzugssteuern*, 78.   [51] Matthew Paris, *Chronica Majora*, iv, 601.

[52] John's activities are described in greater detail by Lunt, *Financial Relations*, 220–5.

[53] *Monumenta Franciscana*, ed. J.S. Brewer, 2 vols. (Rolls Series 4; London 1858, 1882), i, 222–3, 385–6.

[54] Matthew Paris, *Chronica Majora*, iv, 599–600; Lunt, *Financial Relations*, 223.

pope appointed another Franciscan, Brother Desiderius, to supervise and coordinate the collections in the whole of the Spanish
peninsula. Some of Desiderius's appointees as subcollectors are
known. The Franciscan guardian of Gerona, Aimerico, was in
charge of the collections in Aragon, where he was assisted by a
fellow Franciscan, Pedro of Tarragona. A certain Brother Martin,
also a Franciscan, supervised the matter in the Archdiocese of
Toledo, while João Martins continued his task in the Kingdom of
Portugal. But the new team also seems to have encountered
difficulties, and in 1248 two new, non-mendicant collectors took
over from Desiderius.[55]

The increasing number of mendicants appointed as papal collectors of taxes and subsidies during the later 1240s was probably the
primary reason for the friars seeking the privilege of exemption
from these tasks at the end of Innocent IV's reign. Such missions
were not in the friars' interest, considering their commitment to a
life in poverty. The activities of tax collectors also seem occasio-
nally to have led to conflict with the local clergy which cast a
negative light on the mendicant friars in general, since the secular
clergy was especially hostile towards the papacy and the papal
collectors when taxes or mandatory subsidies were levied.[56] It is
also not surprising that the requests from the mendicants to be
relieved of such tasks came at a time when their exempt status came
under attack during a serious conflict with the seculars at the
University of Paris.[57] In the Franciscan order the pontificate of
Innocent IV was also a period of renewed discussion about the
meaning and practice of poverty.[58] The privilege of exempting
individual friars might have been important in trying to reconcile
rigourists amongst the Franciscan friars.

After the mid 1250s the papacy seems to have respected the
mendicant friar's unwillingness to act as papal tax collectors. In
fact, there is only one known case of a friar who became involved
in the collection of crusading taxes after the end of Innocent IV's
pontificate. In 1274 the Dominican John of Darlington – together
with Master Raymond of Nogaret, a papal chaplain – was chosen as
collector of the tenth in England. John's activities as papal collector

[55] Linehan, *Spanish Church*, 195–7.
[56] Lunt, *Financial Relations*, 175–365 *passim*; Housley, *Italian Crusades*, 190–206.
[57] For this conflict, see M.-M. Dufeil, *Guillaume de Saint-Amour et la polémique universitaire parisienne 1250–1259* (Paris 1972). [58] Lambert, *Franciscan Poverty*, 103–25.

are well recorded and have been dealt with elsewhere.[59] Little is known about John's origins or his life other than as papal collector. His appointment was in all probability instigated by King Edward I because of John of Darlington's long-standing, close connection with the royal family. John had been one of Henry III's confessors and in 1256 became a member of the king's council.[60] During his term as collector, in 1279, he was made archbishop of Dublin, and in 1283 the pope relieved him of his duties as collector in order to allow him to devote his full time and energy to his archiepiscopal office.[61]

Nevertheless, the friars were still involved in the administration of crusading taxes and subsidies in the second half of the thirteenth century. When the crusading tenth was re-instituted at the Second Council of Lyons for the duration of six years, the collection of the tax was re-organized and made more systematic, with the establishment of twenty-six permanent tax districts with collectors and subcollectors.[62] The introduction of a specific bureaucracy of tax collection throughout Europe involved the mendicant orders in that their convents were commonly used as safe places for the storage of money in a more systematic manner than before. There is evidence of the storage of money at mendicant convents for the crusade from as early as 1238; for the period after 1274, however, evidence of the safekeeping of crusade taxes in mendicant houses becomes much more plentiful.[63] There is also evidence that after 1260 the friars in various parts of Europe were commissioned to assist papal collectors in certifying the receipt, and organizing the payment, of money from crusading taxes.[64] In addition, the papacy commonly used the heads of individual mendicant houses as papal representatives and judge delegates in connection with the assignment of money to individuals and in order to deal with

---

[59] W.E Lunt, 'A Papal Tenth Levied in the British Isles from 1274 to 1280', *English Historical Review*, xxxii (1917), 49–89; Lunt, *Financial Relations*, 313–42, 641–65. W.E. Lunt, *Papal Revenues in the Middle Ages*, 2 vols. (Records of Civilization. Sources and Studies 19; New York 1934), i, no. 93.   [60] Matthew Paris, *Chronica Majora*, v, 549.

[61] *Mar.IV R*, no. 385.

[62] Gottlob, *Kreuzzugssteuern*, 94–116; Lunt, *Financial Relations*, 311–46.

[63] *Gre.IX R*, no. 4697; *Urb.IV RCam.*, no. 503; *Hon.IV R*, nos. 428, 429; *BF*, iii (Joh.XXI) no. 22 (= *Joh.XXI*, no. 113); *Nic.III R*, no. 126; *Diplomatarium Danicum*, ii, 2, no. 371 (= *Nic.III R*, no. 538); *BF*, iii (Nic.III) no. 104 (= *Nic.III R*, no. 449); *Mar.IV R*, no. 4; see also *Mar.IV R*, no. 5; *Joh.XXI R*, no. 89; *Joh.XXI R*, no. 99.

[64] *Urb.IV RCam.*, no. 462; *BF*, iii (Mar.IV) nos. 34, 35 (= *Mar.IV R*, nos. 242, 243); *Gre.X R*, no. 968; *BF*, iv (Nic.IV) no. 438 (= *Nic.IV R*, no. 6668).

disputes concerning money for the crusade.[65] And lastly, the papacy ordered the Dominicans to buy the houses of the Order of the Penitents of Jesus Christ, when it was dissolved in the mid 1280s, and forward the purchasing price as a subsidy for the defence of the Holy Land.[66] It seems that at times the mendicant houses where crusading funds were stored came under pressure from papal collectors. The increasing efficiency of the collecting apparatus demanded accuracy, expediency, and reliability at the local level. Several times during the 1270s Dominican provincial chapters in Provence reminded the friars to be cautious about any money they received for the subsidy of the crusade and to make sure that the accounts were accurate, lest the collectors force them to pay money that was missing. Money which individual friars received, therefore, was to be put in safe places for storage and transmission as quickly as possible.[67] Significantly it was around this time that one mendicant house was even excommunicated during a conflict over crusading funds.[68]

The friars clearly resented papal assignments purely concerned with the collection of money and were, therefore, allowed to withdraw from the collection of crusade taxes after 1250. But throughout the second half of the thirteenth century the friars still collected donations and vow redemption whenever they preached the cross, and they did not apparently mind storing money from taxes collected by others at their convents. The issue of absolute poverty seems to have been only one, probably minor, reason for refusing to collect taxes. Money which the friars collected or stored could never be considered their own, but belonged to the Holy See. Another, probably more important, reason for refusing to collect taxes seems to have been the friars' desire not to get into conflict with the secular clergy by advancing financial claims on behalf of the papacy. Significantly, there is no conclusive evidence, either from within or outside the orders, to suggest that dealing with crusade finance in whatever form was considered to go

---

[65] *Gre.X R*, nos. 368, 369, 454; *BF*, iii (Gre.X) no. 101 (= *Gre.X R*, no. 602); *Mar.IV R*, no. 25; *BF*, iii (Mar.IV) no. 8 (= *Mar.IV R*, no. 86); *BF*, iii (Hon.IV) no. 48 (= *Hon.IV R*, no. 532)

[66] *Hon.IV R*, nos. 77, 81, 83, 84; *Nic.IV R*, no. 461. In a similar case, the Dominicans at Lausanne were asked to purchase the house of the Order of Sta. Maria in Valle Viridis at Solothurn. See *Hon.IV R*, no. 82.

[67] *Acta Capitulorum Provincialium*, 178, 229.

[68] *Gre.X R*, no. 442.

against the kind of apostolic poverty practised by the vast majority of mendicant friars in the thirteenth century. Generally speaking, there cannot have been any doubt, among the friars as elsewhere, that crusading without sufficient financial resources was simply not possible.

Chapter 7

THE FRIARS AND THE REDEMPTION OF CRUSADE VOWS

The crusade vow differed from most other religious vows in two principal ways. Firstly, it was accompanied by the promise of a plenary indulgence, and, secondly, its execution was not merely an individual act of devotion and penitence, but it was also part of a collective effort in the context of the *negotium crucis*. By taking the vow, the *crucesignatus* made a promise not only to God, but also to his fellow Christians. The redemption of a crusade vow was technically a form of vow commutation substituting an adequate penitential exercise *in lieu* of crusading, in this case the payment of a certain amount of money in aid of the crusade. This was primarily intended for those who sincerely wished to go on crusade but were physically incapable of doing so because of illness, old age, poverty, or other serious impediment. Since, by virtue of his vow, the crusader had taken on an obligation of service to the whole of Christian society, the only way to commute his vow was to support the business of the cross in some other way, either by joining a different crusade or by making a financial payment for the benefit of the crusade. The commutation to other forms of purely individual penance was not possible. This particular situation was dealt with by reserving the powers to redeem (or commute) a crusade vow, unlike that of other vows, to the pope and his appointed agents alone. The 'natural' rate for the redemption of a crusade vow was the donation of enough money to finance a substitute crusader of equal status. But if a crusader would have been accompanied by a retinue, the redeeming *crucesignatus* was expected to pay for a military force equal to his own. A poor crusader, on the other hand, was allowed to contribute less than the 'natural' rate, as long as he donated a substantial part of his material belongings, that is to say as long as the payment constituted a sacrifice which underlined its penitential character. To negotiate the right amount of money for a redemption was a matter of discussion in each individual case. In the second half of the twelfth century it seems to have been common practice to examine the crusader's ability to fulfil a vow in person before taking the cross. Those deemed unfit to crusade in person were offered a partial indulgence in return for paying a certain amount of money in aid of the crusade. This practice restricted the cases of vow redemption to those who fell ill or were struck by sudden poverty between the time of taking the cross and leaving on crusade.[1]

But this was not altogether satisfactory. The examination of a crusader's military ability and financial means seems to have been a difficult and lengthy business, for which crusade preachers were not always equipped and did not always have time. In *Quia major* of 1213 Innocent III, therefore, encouraged the preachers of the Fifth Crusade to let everyone take the cross and deal with the question of redemption afterwards.[2] His aim presumably was to speed up the process of recruiting crusaders rather than to create a situation in which everybody would take the cross. In principle a *crucesignatus* was still expected to pay for at least one soldier to crusade in his stead. A contemporary canon lawyer commented on the issue of vow redemption by suggesting that a 'poor' *crucesignatus* ought to pay one pound, which he probably meant as the lower limit of a redemption.[3] But a person who was able to dispose of a pound was certainly not poor, in the sense of living near or below the subsistence level. The instructions in *Quia major* probably did not mean that people who were quite obviously unable to go on crusade should be given the cross. Innocent III did not perhaps foresee the results which the new regulations concerning vow redemptions created in practice. One chronicler reported that Cardinal Robert Courzon and other crusade preachers in the French kingdom gave the cross indiscriminately to anyone who wished to take it, including children, old people, women, and the disabled. The majority of these would-be crusaders, however, were reluctant to redeem their vows. Most of them, in fact, wanted to crusade in person. But the French nobility was dismayed and refused to be accompanied by a crowd of useless fighters. This situation led to crusade preachers being attacked in public, and

[1] For the discussion of the crusading vow redemption in general, see Brundage, *Canon Law*, *passim*, esp. 68– 114, 131–8; Purcell, *Papal Crusading Policy*, 99–132.
[2] G. Tangl, *Studien zum Register Innocenz' III.* (Weimar 1929), 88–97. See also Innocent III's instructions to the dean of Speyer, in: Innocent III, *Opera Omnia*, 4 vols., *PL*, ccxiv–ccxvii, iii, cols. 904–5.   [3] Brundage, *Canon Law*, 76.

complaints against them were lodged with the pope.[4] Neither the exact nature nor the extent and outcome of these disputes are known. But the incident illustrates that the indiscriminate distribution of the cross was only beneficial if it was accompanied by efficient means of enforcing vow redemptions from those who, from a military point of view, were unwelcome on crusade.

The Fifth Crusade appears to have been the first crusade for which vow redemptions provided a substantial source of finance. The great advantage over other types of crusading subsidies was that vow redemptions could be enforced quickly and the money passed on to crusaders directly for the financing of poor crusaders and mercenary troops. The collection of taxes on clerical income, which was the papacy's other major financial resource for the crusade, usually took years to enforce and collect. In addition, the promise of vow redemption money could be used by the papacy to attract crusaders by offering them financial support as soon as the preaching of the cross started. But even if the returns from crusading vow redemptions were greatly increased by the introduction of the new regulations, their financial efficacy made them prone to exploitation from the start. Frederick II was said to have forced crusaders who planned to join him to redeem their vows after it had become clear that he himself would not go to the East.[5] As a secular person, however, the emperor was not entitled to do so since dealing with vows was a matter for the church. Innocent III certainly did not intend to turn the redemption of crusade vows into a purely financial venture. But the technical changes which he introduced to ease redemptions pointed in that direction.[6] People who would previously have paid a financial subsidy in support of the crusade in order to obtain a partial indulgence, were now tempted to take the cross and redeem it for a plenary indulgence. There was nothing wrong with this as long as the redemption payment was sufficiently high, but the danger of abuse was great.

Little is known about how and by whom the majority of vow redemptions was handled. Only the cases of more prominent crusaders which were referred to the pope are documented.[7] Caesar of Heisterbach recounted a story from the time of the

---

[4] William the Breton, 'Gesta Philippi Augusti', *Oeuvres de Rigord et de Guillaume le Breton*, ed. H.-F. Delaborde, 2 vols. (Paris 1882, 1885), i, 168–333, here 303–4.
[5] Powell, *Anatomy*, 164–5.   [6] Lunt, *Financial Relations*, 426–8.
[7] Lunt, *Financial Relations*, 427; Powell, *Anatomy*, 92–4.

preaching of the Fifth Crusade in which a rich peasant got away with paying five marks for a vow redemption, although he could have paid at least forty marks without even touching his patrimonial possessions.[8] Caesar's story makes it clear that Innocent's new regulations, even though they speeded up the recruitment of crusaders, simply postponed the problem of having to examine the *crucesignatus* until after the cross was taken. In another story from around the same time, Caesar explained that a *crucesignatus*, who could have gone on crusade in person, was not allowed to redeem his vow in his native Dalmatia, where people knew him well, and went to Rome to get his vow redeemed at the Curia by feigning blindness.[9] Generally speaking, however, it seems that standards were applied with care and rigour even if people tried to take advantage of the new system and there is no evidence to suggest that abuses were widespread. In both his stories, Caesar of Heisterbach mentioned a *dispensator* as the person in charge of redemptions. The word does not appear in the papal documents and judging from later evidence it could refer to either a crusade preacher, a personal *executor* of one of the more powerful crusaders or a papal agent especially commissioned to deal with vow redemptions. In any case, the fact that probably more people than ever before took the cross in the late 1210s and 1220s meant that more personnel was needed to administer the new system of vow redemptions. It is doubtful whether the Curia was able to provide enough people initially. A letter written by Oliver of Cologne in the mid 1220s shows that no one empowered to deal with crusade vows had visited some parts of Germany for several years. This, in turn, had led to the occasional appearance of unauthorized crusade preachers who had fraudulently collected vow redemptions.[10] It may have been this situation which allowed Frederick II to control vow redemptions himself in the late 1220s. This, however, was clearly unacceptable to the papacy, and Gregory IX is known to have taken measures to prevent the emperor from doing so.[11] First indications that vow redemptions were handled in a more systematic manner only appear with Gregory IX's widespread use of

---

[8] Caesar of Heisterbach, *Dialogus*, i, 70–2.

[9] Caesar of Heisterbach, *Die Fragmente der Libri VIII Miraculorum*, ed. A. Meister (Römische Quartalschrift für Christliche Alterthumskunde und Kirchengeschichte. Supplementheft 13; Rome 1901), 23–4.

[10] *Die Schriften des Kölner Domscholasters, späteren Bischofs von Paderborn und Kardinal-Bischofs von S. Sabina Oliverus*, ed. H. Hoogeweg (Bibliothek des Literarischen Vereins in Stuttgart 202; Tübingen 1894), 316.   [11] Richard of S. Germano, 'Chronica', 349.

mendicant crusade preachers in the mid 1230s. When Matthew Paris mentioned the friars preaching the cross in the 1230s and 1240s, he pointed out that huge numbers of people who took the cross and redeemed their vows almost immediately; these were mostly old and sick people, women, children, and disabled persons.[12] The friars, in fact, seem to have adopted the policy of making people who were obviously unfit to go on crusade redeem their vows more or less on the spot. This would have reduced the cases of doubtful crusaders whose ability to fulfil their vows in person would have to be examined. It would also have avoided the danger of involuntarily creating a large non-combatant crusading force as happened to Robert Courzon in 1213. But in order to achieve this, it was necessary to convince people that the plenary indulgence was valid, despite the fact that it was acquired in such an apparently easy way. According to Matthew Paris it was exactly this that the friars were so successful at doing.[13]

There is no doubt that the business of crusade vow redemptions continued to be prone to irregularities and abuse. But the following survey will show that the papacy was eager to deal firmly with these, often by seeking assistance from the mendicants. Problems must have arisen early on in the propaganda drive for the crusades of 1239–41. Matthew Paris reported that Gregory IX sent Brother Thomas, a Templar and member of the papal household, to England in 1236 in order to deal with crusading vow redemptions in particular.[14] No other sources mention Thomas and it is, therefore, unknown what exactly he did. But it seems that he was fulfilling a similar function to that of the Franciscan William of Cordelle in the French kingdom. William was not only in charge of coordinating the distribution of crusading funds,[15] but also had to deal with a number of irregularities and abuses. In 1238 William of Cordelle was asked to look into the matter of the *executores* of a number of French noblemen who were forcing crusaders, as well as Jerusalem pilgrims, to redeem their vows.[16] An earlier letter from the pope to the Dominican William of Oléron, who was preaching the cross in western France,[17] illustrates that this practice was likely to deprive the crusading army of man power: crusaders who were obviously capable of making the journey and fighting were

---

[12] Matthew Paris, *Chronica Majora*, iv, 133–4, v, 73–4.
[13] Matthew Paris, *Chronica Majora*, iii, 374.
[14] Matthew Paris, *Chronica Majora*, iii, 374.
[15] See above, 39–41, 124–6. [16] *Gre.IX R*, no. 4222. [17] See above, 42, 127.

apparently leaving for the Holy Land before the general passage in order not to be pressurized into redeeming their vows.[18] Another frequent problem seems to have been that people tried to take advantage of the lack of a proper investigation, prior to taking the cross, of their resolve and capability to crusade in person. This could result in a *crucesignatus* either attempting to redeem a vow for less than his financial situation allowed or to avoid fulfilling his vow in person or redeeming it altogether, while enjoying the legal and financial privileges of a crusader.[19] Thus in 1238 William of Cordelle – and the archbishops of Sens and Rouen – were reminded by the pope that weak and old crusaders had to redeem their vows, ideally by paying what they would have spent on crusade. The pope suggested that, in addition, these *crucesignati* ought to take up other laborious penitential exercises in order to prove their pious intentions.[20] William of Cordelle was also ordered to resolve a dispute between two crusaders over funds. Geoffrey of Argentan had been conceded crusading taxes from the Diocese of Poitiers to finance his crusade, although the money had already been promised to Peter of Brittany at some earlier stage. The pope, therefore, ordered William of Cordelle to make sure that Geoffrey would instead be given an appropriate amount from the vow redemption money of that diocese payable after he had left for Palestine.[21] The papacy was thus able to resolve disputes over crusading finance by drawing on vow redemption money, which was much more readily available than, for example, crusading taxes.

Problems with crusading vow redemptions became once more apparent during the preparatory phase of Louis IX's first crusade. But like his predecessor, Pope Innocent IV was intent on dealing with abuses firmly. In July 1247, two years after the preaching of the cross had started, Innocent IV ordered his agents – one of whom was the Franciscan John of Limoges – to stop collecting redemptions and testamentary legacies in the Kingdom of France for the time being and to deposit the sums safely, while letting the pope know the amount and whereabouts of the money.[22] It seems that the pope wanted to clarify how the redemption of vows was proceeding and how much money had been collected already. It

---

[18] *Gre.IX R*, no. 3945.   [19] Brundage, *Canon Law*, 187–9.
[20] *BF*, i (Gre.IX) no. 282 (= *Gre.IX R*, no. 4640). The same order, sent to the papal legate in Britain, has survived for Scotland. See *Gre.IX R*, no. 4220.
[21] *Gre.IX R*, no. 4107.   [22] *Inn.IV R*, no. 3059.

may well be that this inquiry was prompted by the scandal over the collection of redemptions by a false crusade preacher in Frisia.[23] Probably as a result of this inquiry, Innocent IV told the French bishops in March 1248 that too many crusaders had been allowed to redeem their vows and that stricter standards should be applied: if there was a suspicion that a crusader had redeemed his vow for too little money, he was to be forced to resume the cross.[24] In future, all vow redemptions in the French kingdom also had to be approved by the bishop of Paris. The collectors of the crusading tenth, however, warned the pope that many mentally and physically handicapped *crucesignati* could not possibly travel to Paris. The collectors, in turn, suggested that vow redemptions be collected by them.[25] It is unclear how the matter was resolved, but the evidence indicates that the centralization of the administration of vow redemptions did not, in fact, take place. In autumn 1248, for example, three vow redemption collectors in western France were still quarrelling amongst themselves over the right to collect in certain areas.[26] Around this time Innocent IV also recommissioned the treasurer of St Hilary of Poitiers to continue collecting vow redemptions for Alfonse of Poitiers's crusade, without reference to the bishop of Paris's supervisory function.[27] The problem in France at the time seemed to be compounded by the fact that too many *crucesignati* had been allowed to redeem their vows, thus causing the number of crusaders to fall short of that expected. Since many redemption payments were also considered too low by the pope, it seems that the French crusaders and their *executores* had learned from the mistakes of the late 1230s, when lesser *crucesignati* were alienated by enforcing too high redemptions. Low payments rather than no payments now seemed to be the order of the day. This, however, was likely to bring vow redemptions in general into disrepute because of the apparent ease with which they could be used to obtain plenary indulgences.

Significantly, it was in the context of the late 1240s that Matthew Paris most harshly accused the papacy over the issue of vow redemptions.[28] Matthew criticized Innocent IV for allegedly preventing crusaders from coming to the aid of Louis IX in the

---

[23] See above, 67.   [24] *Inn.IV R*, no. 3708.
[25] 'Triennis et biennis decima ab anno MCCXLVIII collecta', *RGHF*, xxi, 533–40, here 540.   [26] *Regestum Visitationum*, 733.   [27] *Layettes*, iii, no. 3726.
[28] Matthew Paris, *Chronica Majora*, v, 196.

Holy Land by making vow redemptions easier after the departure of the royal army.[29] In the context of the pope's refusal to make peace with Frederick II, Matthew repeated his accusations by saying that Innocent had given way to the requests of magnates, especially in the south-west of France, by allowing the indiscriminate redemption of crusade vows. He even suggested that this was one of the main reasons why Alfonse of Poitiers was unable to provide adequate support for his brother on crusade.[30] But there are doubts over how well informed Matthew Paris was about this matter, and whether he was too prejudiced to investigate the papacy's motives thoroughly. He also criticized the friars for forcing crusaders, after the departure of the French crusading army, to execute or redeem their vows immediately under threat of excommunication. Matthew did not realize that this practice had been established by Gregory IX and was aimed at those crusaders who had taken the cross without the intention of fulfilling their obligations.[31] There is sufficient evidence to show that Matthew Paris's accusations were quite unjustified. King Louis IX, in fact, left behind a fair section of his army when he sailed from Aigues Mortes in August 1245, and it seems that some of these crusaders were seeking to redeem or commute their vows.[32] But there is no indication that the pope gave in to such requests anywhere outside Frisia.[33] Immediately before the French king's departure to the Holy Land, in June 1248, Eudes of Châteauroux was ordered to make sure that no one in Marseille or other maritime cities commuted their vows without his approval.[34] In addition, the papal legate was asked to make sure that the cross continued to be preached after the departure of the main army.[35] The bishops of Evreux and Senlis received the same directives and were reminded that all French crusaders, clerics, and seculars, must either join Louis' army in the East or, if they had sufficient justification, redeem their vows by paying the money they would have needed on crusade.[36] Shortly before Alfonse of Poitiers left with the last section of the French crusading army, the pope once more issued direct appeals to those involved in the recruitment of crusaders. Thus, Eudes Rigaud, archbishop of Rouen and a former

---

[29] Matthew Paris, *Chronica Majora*, v, 24–5.
[30] Matthew Paris, *Chronica Majora*, v, 188–9; Purcell, *Papal Crusading Policy*, 127.
[31] Matthew Paris, *Chronica Majora*, v, 67; see above, 124.
[32] Matthew Paris, *Chronica Majora*, v, 24–5.   [33] See above, 67.
[34] *Inn.IV R*, no. 3966.   [35] *Inn.IV R*, nos. 4662, 4663.
[36] *Inn.IV R*, nos. 3968, 3975, 3976.

Franciscan, and John of Limoges, a Franciscan and a papal penitentiary, were told to oblige on oath ten crusaders to join Alfonse's army. These crusaders had to make themselves known publicly by wearing the cross and were allowed to redeem their vows only if legitimate reasons arose before departure.[37] The death of Raymond of Toulouse, however, caused many crusaders from south western France to abandon the royal crusade for political reasons.[38] This may have created the impression that too high a number of vow redemptions was taking place. But there is no reason to believe that Innocent IV supported this. He was merely accepting that he could not force the nobility of south western France to join the hated Capetian king without a leader of their own, and he tried to make the best of the situation by at least gaining some financial support in Languedoc for Louis's crusade. After Alfonse of Poitiers had left, Innocent IV, in a final attempt to make *crucesignati* fulfil their obligations, again ordered the bishops of Evreux and Senlis to put before crusaders in the County of Toulouse and the March of Provence a final ultimatum either to join the next general passage or to redeem their vows.[39]

One particular case of a vow redemption in Languedoc shows quite clearly that the business was, in fact, handled in a responsible and regular manner. It concerns Count Hugh IV of Rodez, a vassal of Raymond VII. Hugh had been one of Raymond's allies in the rebellion against the king in 1242 and later agreed to take the cross for Louis IX's crusade as a gesture of reconciliation, together with other noblemen from Languedoc.[40] For reasons unknown, he redeemed his vow in October 1248, even before the death of Raymond of Toulouse. Nevertheless, the pope ordered an inquiry into Hugh of Rodez' case in autumn 1249, as part of his campaign to make sure that all remaining crusaders fulfilled their obligations. The result of this inquiry has been recorded in a unique document. This legal document was drawn up on 19 May 1250 by Raymond of Amiliavo, archdeacon of Agen, in order to prove the lawfulness of Hugh of Rodez' vow redemption.[41] In the first section of the document Raymond of Amiliavo copied out a papal letter of 21 November 1249, addressed to himself in which he was ordered to

---

[37] *Regestum Visitationum*, 736.   [38] Richard, *Saint Louis*, 198.
[39] *Inn.IV R*, no. 4926. The same letter was also sent to the two mendicant orders in Germany with regard to crusaders from Frisia and Norway. See *ES*, iii, no. 20 (= *Inn.IV R*, no. 4927).
[40] De Vic and Vaisette, *Histoire*, vi, 736–7, 754–5; Jordan, *Louis IX*, 16–17.
[41] Delorme, no. III.

demand publicly that Hugh of Rodez and other crusaders in the Diocese of Rodez join the next general passage or redeem their vows for money while restoring any papal grants that they had received for the crusade. The second section of the document was headed by the rubric 'Super forma crucis assumptae'. It contained two letters from the bishop of Toulouse and two letters from the bishop of Rodez which confirmed that Hugh of Rodez had taken the cross together with Raymond of Toulouse on 6 January 1248. The third section was entitled 'Super depositione vero crucis'. Here, the archdeacon quoted a letter confirming the redemption of Hugh of Rodez' vow with a full crusading indulgence. This letter is dated 16 October 1248 and shows that the redemption had been authorized by Raymond of Amiliavo himself on behalf of Hugh of Turenne, the Franciscan crusade preacher in charge of recruitment in the lands of Raymond of Toulouse.[42] Raymond of Amiliavo clarified the situation by citing a letter addressed to him from Hugh of Turenne. In this, Hugh set out his powers by copying the papal letters which gave him the right to grant and collect vow redemptions. Hugh of Turenne then authorized Raymond of Amiliavo to act in his stead, in accordance with these powers, in a letter of 14 September 1248, written at the request of Count Raymond of Toulouse. The fourth section of the document is entitled 'Super redemptione vero crucis' and consists of the letter by Raymond of Toulouse to Hugh of Turenne in which he asked him to grant a vow redemption to Hugh of Rodez in return for the financing of one 'miles' on crusade. There follows another letter by Raymond of Toulouse to Hugh of Turenne which stated that Raymond had received from Hugh certain sums on 10 October 1248, including 200 *lib. tour.* paid on behalf of the count of Rodez. The account was confirmed by an *inspeximus* of 17 November 1249 by the papal chamberlain Nicholas, which in turn was corroborated by Hugh of Turenne in an *inspeximus* of 23 April 1250. The whole document was written by William Mainnani, a public notary, at the request of Raymond of Amiliavo who confirmed it on 19 May 1250 together with a number of other witnesses, laymen, and clerics, including several 'iurisprudenti' and 'notarii'.

It is not known why Hugh of Rodez wanted to redeem his vow. The sum offered by Hugh of Rodez for his remission was minimal, because it would at most have allowed to finance one substitute

---

[42] See above, 68.

crusader without retinue to serve for one year.[43] It is also interesting that Raymond of Toulouse wrote a covering letter to Hugh of Turenne about the matter. It appears that it may have been considered proper to obtain the consent of the crusader under whose command the redeeming *crucesignatus* had intended to serve, at least in the case of knightly crusaders. Another point which is illustrated by this document is the fact that Hugh of Turenne seems to have recovered the money which he collected for Raymond's crusade after the latter's death on 27 September 1249.[44] Hugh handed over the money mentioned in the document to Raymond of Toulouse in autumn 1248, at a time when the count was still expected to join King Louis in the East. But he seems to have transferred the money to the papal coffers shortly after Raymond's death. This makes sense in the light of Raymond of Toulouse's testament which stipulated that fifty well-armed soldiers be sent to the Holy Land for one year in case of his death occurring before his having fulfilled his crusading vow.[45] Whatever the scale of abuse, which is difficult to establish, there is no indication that people generally became suspicious of the business of vow redemptions. The case discussed here bears witness of the painstaking accuracy and care which was applied if vow redemptions were handled properly.[46] The papacy's efforts in trying to contain abuses and to stop any attempt to exploit vow redemptions seems to have contributed to the fact that plenary indulgences acquired in this manner remained popular.

It appears that vow redemptions had by the mid 1240s become valued assets for the financing of the crusade, particularly in connection with testamentary legacies. At the First Council of Lyons Innocent IV called upon the prelates of the church and all who were involved in the preaching of the cross to induce people to make testamentary donations in aid of the crusade to the Holy Land and for the defence of the Latin Empire. He stipulated that special indulgences be given for such contributions.[47] The text of the conciliar constitution does not clarify what these special

---

[43] This is an approximate estimate derived from a comparison with the figures quoted by Jordan (*Louis IX*, 67–8).   [44] De Vic and Vaisette, *Histoire*, vi, 804.

[45] Delorme, no. II.

[46] As point of comparison there is one other known case of a thirteenth-century crusading vow redemption which was ordered by the pope to be confirmed by a notarial act. It concerned an excommunicated Italian nobleman, Philip of Marerio, who had agreed to take the cross against Manfred in 1265. See Housley, *Italian Crusades*, 135.

[47] *Conciliorum Oecumenicorum Decreta*, 296.

indulgences were supposed to be. Neither is there much evidence for the way in which it was translated into practice. The different laws and customs of inheritance across Europe must have meant that there could not be one uniform interpretation. Evidence as to how the constitutions were put into practice during the late 1240s has survived for the Diocese of Lincoln in 1247, illustrating the central role which the friars as crusade preachers could, at times, play in this. The document in question is dated 1 August 1247 and consists of an instruction from Bishop Robert Grosseteste of Lincoln to the archdeacons of his diocese.[48] The order dealt with two separate issues, both concerning the business of crusade vow redemption. In the first place, Grosseteste passed on a summons from the papal collectors John Sarracenus and Berard of Nimphia. In a letter of 4 June, they had ordered him, along with other English bishops, to instruct all archdeacons to gather at London on 19 August. They were to bring with them any money from crusade vow redemptions that had been collected in their archdeaconries for Richard of Cornwall's crusade of 1240–1. In the same letter Grosseteste also sent instructions to his archdeacons concerning the collection of vow redemptions for the present crusade, that is Louis IX's first crusade. He ordered them to send trustworthy crusaders in the company of priests to each parish in order to record the names of those crusaders who were close to death or had died recently. They were to note down how much money these crusaders had planned to leave for the subsidy of the crusade in their testaments, while instructing them, or their testamentary executors, to have the money ready for collection. These lists had to be confirmed by witnesses in signature and seal and were to be sent to the rural deans. The deans then were to contact the Dominican and Franciscan friars who had preached the cross in their respective deaneries and instruct them, or their deputies, to go to each parish and demand the money as stated in the lists. If no testament had been made, the friars, together with the friends of the dead crusaders, were to fix a sum which was sufficient for the attainment of a plenary indulgence 'without causing scandal'. What exactly this last phrase meant is unclear, but it was probably aimed at preventing sums which were too large from being exacted for fear of upsetting the heirs to whom the money would otherwise have gone. At the same time the friars were to admonish other crusaders to redeem their vows if and when it seemed fit, and to induce the

[48] Matthew Paris, *Chronica Majora*, vi, 134–8; Lunt, *Financial Relations*, 433, 437.

sick and the dying who had not taken the cross to do so. In both cases they were reminded to be strict about the indulgences they granted. Only the payment of a large proportion of a crusader's possessions could warrant a plenary indulgence; lesser contributions were to be rewarded proportionately. In the case of the dying these agreements had to be made in the presence of those who had witnessed their testaments, possibly in order to facilitate the collection of the money after the death of the crusader. The money thus collected had to be deposited in sealed bags at churches or monasteries to await the arrival of Robert Grosseteste or Walter Cantilupe, bishop of Worcester, who as papal agents were empowered to collect vow redemptions, or their deputies. In this case, it seems, the canon of the First Council of Lyons was understood to mean that testamentary legacies could be used as vow redemption payments, thus allowing the testator to take the cross and to promise the redemption payment for the vow after his or her death. This would have allowed those who could not, or would not, afford to pay sufficient crusading aid for the redemption of a crusading vow to acquire a plenary indulgence by disposing of patrimonial goods which they could not do during their lifetime. Evidence of about the same time from the Diocese of Ely, which reported a similar practice, suggests that this may have been common at least in England.[49]

In his famous deathbed speech, as reported by Matthew Paris, Grosseteste was said to have sharply criticized the friars for persuading sick and dying people to take the cross and to make testamentary donations for the subsidy of the crusade. This practice allegedly led to sick crusaders who recovered having to pay substantial parts of their possessions and deprived the heirs of dead crusaders of large parts of their inheritance.[50] These allegations, however, seem to be Matthew Paris's rather than those of Robert Grosseteste. Similarly, the attacks against the friars – at the beginning of the deathbed speech they are even accused of heresy – and against financial abuses in connection with the preaching of the cross are totally out of line with everything else known about Robert Grosseteste.[51] He was an ardent supporter of both the

---

[49] See below, 173, nos. 29, 31, 32.
[50] Matthew Paris, *Chronica Majora*, v, 401–7, esp. 405.
[51] There has been much discussion about the authenticity of the speech. See R.W. Southern, *Robert Grosseteste: The Growth of an English Mind in Medieval Europe* (Oxford 1986), 291–5.

crusade and the mendicant orders. He officially taught the Franciscans when they first came to Oxford and his relationship with them thereafter remained a good one. They helped Grosseteste during his election to the see of Lincoln, and he, in turn, left them his valuable library. Both Dominican and Franciscan friars were among the members of his household.[52] After his election as bishop of Lincoln, Grosseteste did, in fact, have several altercations with the papacy, but these never touched on the business of the cross in any principal way.[53] On the contrary, Grosseteste was a faithful servant of the pope in matters of the crusade. From 1246 to 1250 he was in charge of collecting vow redemptions and testamentary legacies in England, together with Bishop Walter Cantilupe of Worcester.[54] Robert Grosseteste's appointment was probably due to the fact that earlier, in 1245-6, he had supported the papacy against King Henry III in a dispute over the payment of a subsidy from the English bishops to the Roman church. While defending the papal rights and insisting on the clergy's duty to obey the pope, Grosseteste helped eventually to overcome the king's resistance.[55] During his time as papal financial agent, between 1246 and 1250, he seems to have executed the papal orders with a similar, strict sense of duty. In fact, Robert Grosseteste was not a critic but a faithful supporter of the very practices Matthew Paris pictured him denouncing on his deathbed. Matthew Paris seems to have constructed Grosseteste's alleged anti-mendicant and anti-vow redemption stance on the latter's known opposition to the Roman Curia in some matters of papal finance and government.

Nevertheless, Matthew Paris criticized the friars for the part they played in the business of vow redemptions. His words were harsh. He called them 'arrogant' and accused them of acting against their precept of poverty.[56] In general, the English chronicler was not a friend of the friars, even though he sympathized with their ideas about poverty and evangelization. He found it difficult to accept that the humble friars used papal and royal support in order to obtain convents against the expressed will of other local religious establishments, including his own monastery of St Albans. He also thought it a paradox that they managed to channel people's charity

---

[52] Southern, *Robert Grosseteste*, 11, 19-20, 27, 74-5, 258-9.
[53] Southern, *Robert Grosseteste*, 8-13, 272-95.
[54] *Inn.IV R*, no. 2961; Lunt, *Financial Relations*, 436.
[55] Lunt, *Financial Relations*, 215-9.   [56] Matthew Paris, *Chronica Majora*, iii, 287.

away from other religious institutions and purposes, allowing themselves to live a life somewhat removed from the asceticism of strict apostolic poverty.[57] But these more general reservations about the mendicant orders must not be confused with the specific points of criticism which Matthew Paris put forward with regard to their role as crusade preachers and financial agents of the pope. It needs pointing out that he never accused them, or any other crusade preachers, of actually mishandling the business of crusade vow redemption. On the contrary, he made it clear that the friars' preaching of the cross was done in strict compliance with the privileges and indulgences of the papal bulls.[58] When revising his *Chronica Majora* in the 1250s he even edited out the fiercer attacks on vow redemptions and the friars and now praised them for the 'many fruits' in connection with their preaching in support of the crusade.[59] His motives for these and other changes are not quite clear, but the result was virtually a total turnaround in the way in which he viewed the friars.[60] What was bothering Matthew Paris in connection with the friars' preaching of the cross was that the papacy seemed to have found yet another way of successfully tapping the purses of the faithful. His attacks were first and foremost aimed at the Curia, which he accused of hypocrisy and false pretence in the way in which it tricked people into paying money to the Apostolic See. Several times Matthew mentioned the friars' involvement in vow redemptions in the context of the collection of taxes and subsidies for the support of the pope's conflict with the emperor.[61] He accused the Curia of keeping such money paid by the English clergy, despite the fact that peace between the pope and the emperor had been established, implying that the money from vow redemptions, too, was kept by the Curia without being used to subsidize the crusade. Using a powerful, if somewhat inconclusive, image, he accused the papacy of having captured the simple and the faithful with 'mousetraps' through the business of vow redemptions.[62] But elsewhere he made it clear that

[57] W.R. Thomson, 'The Image of the Mendicants in the Chronicles of Matthew Paris', *AFH*, lxx (1977), 3–34.

[58] Matthew Paris, *Chronica Majora*, iii, 373–4, iv, 133–4, v, 73.

[59] Matthew Paris, *Historia Anglorum*, ed. F. Madden, 3 vols. (Rolls Series 44; London 1866–9), iii, 51–2; see also Siberry, *Criticism*, 151–2.

[60] For the nature, the chronology and the motivations for the abridgements and expurgations in Matthew's chronicles, see R. Vaughan, *Matthew Paris* (Cambridge Studies in Medieval Life and Thought 6; Cambridge 1958), 110–24.

[61] Matthew Paris, *Chronica Majora*, iii, 287–8, iv, 9–10, v, 67.

[62] Matthew Paris, *Chronica Majora*, iv, 9.

in his opinion it was the papacy who had forced the mendicants into their role as financial agents for the Curia against their own will.[63]

There was, however, a specifically English context for Matthew Paris's criticism. His verbal attacks must be seen against the background of repeated attempts to collect vow redemptions for Richard of Cornwall during the 1240s and into the 1250s.[64] Matthew Paris indirectly accused the latter of despoiling the poor by 20,000 marks, in complicity with the Roman pontiff.[65] Richard of Cornwall had, in fact, been promised the vow redemption money from his own lands in order to finance his crusade of 1240–1. At the same time he also received large sums from the English Jewish community, from the king's feudal revenues, and from the tax of one thirtieth levied on clerical incomes.[66] Matthew Paris thought it scandalous that Richard, who so obviously seemed capable of financing his crusade from his own resources, should be given more money not only while he was on crusade, but also years after his return. It is unknown how much Richard of Cornwall spent on crusade and whether the money raised from royal and papal resources was sufficient. But there was no doubt that payments made to him after the crusade had the air of being unnecessary and unjustified. And even if Richard had spent more money on his crusade than he had been able to raise, it must have seemed mean of him to expect vow redemption payments, many of which came from the poor, to make up the difference. There is, however, no indication that the redemption of crusading vows was in any way administered fraudulently, nor is there reason to believe that people generally, whether poor or rich, took and redeemed their vows involuntarily.

Matthew Paris was also deeply suspicious of King Henry III's motives when he was granted crusading funds from the papacy in the 1250s. When the king took the cross himself in March 1250, Matthew accused him of using it as a pretence, believing that the king was not seriously thinking of crusading in person. In 1247 Henry had already unsuccessfully tried to obtain papal grants of crusading subsidies, allegedly in order to sponsor English crusaders, and his attempt to stop the English crusading contingent from joining Louis IX's first crusade in 1249 was throwing a doubtful

---

[63] Matthew Paris, *Chronica Majora*, iv, 635; Matthew Paris, *Historia Anglorum*, iii, 93.
[64] Lunt, *Financial Relations*, 430–4.   [65] Matthew Paris, *Chronica Majora*, iv, 133–4.
[66] Lloyd, *English Society*, 178.

light on the king's intentions. Such fears may not have been
justified at the time, but they were borne out by events to come and
echoed by other contemporaries, who, like Matthew, wrote with
the benefit of hindsight.[67] In addition, Matthew Paris probably
thought that the grant of substantial crusading revenues to Henry
III was unjust. In the mid and late 1240s the royal treasure had been
considerably augmented, probably because Henry was by then
already planning to go on crusade.[68] Additional papal grants must
have seemed unnecessary and and could have been more profitably
used to finance less well-off crusaders. Innocent IV, in fact,
promised King Henry III all crusading taxes, vow redemption
money, and other crusading subsidies of the kingdom in March
1250.[69] English crusaders, however, who had taken the cross
before this date and who were eager to join Louis IX in the East,
were concerned that the money which the pope had granted them
would be claimed by the king. But the pope was well aware of the
problem, which he probably discussed with the English crusaders
who came to see him at Lyons in the same year.[70] As a result, he
took precautions to make sure that the money assigned to crusaders
prior to March 1250 remained at their disposal. Money for the
king's benefit was to be collected by a new set of papal agents
starting with empty bags, as it were, so as to distinguish clearly vow
redemption money collected before and after Henry III's assumption of the cross. To the same end, Innocent IV planned to ascertain
the exact amount of money collected before this date. In autumn
1250 the pope sent Brother John the Englishman, the Franciscan
provincial minister of Provence, who had been used successfully by
the pope as a trouble-shooter in England in 1246–7,[71] as papal
nuncio to England. In the first instance, John was to make sure, with
the help of Bishop Grosseteste of Lincoln, that vow redemptions
and other donations for the Holy Land were set aside for the
crusade of Bishop Walter Cantilupe of Worcester.[72] At the same
time John was ordered to check the accounts of Walter Cantilupe,

[67] Lloyd, *English Society*, 208–32; Tyerman, *England*, 111–123.
[68] D.A. Carpenter, 'The Gold Treasure of King Henry III', *Thirteenth Century England I: Proceedings of the Newcastle upon Tyne Conference 1985*, ed. P.R. Coss and S.D. Lloyd (Woodbridge 1986), 61–88, here 62–71.
[69] For the money assigned to King Henry, see Matthew Paris, *Chronica Majora*, v, 101–2; Lunt, *Financial Relations*, 254–5, 439; Lloyd, *English Society*, 151–2.
[70] Matthew Paris, *Chronica Majora*, v, 117–8.
[71] Lunt, *Financial Relations*, 220–5; see also above, 130.
[72] *BF*, i (Inn.IV) no. 342 (= *Inn.IV R*, no. 4873); Lloyd, *English Society*, 149.

who had been collecting alongside Robert Grosseteste since 1246; the bishop of Chichester and the archdeacon of Essex, who were to take over as collectors, were to be present at the audit.[73] These new collectors were given special papal letters authorizing them to override provisions made to the king in the case of crusaders who had been promised money before March 1250.[74]

All this points to the conclusion that the papacy made every attempt to avoid abuse of the business of vow redemptions and that, as a way of raising money, vow redemptions were effective. Indeed, during the siege of Aachen, for example, they proved a convenient means of quickly raising money which was needed urgently by William of Holland's army. The priors of the Dominican houses at Louvain and Antwerp were told to organize the collection of money from vow redemptions of both Holy Land and anti-Hohenstaufen crusaders in the Archdiocese of Cologne and in the imperial regions of the Dioceses of Cambrai and Tournai.[75] When soon afterwards William of Holland's financial requirements proved to be once more great and urgent, the king's chaplains, William of Maaseik and John of Diest,[76] were also commissioned to collect vow redemptions, among other subsidies, in Germany and adjacent areas. By the same token, a commission of 11 May 1249 required William of Maaseik to organize the collection of vow redemptions and other donations both for the crusade to the Holy Land and against Frederick II. The Holy Land money was to be stored in a safe place until further papal instructions, while the anti-Hohenstaufen subsidies were to be paid to William of Holland directly.[77] Three days later, however, this order was changed. The pope now ordered both chaplains to assign the money from vow redemptions to the Holy Land also to King William.[78] A repetition of the order to collect vow redemptions of Holy Land crusaders went to John of Diest in August 1253 and in March 1254.[79] As in other cases the task of collecting vow redemptions was given directly to the *executores* of the crusaders to whom such money had been conceded, in order to speed up the collection and, at the same time, protect the papacy from accusations of misappropriating crusading funds.

[73] *BF*, i (Inn.IV) no. 349 (= *Inn.IV R*, no. 4875); Lunt, *Financial Relations*, 439.
[74] *Inn.IV R*, nos. 4880, 4881. The same provision was made for Scottish crusaders in 1251. See Macquarrie, *Scotland*, 51. [75] *ES*, ii, no. 589 (= *Inn.IV R*, no. 4166).
[76] See above, 73–6.   [77] *ES*, ii, no. 718 (= *Inn.IV R*, no. 4525).
[78] *ES*, ii, nos. 719, 721 (= *Inn.IV R*, nos. 4508, 4510).
[79] *ES*, iii, no. 225 (= *Inn.IV R*, no. 6910); *BF*, i (Inn.IV) no. 526 (= *Inn.IV R*, no. 7357).

The friars and the redemption of crusade vows

It was around this time that the friars, and other clerics, came under attack for having preached Louis IX's unsuccessful crusade. The news of the disaster of Mansurah in spring 1250 triggered a popular movement known as the Crusade of the Shepherds. Owing to the nature of the sources, there are more questions to be asked about this popular movement than can be answered.[80] Still, there is a possibility that the business of vow redemptions was one of the reasons for the Shepherds' attacks against the clergy, and especially against the friars, which was one of the most striking features of this revolt.[81] Salimbene made clear that these attacks were a result of the clergy's preaching of the cross.[82] They had been responsible for giving the cross and for allowing vow redemptions and commutations, and they were thus indirectly responsible for the recruitment and the composition of an army which had so miserably failed. The Crusade of the Shepherds was clearly designed as a crusade of the underdogs. The mood of the movement was one of evangelical awakening, stemming from the belief that God had assigned to the poor and powerless the task of liberating the Holy Land. Underlying the religious motivation of the Shepherds there was a strong undercurrent of frustration and a sense of social inadequacy. By taking on the business of the crusade, the poor and powerless usurped an activity apparently reserved to the fighting classes. Hence the context of the inception of the movement was the defeat of Louis IX's army, which was largely supported by the French nobility, and hence the composition of the movement, which seems to have been made up primarily of genuinely poor people.[83] In contrast to the way in which the crusade to the Holy Land was usually preached, namely as a war initiated by Christ for the recovery of his patrimony, the Shepherd's leader, the so-called Master of Hungary, claimed to have been given a letter commanding the crusade by the Virgin Mary.[84] This must be seen as a statement against those who had preached

[80] The most complete modern account is: M. Barber, 'The Crusade of the Shepherds in 1251', *Proceedings of the 10th Annual Meeting of the Western Society for French History*, ed. J.F. Sweet (Lawrence 1984), 1–23. Two recent attempts to reconstruct a wider historical context for the Crusade of the Shepherds are largely hypothetical: G. Dickson, 'The Advent of the *Pastores* (1251)', *Revue Belge de Philologie et d'Histoire*, lxvi (1988), 249–67; A. Tuilier, 'La Révolte des pastoureaux et la querelle entre l'université de Paris et les ordres mendiants', *La Piété Populaire au Moyen Age* (Actes du 99e Congrès National des Sociétés Savantes (Besançon 1974). Section de philosophie et d'histoire jusqu'à 1610; Paris 1977), 353–67.   [81] Barber, 'Crusade', 8–10.
[82] Salimbene de Adam, 'Cronica', 444–5.   [83] Barber, 'Crusade', 2–3, 16.
[84] Barber, 'Crusade', 2–3, 7.

the king's crusade, that is the clergy in general, and foremost amongst them the friars. The Shepherds were, however, aware of the irregularity of their undertaking and, therefore, approached Louis IX's mother and regent, Blanche of Castile, at Paris. Their claim that they could help the king where the nobility of the realm had failed was made in the hope that Blanche would legitimize and support their crusade.[85]

It has been argued that the main reason for the Crusade of the Shepherds was the diversion of crusading resources from the Holy Land crusade to the anti-Hohenstaufen crusade, which reached its height at exactly the time when the news of Louis's defeat at Mansurah reached France. The geographical framework suggests such a connection, since the region where the Crusade of the Shepherds most certainly originated was one where the cross for the anti-Hohenstaufen campaign was preached more vigorously than elsewhere.[86] But this cannot be the whole story, since there is no evidence that forcible commutations of vows took place. There is also no evidence that the enthusiasm for the anti-Hohenstaufen crusade in the borderlands between the Empire and France was not genuine. This argument also does not explain the element of social frustration and revolt of the movement. If, on the other hand, Matthew Paris was right in reporting that crusade preachers, and particularly the friars, were rigorously observing the regulations about the redemption of vows, this might be a more appropriate explanation: it may well be that the participants of the Crusade of the Shepherds were exactly those people who, by the mid-1250s, were denied the status of real crusaders by the common efforts of the military elite, who rejected their services, and the clergy who, as it were, sanctioned their exclusion from the crusade by encouraging them to redeem their vows. No one had any doubt that these people were useless for the business of the cross in a military sense. As Matthew Paris suggested, these people were in most cases made to redeem their vows on the spot.

It may have been relatively easy to accept the validity of a vow redemption for those who felt that their money payments made a substantial contribution to the crusade in military terms, most significantly those who financed substitutes to crusade in their stead. It may also have been possible for the educated clergy to believe that their spiritual support of the crusade in the form of

[85] Barber, 'Crusade', 3–4.   [86] Dickson, 'Advent', passim.

prayers was equal to the contribution of a knight in battle and that, therefore, the redemption of their crusading vows was justified. It is, of course, right to say that even the poorest *crucesignati* acquired the spiritual benefit of a plenary indulgence and that they probably believed in its value. But even if they were allowed to enjoy the full spiritual benefits of a *crucesignatus*, they were barred from enjoying the pride and sense of purpose pertaining to the status of crusaders, and no one was likely to honour their tiny financial contribution to the business of the cross. As mentioned at the beginning of this section, the crusade did have a distinct, worldly context. And it was from this context that the very poor seem to have been excluded. For them the experience of being allowed, and most certainly encouraged, to take the cross without being given the opportunity of making a valid contribution to the business of the cross must have been one of frustration, especially after the dismal failure of an army of knights and nobles. Significantly, it was after having been refused support from Blanche of Castille that, realizing that they were unable to organise their own crusade, the Shepherds abandoned the original aim and transformed the movement into a social revolt.[87] The spiritual reward of a redemption may have been some sort of consolation to them, but they lacked any tangible reward for their own, very sincere crusading enthusiasm. Their role in the business of the cross was one on the very fringe, ridiculed rather than honoured. At first sight it seemed that the new practice of vow redemptions of the thirteenth century broadened the social base of the crusading movement. But as a matter of fact, it excluded wide parts of society from any form of serious participation in the crusade.

Vow redemptions caused problems because they had become such an important financial resource for the crusades. In particular, the sums demanded for vow redemptions were the subject of serious and persistent controversy throughout the thirteenth century. In a letter written in the mid 1250s to the Dominican prior of Bristol, King Henry III, for example, considered it necessary to restore confidence in prospective crusaders by guaranteeing that no one would be forced to redeem their vows for more than they had promised when taking the cross.[88] In contrast, Thomas of Cantimpré complained that some gave as little as one tenth, one

---

[87] Barber, 'Crusade', 4–6, 10–11, 16.
[88] *Calendar of the Patent Rolls of the Reign of Henry III Preserved in the Public Record Office*, 6 vols. (London 1901–8), iv [1247–58], 84.

twentieth, or even one hundredth of the value of their moveable goods without ever having to touch patrimonial possessions. To him this seemed absurd, not because he thought that a plenary indulgence acquired in this way would not be of value, but because he could not understand that so small a sacrifice should be demanded of these people. Thomas found it difficult to accept that these *crucesignati* could gain a plenary indulgence with comparative ease whereas members of religious orders – he specifically mentioned the Cistercians, Franciscans, and his own order the Dominicans – did not receive a comparable spiritual reward for their harsh and austere everyday life.[89] The papacy certainly listened to these critics and took their concerns seriously. Thus Pope Clement IV reminded his papal legate in France to be stricter in the application of the regulations, since too many crusaders had been allowed to redeem their vows,[90] and later he suggested that vow redemptions with plenary indulgences should not be granted for less than one quarter of a crusader's annual income.[91] Another way of preventing abuse was to fix the sums for which crusaders might redeem their vows at the time of taking the cross. This practice appears at the end of Innocent IV's pontificate.[92] How common this became during the remainder of the thirteenth century is unclear, but three copies of such agreements have survived. One concerned the vow redemption of an English crusader in 1282,[93] the two other ones were drafted by Franciscan crusade preachers for crusaders in Marseille and probably Bologna in 1290.[94] On the one hand, the practice of having written agreements protected crusaders from unjustifiably high demands for vow redemptions. But, on the other hand, it could always be used by a crusader in an attempt to acquire a plenary indulgence for less than he could have paid. Thus the Dominican provincial chapter of Provence warned crusade preachers in 1275 not to overstep their powers of granting indulgences and to be cautious about giving the cross in return for fixed sums of money.[95] Nevertheless, the practice of fixing sums in advance did, at times, lead to a tendency to overcharge crusaders for a redemption. Around 1270, the Franciscan Gilbert of Tournai

---

[89] Thomas of Cantimpré, *Bonum universale de apibus* (Douais 1627), 138–9.
[90] *Cle.IV R*, nos. 1608, 1676.
[91] *Thesaurus novus anecdotorum*, ed. E. Martène and U. Durand. 5 vols. (Paris 1717), ii, cols. 196–9.   [92] *Inn.IV R*, no. 6419.
[93] *Letter Book of William of Hoo, Sacrist of Bury St Edmunds*, ed. A. Gransden (Suffolk Record Society 5; [Ipswich] 1963), 57.   [94] 'Documents inédits', 33–4; AFB, no. 466.
[95] *Acta Capitulorum Provincialium*, 199.

criticized those who tried to extort too high sums from sick and old crusaders and especially from those who had fixed a certain sum for redemption in advance. According to Gilbert this undermined the credibility and authority of crusade preachers in general, and caused many people to be reluctant to take the cross in the first place.[96]

The fact that abuses were almost impossible to do away with made vow redemptions an easy target for criticism. It came up regularly as a theme in crusading chansons which complained about the failure of specific crusading ventures. Huon of St Quentin attacked the practice of vow redemption in the wake of the Fifth Crusade.[97] An extended version of the same poem, advancing the same criticism, was written either by himself or by some other troubadour after the defeat of Louis IX's army in Egypt.[98] After the fall of Arsuf and Caesarea in 1265 the troubadour and Templar brother, Ricaut Bonomel, also criticized the diversion of money from vow redemptions,[99] whereas Raimon Gaucelm of Béziers spoke out against vow redemptions in general after the failure of Louis IX's second crusade at Tunis.[100] These criticisms were doubtless justified and serious, but it must not be forgotten that in all these chansons the redemption of crusading vows was only one amongst many other points of criticism, and it never was the most prominent or the most elaborate.[101] The authors, all of them crusading enthusiasts trying to account for the failure of a crusade, must have considered the business of vow redemptions a convenient scapegoat because of the recurring cases of abuse.

This is, however, not to deny that some of these critics attacked vow redemptions from a more fundamental, theological aspect. Huon of St Quentin thought that the disaster of the crusaders in Egypt showed clearly that God did not approve of vow redemp-

---

[96] Gilbert of Tournai, 'Collectio de Scandalis Ecclesiae. Nova Editio', ed. A Striock, *AFH*, xxiv (1931), 33–62, here 39–40.

[97] 'Jerusalem se plaint et li pais', *Les Chansons de Croisade*, ed. J. Bédier and P. Aubrey (Paris 1909), 146–9.

[98] 'La complainte de Jérusalem contre la cour de Rome', *La Langue et la Littérature Françaises depuis le IXe siècle jusqu'au XIV siècles*, ed. K. Bartsch (Paris 1887), cols. 373–80.

[99] 'Ir' e dolors s'es e mon cors asseza', *Poesie provenzali storiche relative all'Italia*, ed. V. De Bartholomaeis, 2 vols. (Fonti per la Storia d'Italia 71, 72; Rome 1931), ii, 222–4; Housley, *Italian Crusade*, 107.

[100] 'Ab grans trebalhs et ab grans marrimens', 'Les troubadours de Béziers', ed. G. Azais, *Bulletin de la société archéologique de Béziers* (2nd series), i (1858), 187–290, here 191.

[101] Siberry, *Criticism*, 196–8.

tions and that those who redeemed their vows, therefore, committed a mortal sin. In the 1260s Rutebeuf reiterated this view with special reference to the friars' activities. A vow redemption, he claimed, constituted an act of treason against God. For him there was no validity in a plenary indulgence procured through vow redemption and he thus accused the friars of deceiving the faithful by pretending 'to sell paradise'.[102] Significantly, Rutebeuf's criticism came at a time of renewed efforts, in summer 1262, by the recently elected Pope Urban IV to make sure that crusading vows were executed either by crusading in person or, with good reason, by the redemption of vows.[103] The variety of instructions contained in these letters suggests that there was a considerable amount of confusion as to the exact way in which the matter was to be handled. As a consequence of this, at various stages throughout the crusading season of spring to autumn 1263, Urban IV supplied the mendicant crusade preachers with a copy of *Ad liberandam* from Innocent III's registers, which contained all the principal crusading indulgences and privileges.[104] In addition, the Franciscan minister general and the Dominican master general were approached by the pope requesting them to make sure that the papal orders were carried out without delay and to clarify specific points about the way the propaganda was to be conducted.[105] Rutebeuf may also have suspected that the friars were collecting money for their own personal gain.[106] In fact, since the early 1230s individual houses of both mendicant orders had at times been conceded money collected for the crusade and other pious purposes for the building of convents and churches, although in general these payments excluded money from the redemption of vows for the Holy Land crusade.[107] But because in the early 1260s no major crusade seemed

---

[102] Rutebeuf, *Oeuvres complètes*, ed. E. Faral and J. Bastin, 2 vols. (Paris 1959, 1960), i, 424–30.

[103] Sevesi, nos. XVI, XVII; Delorme, nos. V, 3, 4, 8, 9; Verci, ii, doc. no. CXVIII; *Urb.IV R*, nos. 2912, 2915; *BP*, i (Urb.IV) no. 14, 20; *Doat*, ff. 47v–48v, 53r–54r; *APP*, ii, nos. 1145, 1147.

[104] *BF*, ii (Urb.IV) no. 51; *Urb.IV R*, nos. 436, 467, 2951; *Urb.IV RCam*, no. 327; *APP*, ii, nos. 1170, 1173, 1199, 1219, 1225.

[105] *APP*, ii, nos. 1119, 1142, 1200; *Urb.IV R*, nos. 365, 2912–15; *BF*, ii (Urb.IV) no. 31; *BSA*, x, 185–6, nos. 171–5.

[106] See the introduction to 'La complainte de Constantinople' in: Rutebeuf, *Oeuvres*, i, 422–4.

[107] *Gre.IX R*, no. 1209; *BF*, i (Gre.IX) no. 201, ii (Ale.IV) nos. 230, 403, 408, 411, 412, 457, 483; *BP*, i (Ale.IV) no. 162; *Codex Diplomaticus sive Anecdotorum Res Maguntinas, Francicas, Trevirenses, Colonienses Finitimarumque Regionum nec non Ius Germanicum et S.R.I. Historiam vel maximam illustrantium*, ed. V.F. de Gudenus et al., 5 vols. (Göttingen 1743–68), ii, 664.

likely to emerge, on which the money which was being collected as a result of the renewed preaching efforts could be spent, the French poet's fears were to some extent understandable. Rutebeuf, however, knew that his own opinion was not shared by everyone. In his chanson *La disputation du croisé et du décroisé* he showed an acute awareness of the fact that vow redemptions could be justified and that many people accepted them as a valid substitution for a crusade.[108] Theologians and canon lawyers of the first half and the middle of the century – amongst them the most eminent scholars of the mendicant orders – had developed the theory and theological foundation of the indulgence in such a way as to allow them to accommodate vow redemptions within the accepted body of the theological learning of the church without major contradiction.[109] This probably accounted for the fact that there was no fundamental criticism of vow redemptions from within the church throughout the whole of the thirteenth century.

The business of crusading vow redemption certainly remained alive and popular during the latter half of the thirteenth century, so that there is no reason to believe that the criticism levelled against it damaged it in any serious way. In England, where the episcopal records of the thirteenth century are much richer than elsewhere in Europe, sufficient documentation has survived to illustrate the point. As a rule, the registers only sporadically recorded specific cases of redemptions when a vow had been taken as an act of penance for a manifest crime, notably the violation of clerical privileges. In these cases the entry of the redemption served as a proof that satisfaction for the crime had been done.[110] However, two entire lists of questions for the examination of *crucesignati* have survived in the episcopal registers of Hereford and Lincoln, dating from the beginning of the 1280s and 1290s respectively. These lists must have been used to screen crusaders with the intention to establish under what circumstances and at what price a vow might be redeemed.[111] There is thus little doubt that vow redemptions were handled frequently and with the necessary care, even though conclusive information about the overall number of vow redemptions has not survived. But it seems that the papacy was trying hard

---

[108] Rutebeuf, *Oeuvres*, i, 470–8.   [109] Purcell, *Papal Crusading Policy*, 99–106.

[110] *Rolls and Registers*, iii, 159–60; *The Registers of Walter Giffard, Lord Archbishop of York, 1266–79*, ed. W. Brown (Surtees Society Publications 109; Durham 1904), 277–286.

[111] *Registrum Ricardi de Swinfield Episcopi Herefordensis AD. MCCLXXXIII–MCCCXVII*, ed. W.W. Capes (Canterbury and York Society Publication 6; London 1909), 78–9; *Rolls and Registers*, iii, 157–9; see also Brundage, *Canon Law*, 131.

to ensure that vow redemptions were administered in a meticulous and responsible manner and to deal firmly with cases of abuse. This certainly contributed to the fact that vow redemptions remained popular throughout the thirteenth century and that they provided the crusades with a valuable source of finance.

CONCLUSION

The friars' involvement in the propaganda for the crusade opens up a new aspect in the history of the mendicant orders. Throughout the thirteenth century, Franciscan and Dominican friars preached the cross for virtually all crusades wherever and whenever they were required to do so by the papacy. Until recently, historians ignored the topic despite the richness of the available source material. A general tendency to view the friars as 'humble', 'pacifist', and preoccupied with the basics of pastoral ministry has in the past caused many historians of the mendicant orders to emphasise the friars' missionary activities at the expense of their involvement in the crusading movement. But the careers of men such as Peter the Hermit, Bernard of Clairvaux and Fulk of Neuilly, who belong to the first century of the crusading movement, make it quite clear that there was a certain tradition of combining a life of apostolic poverty, asceticism, and popular preaching with an enthusiastic, and sometimes even fanatical, support for the crusade. In addition, few people in the thirteenth century viewed mission and crusade as mutually exclusive. This is also made clear by the fact that, despite the friars' involvement in missionary activities, the voices against the crusades from within the mendicant orders were few and isolated, and certainly not representative of the majority of friars.[1]

In lending their support to the crusades the mendicant friars followed in their founder saints' footsteps. By looking at the available source material in a new light it can be shown that both St Dominic and St Francis openly supported the crusades. Although Dominic persisted in his efforts to convert Albigensian heretics by preaching once the crusade against them had started, he can be shown to have been in close contact with the crusading army and its leader, Simon of Montfort. Francis of Assisi's support for the

[1] Kedar, *Crusade*, 136–203 *passim*.

business of the cross is even more apparent. His attempt, at Damietta, to convert Sultan al-Kamil and his army to the Christian religion was by no means a sign of disapproval of the crusade. On the contrary, the sources for his encounter with al-Kamil clearly indicate that Francis had no doubts whatsoever that, after the Muslims' refusal to embrace Christianity, the crusade was not only justified but that it was ordained by God. The mendicant friars thus followed their founder saints' vocation when lending their support to the crusade by preaching the cross.

Given the need for widespread and accurate propaganda for the crusades, the mendicant friars could, however, not be involved in the preaching of the cross effectively until their orders were established throughout Europe and until the papacy could trust the friars to execute orders issued by the Roman Curia faithfully. The person ultimately responsible for involving the friars in the propaganda for the crusade was Cardinal Ugolino of Ostia, later Pope Gregory IX. He was crucial in helping the Franciscan order to overcome its internal conflicts during the late 1210s and early 1220s, which despite its immense popularity had prevented the order's expansion beyond the Italian peninsula. Similarly, he was instrumental in creating the conditions which allowed the Dominican order to establish study centres at the Universities of Bologna and Paris, which, in turn, marked the beginning of the Dominicans' expansion into most other parts of Europe. Following the two orders' spectacular growth during the early 1220s, Gregory IX successfully tested their loyalty and reliability as papal negotiators and agents in Italy during his quarrels with Frederick II. He thus prepared the ground which led the papacy to employ the friars all over Europe for the preaching of virtually all thirteenth-century crusades after 1230.

The great number of trained preachers made available by the mendicant orders allowed the papacy to choose preachers and target crusade propaganda in a way which had been impossible before 1230. The most significant change brought about by the use of mendicant friars as crusade propagandists was that individual crusade preachers, personally commissioned by the papacy, were no longer the mainstay of papal crusade propaganda. The Curia now relied on the mendicant friars *en bloc* as the principal preaching force. The great number of mendicant houses all over Europe and the fact that the friars covered outlying areas and regions by itinerant preaching ensured the widest possible spread of the propaganda for the crusades. Individual preachers who were known to be particularly adept at broadcasting propaganda were now only sent to areas where the preaching of a specific crusade proved difficult or where special recruitment efforts were thought to be necessary. Since often two or more crusades were being preached at the same time, it was crucial that propaganda was organized in such a way that the individual crusades benefited according to their particular needs. The crusade to the Holy Land was, in this respect, considered the most important one by the papacy. Whenever the cross to the Holy Land was preached, popes commissioned the clergy all over Europe, including the mendicant friars. The preaching for other crusades was usually more limited in terms of the geographical area and the number of preachers. But it was in those cases that the friars proved to be most useful to the papacy. The great numbers of preachers available from the mendicant orders made it possible to conduct the propaganda for these crusades effectively even if other crusades were being preached at the same time. Thus, for example, in the late 1230s the pope was able to commission the Dominicans of northern France to preach the cross for the defence of the Latin Empire without endangering the recruitment of crusaders to the Holy Land. And in the 1240s the friars of both mendicant orders were in a position to supply the papacy with the additional preaching force necessary to sustain a minimal level of propaganda in support of the Latin Empire at a time when the main crusading enthusiasm and support was once more directed towards the crusades to the Holy Land. The earliest and most striking example, however, concerned the preaching of the cross for the Baltic crusades. Gregory IX and Innocent IV used the Dominicans of northern and north-eastern Europe to spread, and at the same time control, propaganda in order to channel crusading support into the hands of the Teutonic Knights. This allowed the latter to spearhead the christianization and colonization of the Baltic which had previously been held up by the rivalries between German and Scandinavian nobles. By restricting the preaching of the cross to the Dominicans alone, the papacy also prevented the immensely popular, and comparatively less expensive, Baltic crusade from soaking up the crusade resources of these areas to the detriment of other crusades. Later, however, as the threat to the Christian Baltic lands increased, the Curia successively extended the preaching of the cross, first to the Franciscans of north-eastern Europe and later also to the Baltic bishops and to members of other orders. The greatest test of the mendicant friars' reliability as crusade preachers came in the 1240s and 1250s when the cross against the Hohenstaufen was preached in Germany. The political circumstances caused the propaganda for this crusade to be conducted in an atmosphere which in certain areas of Germany posed an outright threat to the lives of those who preached it. Nevertheless, the vast majority of friars lived up to their duty of obedience towards the pope, and it was they who seem to have recruited most of the crusaders during that time. Even after the papacy changed its propaganda strategy away from public preaching towards diplomatic missions to key figures amongst potential anti-Hohenstaufen supporters, individual mendicant friars were prominent among the propagandists. As the focus of the anti-Hohenstaufen crusade shifted across the Alps to Italy, the mendicant friars remained involved in the preaching of the cross in both Italy and France, where they preached the cross alongside papal legates. In northern Italy they also recruited anti-Hohenstaufen crusaders as part of their inquisitorial activities during the 1250s.

Given the nature of the sources it is, of course, difficult to evaluate the friars' success in recruiting crusaders in quantitative terms. Chronicles only sporadically mention the preaching of the cross and they hardly ever present reliable figures. But looking at the evidence available for the organization of the preaching, it becomes clear that the volume of propaganda broadcast by the friars must have been considerable. Communications between the Curia and the provinces of the mendicant orders seem to have functioned reasonably well, and there are indications that the heads of the provinces were efficient in the way in which they passed on papal commissions. As to the overall number of preachers in each province, only limited information has survived. Initially, the papacy expected two friars per province to preach the cross, whereas towards the end of the century this figure was in some cases increased to as many as forty. These are only rough guidelines as to the actual number of preachers of the cross, but evidence from England in the 1290s suggests that the latter figure was not unrealistic. If applied to the whole of Europe, this means that, at times, many hundreds of friars would have been preaching the cross throughout Europe. But altough we have a great deal of information about the preaching of the cross, it is impossible to say exactly what proportion of the propaganda for the crusade was broadcast by the friars. There are some indications that mendicants far outnumbered the secular clergy as preachers of the cross by the end of the thirteenth century. But a reliable comparison can only be made once there has been more systematic research into the crusade propaganda efforts of the secular clergy. In the course of this study it has, however, become clear that the tensions between the friars and the secular clergy, which are seen by many historians as a major determining factor in the development of the mendicant orders in the thirteenth century, must not be overemphasized with regard to crusade propaganda. The general level of education among local clerics and the increasing burden of diocesan administration probably prevented many bishops from organizing the preaching of the cross successfully from their own resources. There is ample evidence that bishops generally supported friars who were preaching the cross in their dioceses and at times called upon local mendicants to support their own efforts in propagating the crusade.

Despite the richness of the source material it is impossible to reconstruct the contents of the mendicant crusade sermons. There are certain indications as to the way in which sermons were put together by using the papal crusading bulls and preaching materials such as model sermons, preaching tracts and exempla. It is also known that there were certain occasions on which crusade sermons might be held, such as special feastdays or tournaments. In addition, there is information about general strategies of persuasion employed by crusade propagandists in trying to draw on their audiences' sense of contrition and revenge. But unfortunately there are no sources revealing what mendicant crusade preachers actually said in their sermons. It is thus not possible to determine a particularly mendicant form of crusade preaching.

Hand in hand with preaching the cross went the collection of money in aid of the crusades. The kind of poverty practised by the vast majority of mendicant friars in the thirteenth century does not seem to have prevented them from collecting money for the crusade in the form of donations and vow redemptions whenever and wherever they preached the cross. Acting as papal financial agents did not, *prima facie*, violate the vow of absolute poverty, since money collected in this way technically belonged to the Roman Curia and never passed into the possession of the friars themselves. However, the friars were loath to take on commissions which were purely concerned with the collection of money, also because it was likely to lead to conflict with the secular clergy. As a result of this, the papacy, from the late 1250s onwards, refrained from involving them in the collection of crusade taxes. With regard to the redemption of crusade vows, the friars even seem to have led the way towards a more efficient administration of the system, introduced by Pope Innocent III, which allowed practically everyone to take the cross and redeem it for money. The friars appear to have been particularly adept at reducing the inherent problem of examining a crusader's ability to fulfil his or her vow in person by making it easy for those who were clearly unable to do so to redeem their vows more or less immediately. Although this practice may have been one of the points of departure for the Crusade of the Shepherds, during which the friars in particular were attacked for their role as crusade preachers, it generally seems to have helped to streamline the crusading armies by excluding vast non-combatant contingents.

This study has attempted to throw new light on certain aspects of the history of the crusades and the mendicant orders in the thirteenth century. The friars' involvement in the preaching of the cross shows them to have been an important link between the papacy and the people of Europe. Being an expression of forceful and ebullient religious belief, the crusade seems to have fitted well into the mendicant orders' pastoral programme of religious renewal which was meant to imbue the faithful with a new Christian spirit. The mendicant friars took on this mediating role early in the development of their orders and it remained important throughout the thirteenth century. This, in turn, allowed the papacy to employ the friars in its attempt to give the crusades a well-organized and efficient propaganda back-up on the home front. The popes had to do this because of the sharp increase in crusading activity in the thirteenth century and they were able to do it because of the emergence and growth of the mendicant orders. Without the friars the papacy would probably have had to surrender control over the crusading movement during this period. Crusaders all over Europe, on the other hand, might have encountered many more serious problems over recruitment and financing their campaigns. The friars thus helped in shaping the crusading movement in a crucial way. Without them the crusades of the thirteenth century might have developed very differently.

Appendix 1

THE CRUSADE AGAINST THE DRENTHER AND THE ESTABLISHMENT OF THE DOMINICAN INQUISITION IN GERMANY

The inquisition had been on the minds of both Gregory IX and Frederick II long before its formal establishment in the Empire at the end of the 1220s and the beginning of the 1230s. Before becoming pope, Cardinal Ugolino of Ostia persuaded Frederick to promulgate a first set of imperial decrees against heretics on the day of his coronation as emperor in 1220.[1] In 1224 Frederick re-inforced legislation against heretics in Lombardy.[2] In turn, Gregory IX, after becoming pope, reconstituted the inquisition in Lombardy in 1227, and at the same time sent Conrad of Marburg, previously a crusade preacher in papal service, as inquisitor to Germany.[3] But despite Conrad of Marburg's efforts, the inquisition in Germany was underdeveloped in the late 1220s. The effective running of the inquisition required close collaboration between the secular and the ecclesiastical powers. Only the latter could conclusively decide who was and who was not a heretic and only the former was in a position to punish those convicted. This fact was brought home to the pope most forcefully in 1227–8, when the conflict surrounding the allegedly heretical Drenther peasants took on warlike dimensions. After the murder of Bishop Otto II of Utrecht by the Drenthers, Willibrand of Oldenburg was elected as his successor in 1227. According to the *Gesta Episcoporum Traiectensium*, Willibrand was chosen because of his close family ties with the counts of Holland and Guelders, who were among the major opponents of the Drenthers, and because of his acquaintance with Emperor Frederick II.[4] Willibrand was expected to be a strong and resourceful avenger and defender of the episcopal rights and honours. The sources for the Drenther crusade are too sparse to determine how exactly this local conflict was turned into a crusade.[5] Willibrand was reported to have preached the cross in Frisia several times in late summer and autumn of 1228, in summer of 1230, and again in winter of 1230–1.[6]

---

[1] K.-V. Selge, 'Die Ketzerpolitik Friedrichs II.', *Probleme um Friedrich II.*, ed. J. Fleckenstein (Vorträge und Forschungen 16; Sigmaringen 1974), 309–43, here 316–21.

[2] Selge, 'Ketzerpolitik', 321–4. It is uncertain whether the decree applied to Lombardy only; but scholars generally seem to assume that it was not valid for Germany. In the light of the later developments of the inquisition in Germany this appears a likely assumption. See Patschovsky, 'Ketzerverfolgung', 692, n. 160.

[3] *ES*, i, no. 362 (= *Gre.IX R*, no. 109); Patschovsky, 'Ketzerverfolgung', 642–3.

[4] 'Gesta Episcoporum Traiectensium', 415–16.

[5] The general background of the war against the Drenther is discussed in: F.H.J. Diepernik, 'De Drenste opstand tegen het bisschoppelijke gezag in 1227', *Bijdragen van het Institut voor middeleeuwse geschiednis der Rijks-Universiteit te Utrecht*, xxvi (1953), 1–36.

[6] 'Gesta Episcoporum Traiectensium', 417, 421, 422–3.

Appendix 1

Even though no papal bull has survived, the *Gesta Episcoporum Traiectensium* makes it clear that from the start Willibrand was acting with papal authority.[7] Since at the time of his election to the see of Utrecht, Willibrand was staying with Frederick II in Italy and is known to have acted as imperial envoy to the Curia, he would have been in a position to obtain the powers to preach the cross by asking the pope in person before returning to take up his bishopric in the Low Countries in 1228.[8] The justification for the crusade was presumably that the Drenther had defied their bishop's authority (*contemptus clavium*) which technically made them heretics.[9] There is, however, no evidence that the pope had the allegations of heresy properly investigated. Gregory IX probably trusted Willibrand as a crusader of longstanding reputation[10] to proceed with the crusade only if he considered these allegations justified. What may have been worrying the pope, however, was the fact that the crusade against the Drenther was initially not very successful and was not finally ended until September 1232.[11]

Following the Peace of S. Germano and Ceprano a new common initiative by the pope and the emperor against heretics in the Empire was begun. In December 1230 Gregory IX asked Frederick II to provide the secular legal framework for the support of the inquisition in the imperial parts of Provence.[12] In the *Regno*, Frederick implemented the anti-heretical statutes in the Constitutions of Melfi which were completed in August 1231.[13] In Lombardy, as in the city of Rome, Pope Gregory had already promulgated new anti-heretical statutes on the basis of the imperial decree of 1224 in the hope that the secular authorities would lend their cooperation voluntarily, since the emperor's power was too weak to create an improved legal framework for the inquisition in northern Italy.[14] The Curia also worked out a new set of inquisitorial statutes for Germany which was first sent to the German archbishops in June 1231.[15] The pope seems to have waited for a reaction from the German episcopate as to the viability of the new statutes before supplying Conrad of Marburg as the existing, and the German Dominicans as the newly selected, inquisitors with the statutes in October and November.[16] Although there are indications that King Henry VII showed a certain willingness to support the new plans for the German inquisition as early as June 1231, his intransigence towards the German princes and the emperor delayed the promul-

---

7 'Gesta Episcoporum Traiectensium', 417.

8 'Gesta Episcoporum Traiectensium', 415–16; J.C.M. Laurent, *Wilbrands von Oldenburg Reise nach Palestina und Kleinasien* (Hamburg 1859), 35–7. There is no justification for supposing that in the latter years he was overspending 'his spiritual capital' and that his 'indulgence was a gimmick', as stated by Kennan ('Innocent III', 27–9). Willibrand would legitimately have used the authority confered upon him in the original papal bull during the entire crusade.

9 O. Hageneder, 'Die Häresie des Ungehorsam und das Entstehen des hierokratischen Papastums', *Römische Historische Mitteilungen*, xx (1978), 29–47, here 42–4.

10 'Gesta Episcoporum Traiectensium', 416; Rüdebusch, *Anteil Niedersachsens*, 23, 45–7, 70–1.   11 'Gesta Episcoporum Traiectensium', 426.

12 *Gre.IX R*, no. 508; Selge, 'Ketzerpolitik', 335.

13 The inquisition in the *Regno* seems to have functioned well, too well in fact for the pope's liking, who accused Frederick two years later of abusing the inquisition for political reasons. See Selge, 'Ketzerpolitik', 334–7.   14 *Gre.IX R*, nos. 535, 539, 540.

15 *Acta Imperii Selecta*, no. 959.   16 Freed, *Friars*, 142–3.

gation of the secular legislation which was needed to make the inquisition effective.[17] After the king's failure to attend the imperial diet at Ravenna in late 1231, Frederick II, in February 1232, proceeded without his son's approval and published the imperial decree which allowed secular judges to pronounce the death sentence on heretics condemned by the inquisition. In March the emperor formally confirmed his support of the inquisition directly with the five Dominican houses of Friesach, Regensburg, Würzburg, Strasbourg and Bremen.[18]

[17] Van Cleve, *Emperor Frederick II*, 357–64.
[18] Selge, 'Ketzerpolitik', 334–5, esp. n. 64.

Appendix 2

A LIST OF THIRTEENTH CENTURY SERMONS AND EXEMPLA FOR THE RECRUITMENT OF CRUSADERS

A CRUSADE SERMONS[1]

James of Vitry

1 'Sermo ad crucesignatos vel crucesignandos'.[2]
2 'Sermo ad crucesignatos vel crucesignandos'.[3]

John of Abbeville

3 'Sermo ad crucesignatos'.[4]

Philip the Chancellor

4 'Sermo de crucesignatione contra Albigenses'.[5]
5 'Sermo de crucesignatione contra Albigenses'.[6]

---

[1] A crusade sermon ascribed to Stephen Langton has been lost. The sermon was part of a section of a compilation of sermons by various early thirteenth-century Paris masters now at Oxford: Ms. Oxford, Magdalen College, 168, ff. 50v–51r mentions a sermon *ad crucesignatos* on the contents sheet of the original collection. But only the first nineteen sermons mentioned there, which do not include this sermon, have survived. See F.M. Powicke, *Stephen Langton* (Oxford 1927), appendix 2, 170–6. There are also five short sermons 'euntibus ad bellum vel accipientibus crucem contra infideles' in an anonymous Franciscan sermon collection now at Barcelona (Ms. Barcelona, Archivo de la Corona de Aragon, *Ripoll 187*, ff. 82r–82v, 82v–83r, 83r, 83v, 83v–84r; Schneyer, *Repertorium*, vii, 147, nos. 56–60). Although the collection is not dated, paleographical evidence suggests that it belongs to the early fourteenth century. Apart from stylistic features, the most important dating evidence is the use throughout of Arabic numerals, which outside mathematical tracts does not appear before the fourteenth century in Spain. See A. Millares Carlo and J.M. Ruiz Ascencio, *Tratado de Paleographia Española*, 3 vols. (Madrid 1983), i, 281–2. [I wish to thank Dr D. Greenway for her expert advice on these matters].
[2] Schneyer, *Repertorium*, iii, 216, no. 413; edited in: *Analecta Novissima*, ii, 421–2.
[3] Schneyer, *Repertorium*, iii, 216, no. 414; edited in: *Analecta Novissima*, ii, 422–30.
[4] Schneyer, *Repertorium*, iii, 538, no. 395b; see Ms. Paris, Bibliothèque Nationale, *Nouv. acqu. lat. 999*, ff. 169r–170r; edited in: Cole, *Preaching*, 222–6.
[5] Schneyer, *Repertorium*, iv, 837, no. 270. The sermon appears amongst a number of additional sermons of Philip's sermons, in: Ms. Troyes, Bibliothèque Municipale, *1099*, ff. 17r–18r.
[6] Schneyer, *Repertorium*, iv, 837, no. 271. The sermon appears amongst a number of additional sermons of Philip's sermons, in: Ms Troyes, Bibliothèque Municipale, *1099*, ff. 18r–19r.

A list of thirteenth-century sermons

Eudes of Châteauroux

6 'Sermo in conversatione beati Pauli et exhortatio ad assumendam crucem'.[7]

7 'Sermo de invitatione ad crucem'.[8]

8 'Sermo de invitatione ad crucem'.[9]

9 'Sermo de invitatione ad crucem'.[10]

10 'Sermo ad invitandum ad crucem'.[11]

11 'Sermo contra hereticos de Albigensibus partibus'.[12]

12 'Sermo de rebellione Sarracenorum Lucherie in Apulia'.[13]

13 'Sermo de rebellione Sarracenorum Lucherie in Apulia'.[14]

14 'Sermo de rebellione Sarracenorum Lucherie in Apulia'.[15]

Gilbert of Tournai

15 'Sermo ad crucesignatos et crucesignandos'.[16]

16 'Sermo ad crucesignatos et crucesignandos'.[17]

17 'Sermo ad crucesignatos et crucesignandos'.[18]

Humbert of Romans

18 'Sermo ad peregrinos crucesignatos'.[19]

Roger of Salisbury

19 'Sermo ad dominicam quartam post epiphaniam domini; Istud potest esse thema ad crucesignatos vel in die parasceves.[20]

Frederick Visconti

20 'Quando idem dominus (= Frederic) predicavit crucem litteraliter clero Pisano de mandato domini pape'.[21]

---

[7] Schneyer, *Repertorium*, iv, 439, no. 562; edited in: *Analecta Novissima*, ii, 310–15.

[8] Schneyer, *Repertorium*, iv, 443, no. 602; edited in: *Analecta Novissima*, ii, 328–31.

[9] Schneyer, *Repertorium*, iv, 443, no. 603; edited in: *Analecta Novissima*, ii, 331–2.

[10] Schneyer, *Repertorium*, iv, 443, no. 604; partly edited in: *Analecta Novissima*, ii, 332.

[11] Schneyer, *Repertorium*, iv, 468, no. 909; partly edited in: *Analecta Novissima*, ii, 332–3. Also in: Ms. Pisa, Biblioteca Cateriniana del Seminario, *21*, ff. 79r–80r.

[12] Schneyer, *Repertorium*, iv, 464, no. 863; Ms. Arras, Bibliothèque Municipale, *137 (876)*, ff. 88v–90r.

[13] Schneyer, *Repertorium*, iv, 465, no. 877; Ms. Arras, Bibliothèque Municipale, *137 (876)*, ff. 108r–109r.

[14] Schneyer, *Repertorium*, iv, 465, no. 878; Ms. Arras, Bibliothèque Municipale, *137 (876)*, ff. 109r–110v.

[15] Schneyer, *Repertorium*, iv, 465–6, no. 879; Ms. Arras, Bibliothèque Municipale, *137 (876)*, ff. 110v–111v.

[16] Schneyer, *Repertorium*, ii, 303, no. 245; Gilbert of Tournai, *Sermones*, ff. 132r–134v.

[17] Schneyer, *Repertorium*, ii, 303, no. 246; Gilbert of Tournai, *Sermones*, ff. 134v–135v.

[18] Schneyer, *Repertorium*, ii, 303, no. 247; Gilbert of Tournai, *Sermones*, ff. 135v–137v.

[19] Humbert of Romans, *Sermones ad omnes status* ([Hagenau] 1508), no. 90.

[20] Schneyer, *Repertorium*, v, 341, no. 9; edited in: Cole, *Preaching*, 227–31.

[21] Schneyer, *Repertorium*, ii, 83, no. 26; Ms. Florence, Biblioteca Medicea-Laurenziana, *Plut.33 sin.1*, ff. 39v–41r.

21 'Quando idem dominus predicavit (here follows the sign of the cross) respondendo nuntiis Tartarorum in clero Pisano'.[22]

John Russel

22 no title [fragment].[23]

B EXEMPLA[24]

Caesar of Heisterbach

1 *Dialogus Miraculorum*, i, 70–2, cap. 7 (abuse of vow redemption).
2 *Ibid.*, i, 136–7, cap. 21 (crusaders at sea).
3 *Ibid.*, i, 181–3, cap. 10 (Oliver of Cologne preaching the cross).
4 *Ibid.*, i, 183, cap. 11 (Arnold of Burgende preaching the cross).
5 *Ibid.*, ii, 3–5, cap. 3 (crusade as punishment for sins).
6 *Ibid.*, ii, 102–3, cap. 27 (crusaders at Damietta).
7 *Ibid.*, ii, 103 (*ditto*).
8 *Ibid.*, ii, 137, cap. 66 (German and Frisian crusaders in Spain).
9 *Ibid.*, ii, 234–5, cap. 22 (Oliver of Cologne preaching the cross).
10 *Ibid.*, ii, 245, cap. 37 (*ditto*).
11 *Ibid.*, ii, 245, cap. 38 (*ditto*).
12 *Ibid.*, ii, 245, cap. 39 (*ditto*).
13 *Ibid.*, ii, 246, cap. 40 (*ditto*).
14 *Ibid.*, ii, 332–5, cap. 13 (*ditto*).
15 'Fragmente', 23–4, no. 14 (abuse of vow redemption).

Stephen of Bourbon

16 *Anecdotes Historiques*,[25] 36–7, no. 29 (crusading for dead parents).

[22] Schneyer, *Repertorium*, ii, 83, no. 27; Ms. Florence, Biblioteca Medicea-Laurenziana, *Plut.33 sin.1*, ff. 41v–42r. I take 'nuntiis Tartarorum' to mean 'news about the Mongols' rather than 'envoys of the Mongols' since no Mongol envoys were known to have visited Pisa in the thirteenth century. D. Herlihy (*Pisa in the Early Renaissance. A Study of Urban Growth* (Yale Historical Publications Miscellany 68; New Haven 1958), 29, n. 34) thought that the reference was to John of Piano Carpini's report about his mission to the Mongols in the second half of the 1240s, since Frederick Visconti owned a copy of this. A date of around 1260, however, fits better because there was a general crusade preaching campaign in Europe at that time. See above, 85.

[23] Ms. Oxford, Bodleian Library, *Digby 154 (1755)*, f. 37v; see Smalley, 'John Russel', 280–1.

[24] This list cannot claim to be complete. It only comprises such *exempla* collections which are published or referred to in publications. It excludes the vast number of *exempla* referring to the cross in general or to military orders or to other themes which have indirect connections with the crusades. The list also excludes *exempla* by anonymous authors which only appear in post thirteenth-century mss. It also does not include *exempla* which form part of model sermons and crusade preaching treatises.

[25] Stephen of Bourbon, *Anecdotes Historiques, Légendes et Apologues Tirés du Recueil Inédit*, ed. A. Lecoy de la Marche (Paris 1877).

17 *Ibid.*, 37–8, no. 30 (Abbot of Murbach preaching the cross).
18 *Ibid.*, 89–90, no. 89 (Eudes of Châteauroux preaching the cross).
19 *Ibid.*, 90, no. 99 (vision during preaching of the cross).[26]
20 *Ibid.*, 91, no. 100 (crusaders in battle).
21 *Ibid.*, 91–2, no. 101 (value of crusading indulgence).
22 *Ibid.*, 92, no. 102 (crusaders in battle).
23 *Ibid.*, 92, no. 103 (*ditto*).
24 *Ibid.*, 373–4, no. 430 (Count Gerard of Mâcon on crusade).

Thomas of Cantimpré

25 *Bonum universale*, 137–8, no. 9 (vision about the different kinds of crusades).
26 *Ibid.*, 140, no. 14 (Childrens' crusade).
27 *Ibid.*, 140–1, no. 15 (Crusade of the Shepherds).

Anonymi

28 *Speculum Laicorum*,[27] 34, no. 147 (old female crusader dying en route).
29 *Ibid.*, 34, no. 149 (Bishop of Ely gives the cross to the dying in 1247).
30 *Ibid.*, 34–5, no. 151 (mason disturbing a crusade sermon).
31 *Ibid.*, 66, no. 324 (sick person given the cross by his confessor).
32 *Ibid.*, 66, no. 325 (dying person given the cross by his bishop).
33 *Ibid.*, 81, no. 420 (crusaders in battle).
34 Ms. Bern, Bürgerbibliothek, *679*,[28] ff. 68v–69r (woman on crusade).
35 *Ibid.*, f. 69r (crusaders in battle).
36 *Ibid.*, f. 69r (servant on crusade).
37 *Ibid.*, ff. 69r–69v (zeal of the crusader).
38 *Ibid.*, f. 70r (papal legate and village priest preaching the cross).
39 *Ibid.*, f. 70v–71r (crusader leaving his family).[29]
40 *Ibid.*, f. 71r (friar preaching the cross).
41 *Ibid.*, f. 71r (*ditto*).
42 Ms. London, British Library, *Add. 27909 B*,[30] f. 11r (dying crusader).

[26] This *exemplum* first appeared James of Vitry's *ad crucesignatos* sermon. See *Analecta Novissima*, ii, 422.

[27] *Le Speculum Laicorum. Édition d'une collection d'exempla composée en Angleterre à la fin du xiiie siècle*, ed. J.T. Welter (Thesaurus Exemplorum 5; Paris 1914).

[28] This ms. dates from the thirteenth century and seems to have been written by a Dominican friar. See J.T. Welter, *L'"Exemplum" dans la littérature religieuse et didactique du Moyen Age* (Paris and Toulouse 1927), 236–44. According to Welter there is an extended version of the same *exempla* collection at Tours which also has more *exempla* about the crusade, dating, however, from the fifteenth century.

[29] This *exemplum* first appeared in one of James of Vitry's *ad crucesignatos* sermons. See *The Exempla or Illustrative Stories from the Sermones Vulgares of Jacques de Vitry*, ed. T.F. Crane (London 1890), 57, no. 124.

[30] For the date (13th c.) of this ms., see *Catalogue of Romances in the Department of Manuscripts in the British Museum*, ed. H.L.D. Ward and J.A. Herbert, 3 vols. (London 1883–1910), iii, 464.

43 Ms. London, British Library, *Royal 7 D i*,[31] f. 63v (Louis VII and St Bernard and defeat on crusade).

44 *Ibid.*, f. 89v (crusader in battle).

45 Ms. Vatican, Biblioteca Apostolica, *Ottob.lat.522*, f. 243r (92r) (St Francis preaching in front of al-Kamil).[32]

46 *Ibid.*, f. 250v (99v) (*ditto*).[33]

---

[31] This ms. might be of Dominican provenance and belongs to the second half of the thirteenth century. See *Catalogue of Romances*, iii, 477–8.

[32] This and the following *exemplum* have been edited in: Golubovich, *Biblioteca*, i, 36–7; 'Liber Exemplorum', 250–1. See also above, 13–6.

[33] For publications of this *exemplum* see previous note and also Kedar (*Crusade*, 218).

BIBLIOGRAPHY

MANUSCRIPT SOURCES

Arras, Bibliothèque Municipale, *137 (876)*.
Barcelona, Archivo de la Corona de Aragón, *Ripoll 187*.
Basel, Universitätsbibliothek, *B.V.7*.
Bern, Bürgerbibliothek, *679*.
Florence, Biblioteca Medicea-Laurenziana, *Plut.33 sin.1*.
Limoges, Archives de la Haute Vienne, *H 9640*.
London, British Library, *Add. 27909 B*.
   Royal 7 D i.
Oxford, Magdalen College, *168*.
   Bodleian Library, *Digby 154 (1755)*.
Paris, Bibliothèque Nationale, *Doat XVI*.
   lat. 18081.
   nouv.acqu.lat.999.
Pisa, Biblioteca Cateriniana del Seminario, *21*.
Troyes, Bibliothèque Municipale, *1099*.
Vatican, Biblioteca Apostolica, *Ottob.lat.522*.

PRINTED SOURCES

'Acta Capitulorum Generalium Ordinis Praedicatorum', *MOPH*, iii.
Acta Capitulorum Provincialium Fratrum Praedicatorum, ed. C. Douais, (Toulouse 1894).
Acta Imperii Selecta. Urkunden deutscher Könige und Kaiser 928–1398, ed. J.F. Böhmer (Innsbruck 1870).
'Acta Franciscana e Tabulariis Bononiensibus Deprompta', *AF*, ix.
[Les] Actes Pontificaux Originaux des Archives Nationales Paris, ed. B. Barbiche, 3 vols. (Vatican 1975–82).
Alain of Lille, *Textes inédits avec une introduction sur sa vie et ses oeuvres*, ed. M.-T. d'Alverny (Études de Philosophie Médiévale 52; Paris 1965).
Albert of Trois-Fontaines, 'Chronicon', *MGHS*, xxiii, 631–950.
Analecta Franciscana [in progress] (Ad Claras Aquas (Quaracchi) 1885ff).
Analecta Hassiaca, ed. J.P. Kuchenbecker, 6 vols. (Marburg 1728–42).
Analecta Novissima, ed. J.P. Pitra, 2 vols. ([Paris] 1885, 1888).
'Annales Basileenses', *MGHS*, xvii, 193–202.
'Annales Capituli Cracoviensis', *MGHS*, xix, 582–608.

Bibliography

'Annales Erphordenses Fratrum Praedicatorum', *MGHSS*, xlii, 72–116.

'Annales Gotwicenses. Continuatio Claustroneoburgensis III', *MGHS*, ix, 628–37.

'Annales Gotwicenses. Continuatio Sancrucensis I', *MGHS*, ix, 626–8.

'Annales Placentini Gibellini', *MGHS*, xviii, 457–581.

'Annales Sancti Pantaleonis Coloniensis', *MGHS*, xxii, 529–47.

'Annales Scheftlarienses Maiores', *MGHS*, xvii, 335–43.

'Annales Stadenses', *MGHS*, xvi, 271–379.

'Annales Wormatienses', *MGHS*, xvii, 34–73.

[Das] Archiv der Oberdeutschen Minoritenprovinz im Staatsarchiv Luzern, ed. A. Gössi (Luzerner Historische Veröffentlichungen, Archivinventare 2; Lucerne and Munich 1979).

Baldric of Bourgueil, 'Historia Jerosolimitana', *RHC oc.*, iv, 1–111.

Bartholomew of Neocastro, 'Historia Sicula', *RSNS*, xiii(3).

[St] Bonaventure, *Opera Omnia*, ed. A.C. Peltier, 15 vols. (Paris 1864–71).

Opera Omnia, 10 vols. (Ad Claras Aquas (Quaracchi) 1882–1902).

'Legenda Major S. Francisci', *AF*, x, 555–652.

Bremisches Urkundenbuch, ed. D.R. Ehmck, 5 vols. (Bremen 1863–93).

Bullarii Franciscani Epitome et Supplementum Quattuor Voluminum Priorum Olim a Johanne Hyacinthio Sbaralea Editorum, ed. C. Eubel (Ad Claras Aquas (Quaracchi) 1908).

Bullarium Franciscanum, ed. J.H. Sbaralea, 4 vols. (Rome 1759–68).

Bullarium Ordinis Praedicatorum, ed. T. Ripoll and A. Bremond, 8 vols. (Rome 1729–40).

'Bullarium Pontificum quod existat in archivo Sacri ordinis Conventus S. Francisci Assisiensis', ed. L. Alessandri and F. Penacchi, *AFH*, viii (1915), 592–617, x (1917), 185–219, xi (1918), 206–50, 442–90.

'Bulles originales du XIIIe siècle conservées dans les Archives de Navarre', ed. L. Cadier, *Mélanges d'Archéologie et d'Histoire*, vii (1887), 268–338.

Caesar of Heisterbach, *Dialogus miraculorum*, ed. J. Strange, 2 vols. (Cologne 1851).

Die Fragmente der Libri VIII Miraculorum, ed. A. Meister (Römische Quartalschrift für Christliche Alterthumskunde und Kirchengeschichte. Supplementheft 13; Rome 1901).

'Epistola in Vitam Sancte Elyzabeth Lantgravie', *Die Wundergeschichten des Caesarius von Heisterbach*, ed. A. Hilka, 3 vols. (Publikationen der Gesellschaft für Rheinische Geschichtskunde 43; Bonn 1933–7), iii, 341–81.

Calendar of Documents Relating to Ireland preserved in Her Majesty's Public Record Office London, 1171–1304, ed. H.S. Sweetman and G.F. Handcock, 5 vols. (London 1875–86).

Calendar of the Patent Rolls of the Reign of Henry III Preserved in the Public Record Office, 6 vols. (London 1901–8).

Cartulaire ou Histoire Diplomatique de S. Dominique, ed. F. Balme *et al.*, 3 vols. (Paris 1893–1901).

Catalogue of Romances in the Department of Manuscripts in the British Museum, ed. H.L.D. Ward and J.A. Herbert, 3 vols. (London 1883–1910).

Bibliography

Catherina Scota, *Toleratio Fratrum et Crucesignatorum*, ed. G.R. Atia (Ad Orientales Aquas 1988–90).

[La] Chanson de Roland, ed. J. Bédier (Paris 1922).

[Les] Chansons de Croisade, ed. J. Bédier and P. Aubrey (Paris 1909).

'[E] Chronicon Normanniae', *RGHF*, xxiii, 212–22.

'[E] Chronicon Sanctae Catharinae de Monte Rothomagi', *RGHF*, xxiii, 397–410.

Chronique d'Ernoul et de Bernard le Trésorier, ed. M.L. de Mas Latrie (Paris 1871).

Close Roll of the Reign of Henry III Preserved in the Public Record Office, 1226–1272, 14 vols. (London 1902–38).

Codex Diplomaticus sive Anecdotorum Res Maguntinas, Francicas, Trevirenses, Colonienses Finitimarumque Regionum nec non Ius Germanicum et S.R.I. Historiam vel maximam illustrantium, ed. V.F. de Gudenus *et al.*, 5 vols. (Göttingen 1743–68).

Codex Diplomaticus Prussicus, Urkundensammlung zur älteren Geschichte Preussens aus dem königlichen Archiv zu Königsberg nebst Regesten, ed. J. Voigt *et al.*, 6 vols. (Königsberg 1836–61).

'Compte d'une mission de prédication pour secours à la Terre Sainte (1265)', ed. Borelli de Serres, *Mémoires de la Société de l'histoire de Paris et de l'Ile de France*, xxx (1903), 243–80.

Conciliorum Oecumenicorum Decreta, ed. J. Alberigo *et al.* (Basel 1962).

Conrad of Scheirn, 'Annales', *MGHS*, xvii, 629–633.

'Continuation de Guillaume de Tyr', *RHC oc.*, ii, 483–639.

Corpus der Altdeutschen Originalurkunden bis zum Jahr 1300, ed. F. Wilhelm *et al.*, 4 vols. (Lahr 1932–63).

Correspondance Administrative d'Alfonse de Poitiers, ed. A. Molinier, 2 vols. (Collection des documents inédits sur l'histoire de France; Paris 1894, 1900).

'Cronica Minor Minoritae Erphordensis', *MGHSS*, xlii, 486–671.

Diplomatarium Danicum, ed. A. Afzelius *et al.* [in progress] (Copenhagen 1938).

Diplomatarium Suecarum, ed. J.G. Liljegren, 2 vols. (Holm 1829, 1837).

[La] Documentacion Pontifica de Urbano IV (1261–1264), ed. I.R.R. De Lama (Monumenta Hispaniae Vaticana. Seccion Registros 6; Rome 1981).

'Documents inédits concernant l'orient Latin et les croisades (XIIe–XIVe siècle)', ed. C. Kohler, *Revue de l'Orient Latin*, vii (1899), 1–37.

'Emonis Chronicon', *MGHS*, xxiii, 465–523.

Epistolae Selectae Saeculi XIII e Regestis Pontificum Romanorum, ed. C. Rodenberg, 3 vols. (Monumenta Germaniae Historiae; Berlin 1883–94).

'[L]'Estoire de Eracles Empereur', *RHC oc.*, ii, 1–481.

Eudes of Châteauroux, 'Sermones sex de sancto Dominico', ed. A. Walz, *Analecta Sacri Ordinis Fratrum Paedicatorum*, xxxiii (1925), 174–233.

[The] Exempla or Illustrative Stories from the Sermones Vulgares of Jacques de Vitry, ed. T.F. Crane (London 1890).

Foedera, Conventiones, Litterae et Cuius-cunque Generis Acta Publica inter Reges Angliae et Alios Quosvis Imperatores, Reges, Pontifices, Principes vel Communitates, ed. T. Rymer *et al.*, 4 vols. (London 1816–69).

Fratris Arnoldi Ordinis Praedicatorum de correctione ecclesiae epistola et anonymi de

Innocentio IV. P.M. Antichristo libellus, ed. E. Winkelmann (Berlin 1865).

Galvagno de la Flamma, 'Cronica Ordinis Praedicatorum', *MOPH*, ii.

Gerald of Wales, *Opera*, ed. J.S. Brewer *et al.*, 8 vols. (Rolls Series 21; London 1861–91).

Gerard of Fracheto, 'Vitae Fratrum ordinis Praedicatorum necnon cronica ordinis', *MOPH*, i.

'Gesta Episcoporum Traiectensium', *MGHS*, xxiii, 400–26.

'Gesta Treverorum Continuata', *MGHS*, xxiv, 368–488.

Gilbert of Tournai, *Sermones ad omnes status de novo correcti et emendati* (Lyon [1510]).

   'Collectio de Scandalis Ecclesiae. Nova Editio', ed. A Striock, *AFH*, xxiv (1931), 33–62.

[Die] Goldene Chronik von Hohenschwangau, ed. J. (Frhr. von) Hormayr-Hortenburg (Munich 1842).

Günther of Pairis, 'Historia captae a Latinis Constantinopoleos', *PL*, ccxii, cols. 226–56.

Henry of Avranches, 'Legenda S. Francisci Versificata', *AF*, x, 405–521.

Hermann of Altaich, 'Annales', *MGHS*, xvii, 381–416.

Historia Diplomatica Frederici Secundi, ed. J.L.A. Huillard-Bréholles, 6 vols. (Paris 1852–61).

'Historia Monasterii Rastedensis', *MGHS*, xxv, 495–511.

'Historia peregrinorum', *MGHS* rg, v, 116–72.

Historical Papers and Letters from the Northern Registers, ed. J. Raine (Rolls Series 61; London 1873).

Humbert of Romans, 'Legenda S. Dominici', *MOPH*, xvi, 353–433.

   De predicatione Sancte crucis ([Nürnberg] 1495).

   Sermones ad omnes status ([Hagenau] 1508).

   Opera de vita regulari, ed. J.J. Berthier, 2 vols. (Turin 1956).

Innocent III, 'Opera Omnia', 4 vols., *PL*, ccxiv–ccxvii.

James of Vitry, *Lettres*, ed. R.B.C. Huygens (Leiden 1960).

   Historia Occidentalis, ed. J. Hinnebusch (Specilegium Friburgense 17; Freiburg i.Ue. 1972).

John of St Arnulf, 'Vita Johannis abbatis Gorzensis', *MGHS*, iv, 335–77.

Jordan of Giano, *Chronica*, ed. H. Boehmer (Collection d'études et de documents sur l'histoire religieuse et littéraire du moyen âge 6; Paris 1908).

Jordan of Saxony, 'Libellus de Principiis Ordinis Praedicatorum', *MOPH*, xvi, 1–88.

Julian of Speyer, 'Vita S. Francisci', *AF*, x, 333–71.

[La] Langue et la Littérature Françaises depuis le IXe siècle jusqu'au XIV siècles, ed. K. Bartsch (Paris 1887).

Layettes du Trésor des Chartes, A. Teulet *et al.*, 5 vols. (Paris 1863–1909).

Liv-, Esth- und Curländisches Urkundenbuch nebst Regesten, ed. F.G. v.Bunge, 12 vols. (Reval 1852–1910).

Letter Book of William of Hoo, Sacrist of Bury St Edmunds, ed. A. Gransden (Suffolk Record Society 5; [Ipswich] 1963).

'Liber Exemplorum Fratrum Minorum Saeculi XIII (Excerpta e cod. Ottob. lat.

Bibliography

522)', ed. L. Oliger, *Antonianum*, ii (1927), 203–76.

Lois et Coutumes de la Ville de Lille, ed. Brun-Lavin and Rosin (Lille and Paris 1842).

'[E] mari historiarum auctore Johannis de Columpna OP', *RGHF*, xxiii, 106–24.

Matthew Paris, *Chronica Majora*, ed. H.R. Luard, 7 vols. (Rolls Series 47; London 1872–83).

Historia Anglorum, ed. F. Madden, 3 vols. (Rolls Series 44; London 1866–9).

Menko, 'Chronicon', *MGHS*, xxiii, 523–61.

'Monumenta Diplomatica S. Dominici', *MOPH*, xxv.

Monumenta Franciscana, ed. J.S. Brewer, 2 vols. (Rolls Series 4; London 1858, 1882).

Monumenta Germaniae Historica. Scriptores, ed. G.H. Pertz *et al.* [in progress] (Hanover 1826ff).

Monumenta Germaniae Historica. Scriptores Rerum Germanicarum in usum scholarum seperatim editi, ed. G.H. Pertz *et al.* [in progress] (Hanover 1840ff).

Monumenta Germaniae Historica. Scriptores Rerum Germanicarum. Nova Series, ed. G.H. Pertz *et al.* [in progress] (Hanover 1922ff).

Monumenta Ordinis Praedicatorum Historia, 25 vols. (Louvain 1897–1966).

Nicholas Trevet, *Annales sex Regum Angliae, 1135–1307*, ed. T. Hog (London 1845).

Opuscula S. Patris Francisci, ed. L. Lemmens (Bibliotheca Franciscana Ascetica 1; Ad Claras Aquas (Quaracchi) 1909).

'Ordinacio de Predicacione S. Crucis in Anglia', *Quinti Belli Sacri Scriptores Minores*, ed. R. Röhricht (Publications de la Société de l'Orient Latin. Série historique 2; Geneva 1879), 2–26.

Patrologiae cursus completus. Series Latina, comp. P. Migne (Paris 1844–64).

Peter Ferrand, 'Legenda S. Dominici', *MOPH*, xvi, 195–260.

Philippe Mouskes, *Chronique rimée*, ed. [F.] de Reiffenberg, 2 vols. (Brussels 1836–8).

Poesie provenzali storiche relative all'Italia, ed. V. De Bartholomaeis, 2 vols. (Fonti per la Storia d'Italia 71, 72; Rome 1931).

Pontifica Hibernica. Medieval Papal Chancery Documents concerning Ireland (640–1241), ed. M.P. Sheeny, 2 vols. (Dublin 1962, 1965).

Preussisches Urkundenbuch, Politische Abteilung, ed. A. Seraphim *et al.* [in progress] (Königsberg 1882ff).

'Raymundiana seu Documenta quae Pertinent ad S. Raymundi de Pennaforti Vitam et Scripta', 2 fasc., *MOPH*, vi.

Recueil des Historiens des Croisades. Historiens Occidentaux, ed. Académie des inscriptions et belles-lettres, 5 vols. (Paris 1844–1895).

Recueil des Historiens des Gaules et de la France, ed. M. Bouquet *et al.*, 24 vols. (Paris 1737–1904).

Regesta Honorii Papae III, ed. P. Pressuti, 2 vols. (Rome 1888, 1905).

Regesta Pontificum Romanorum, ed. A. Potthast, 2 vols. (Berlin 1874, 1875).

Regestum Visitationum Archiepiscopi Rothomagensis, ed. T. Bonin (Rouen 1852).

[The] Register of John le Romeyn. Lord Archbishop of York 1286–1296, ed. W. Brown, 2 vols. (Surtees Society 123, 128; Durham 1913, 1916).

[The] Registers of Walter Giffard, Lord Archbishop of York, 1266–1279, ed. W.

Bibliography

Brown (Surtees Society Publications 109; Durham 1904).

[Les] Registres d'Alexandre IV, ed. C. Bourel de la Roncière *et al.*, 3 vols. (Bibliothèque des Écoles françaises d'Athènes et de Rome (2nd ser.); Paris 1895–1959).

[Les] Registres de Clément IV, ed. E. Jordan (Bibliothèque des Écoles françaises d'Athènes et de Rome (2nd ser.); Paris 1893–1945).

[Les] Registres de Grégoire IX, ed. L. Auvray, 4 vols. (Bibliothèque des Écoles françaises d'Athènes et de Rome (2nd ser.); Paris 1890–1955).

[Les] Registres de Grégoire X et de Jean XXI, ed. J. Guiraud and E. Cadier (Bibliothèque des Écoles françaises d'Athènes et de Rome (2nd ser.); Paris 1892–1960).

[Les] Registres de Martin IV, ed. F. Olivier-Martin *et al.* (Bibliothèque des Écoles françaises d'Athènes et de Rome (2nd ser.); Paris 1901–35).

[Les] Registres de Nicolas III, ed. J. Gay and S. Clémencet-Witte (Bibliothèque des Écoles françaises d'Athènes et de Rome (2nd ser.); Paris 1898–1938).

[Les] Registres de Nicolas IV, ed. E. Langlois (Bibliothèque des Écoles françaises d'Athènes et de Rome (2nd ser.); Paris 1886–1906).

[Les] Registres de Urban IV, ed. J. Guiraud, 4 vols. (Bibliothèque des Écoles françaises d'Athènes et de Rome (2nd ser.); Paris 1899–1958).

[Les] Registres d'Honorius IV, ed. M. Prou (Bibliothèque des Écoles françaises d'Athènes et de Rome (2nd ser.); Paris 1886–8).

[Les] Registres d'Innocent IV, ed. É. Berger, 3 vols. (Bibliothèque des Écoles françaises d'Athènes et de Rome (2nd ser.); Paris 1884–1921).

Registrum Ricardi de Swinfield Episcopi Herefordensis AD. MCCLXXXIII–MCCCXVII, ed. W.W. Capes (Canterbury and York Society Publication 6; London 1909).

Rerum Italicarum Scriptores (new series), ed. C. Carducci *et al.* [in progress] (Città di Castello-Bologna 1900).

Richard of St Germano, 'Chronica', *MGHS*, xix, 321–84.

Roger of Howden, *Chronica*, ed. W. Stubbs, 4 vols. (Rolls Series 51; London 1868–71).

[The] Rolls and Registers of Bishop Oliver Sutton 1280–1299, ed. R.M.T. Hill, 8 vols. (Hereford 1948–86).

Rutebeuf, *Oeuvres complètes*, ed. E. Faral and J. Bastin, 2 vols. (Paris 1959, 1960).

Salimbene de Adam, 'Cronica', *MGHS*, xxxii.

[Die] Schriften des Kölner Domscholasters, späteren Bischofs von Paderborn und Kardinal-Bischofs von S. Sabina Oliverus, ed. H. Hoogeweg (Bibliothek des Literarischen Vereins in Stuttgart 202; Tübingen 1894).

Scripta Leonis, Rufini et Angeli Sociorum S. Francisci. The Writings of Leo, Rufino and Angelo Companions of St Francis, ed. and trans. R.B. Brooke (Oxford 1970).

[Le] Speculum Laicorum. Édition d'une collection d'exempla composée en Angleterre à la fin du xiiie siècle, ed. J.T. Welter (Thesaurus Exemplorum 5; Paris 1914).

Stephen of Bourbon, *Anecdotes Historiques, Légendes et Apologues Tirés du Recueil Inédit*, ed. A. Lecoy de la Marche (Paris 1877).

Stephen of Salagnac, 'De quatuor in quibus Deus praedicatorum ordinem insignivit', *MOPH*, xxii.

Bibliography

Thesaurus novus anecdotorum, ed. E. Martène and U. Durand. 5 vols. (Paris 1717).

Thomas of Cantimpré, *Bonum universale de apibus* (Douais 1627).

Thomas of Celano, 'Vita Prima S. Francisci', *AF*, x, 1–117.

'Vita Secunda S. Francisci', *AF*, x, 127–268.

Thomas Wykes, 'Chronicon', *Annales Monastici*, ed. H.R. Luard, 4 vols. (Rolls Series 36; London 1864–9), iv, 6–352.

'Triennis et biennis decima ab anno MCCXLVIII collecta', *RHGF*, xxi, 533–40.

'[Les] troubadours de Béziers', ed. G. Azais, *Bulletin de la société archéologique de Béziers* (2nd. ser.), i (1858), 187–290.

Ungedruckte Dominikanerbriefe des 13. Jahrhunderts, ed. H. Finke (Paderborn 1891).

Vetera Monumenta Historica Hungariam Sacram Illustrantia, ed. A. Theiner, 2 vols. (Rome 1859, 1860).

Vetera Monumenta Poloniae et Lithuaniae gentiumque finitimarum Historiam illustrantia, ed. A. Theiner, 4 vols. (Rome 1860–4).

William of Nangis, 'Chronicon', *RGHF*, xx, 543–82.

William Peyraut, *Sermones dominicales ex epistolas et evangelys atque de sanctis secundum ecclesie ordinem* (Tübingen 1499).

William the Breton, 'Gesta Philippi Augusti', *Oeuvres de Rigord et de Guillaume le Breton*, ed. H.-F. Delaborde, 2 vols. (Paris 1882, 1885), i, 168–333.

Writings and Early Biographies. English Omnibus of the Sources for the Life of St Francis, ed. M.A. Habig (4th edition; Chicago 1983).

SECONDARY WORKS

Abulafia, D., *Frederick II. A Medieval Emperor* (London 1988).

Altaner, B., *Die Dominikanermissionen des 13.Jahrhunderts* (Breslauer Studien zur historischen Theologie 3; Habelschwerdt 1924).

[The] Atlas of the Crusades, ed. J.[S.C.] Riley-Smith (London 1991).

Baethgen F., Review of H. Kroppmann: Ehedispensübung und Stauferkampf unter Innozenz IV., *Zeitschrift der Savigny Stiftung für Rechtsgeschichte*, lix (*Kanonische Abteilung*, xxviii) (1939), 511–14.

Barber, M., 'The Crusade of the Shepherds in 1251', *Proceedings of the 10th Annual Meeting of the Western Society for French History*, ed. J.F. Sweet (Lawrence 1984), 1–23.

Benninghoven, F., *Der Orden der Schwertbrüder. Fratres Milicie Christi de Livonia* (Cologne and Graz 1956).

Berg, D., *Armut und Wissenschaft. Beiträge zur Geschichte des Studienwesens der Bettelorden im 13. Jahrhundert* (Bochumer Historische Studien 15; Düsseldorf 1977).

Bernet, X., 'Beiträge zur Geschichte der Kreuzzüge gegen die Mongolen im 13. Jahrhundert', *Geschichtsfreund*, i (1843), 351–64, 376–8.

Bishko, C.J. 'The Spanish and Portuguese Reconquest 1095–1492', *A History of the Crusades*, iii, 396–456.

Bleck, R. 'Ein oberrheinischer Palästina-Kreuzzug 1267', *Basler Zeitschrift für Geschichte und Altertumskunde*, lxxxvii (1987), 5–28.

Bibliography

Böhm, L., *Johann von Brienne, König von Jerusalem, Kaiser von Konstantinopel* (Heidelberg 1938).

Boockmann, H., *Der Deutsche Orden. Zwölf Kapitel aus seiner Geschichte* (Munich 1981).

Brett, E.T., *Humbert of Romans. His Life and Views of Thirteenth-Century Society* (Studies and Texts 67; Toronto 1984).

Brooke, R.B., *Early Franciscan Government. Elias to Bonaventure* (Cambridge Studies in Medieval Life and Thought [new series] 7; Cambridge 1959).

Brundage, J.A., 'The Crusader's Wife: a Canonistic Quandary', *Studia Gratiana*, xii (1967), 425–41.

Canon Law and the Crusader (Madison 1969).

Cardini, F., 'Nella presenza del Soldan superba: Bernardo, Francesco, Bonaventura e il superamento spirituale dell'idea di crociata', *Studi Francescani*, lxxi (1974), 199–250.

'Gilberto di Tournai. Un Francescano Predicatore della Crociata', *Studi Francescani*, lxxii (1975), 31–48.

Carpenter, D.A., 'The Gold Treasure of King Henry III', *Thirteenth Century England I: Proceedings of the Newcastle upon Tyne Conference 1985*, ed. P.R. Coss and S.D. Lloyd (Woodbridge 1986), 61–88.

Charasson, A., *Un curé plébeien au xiie siècle. Foulque curé de Neuilly-sur-Marne 1191–202. Prédicateur de la IVe croisade, d'après ses contemporains et chroniques du temps* (Paris 1905).

Chazan, R., *Medieval Jewry in Northern France. A Political and Social History* (John Hopkins University Studies in Historical and Political Sience 91st series 2; Baltimore and London 1973).

Christiansen, E., *The Northern Crusades, The Baltic and the Catholic Frontier 1100–1525* (London and Basingstoke 1980).

Cole, P.J., *The Preaching of the Crusades to the Holy Land, 1095–1270* (Medieval Academy Books 98; Cambridge, Mass. 1991).

Cramer, V., *Albert der Grosse als päpstlicher Kreuzzugs-Legat für Deutschland 1263/64 und die Kreuzzugsbestrebungen Urbans IV*. (Palästina-Hefte des Deutschen Vereins vom Heiligen Lande 7, 8; Cologne 1933).

D'Alatri, M. 'I francescani e l'eresia', *Espansione del Francescanesimo tra Occidente e Oriente nel secolo XIII. Atti del VI Convegno Internazionale, Assisi 12–14 Ottobre 1978*, ed. Società Internazionale di Studi Francescani (Assisi 1979), 241–70.

D'Avray, D.L., *The Preaching of the Friars. Sermons diffused from Paris before 1300* (Oxford 1985).

Delorme, F.M, 'Bulle d'Innocent IV pour la croisade (6 février 1245)', *AFH*, vi (1913), 386–9.

'Bulle d'Innocent IV en faveur de l'empire latin de Constantinople', *AFH*, viii (1915), 307–10.

'De praedicatione cruciatae saec. XIII per fratres minores', *AFH*, ix (1916), 99–117.

'Trois bulles à frère Hugues de Turenne', *AFH*, xviii (1925), 291–5.

De Vic, C. and Vaisette, J., *Histoire Générale de Languedoc aves des notes et les pièces*

Bibliography

justificatives, 16 vols. (Toulouse 1872–1905).

Dickson, G., 'The Advent of the Pastores (1251)', *Revue Belge de Philologie et d'Histoire*, lxvi (1988), 249–67.

Diepernik, F.H.J., 'De Drenste opstand tegen het bisschoppelijke gezag in 1227', *Bijdragen van het Institut voor middeleeuwse geschiednis der Rijks-Universiteit te Utrecht*, xxvi (1953), 1–36.

Donner, G.A., *Kardinal Wilhelm von Sabina. Bischof von Modena 1222–1234. Päpstlicher Legat in den Nordischen Ländern (t 1251)* (Societas Scientiarum Fennica. Commentationes Humanorum Litterarum II, 5; Helsingfors 1929).

Douais [C.], 'Les frères Prêcheurs de Limoges (1220–1693)', *Bulletin de la Société Archéologique et Historique du Limousin*, xl (1892/1893), 270–363.

Dufeil, M.-M., *Guillaume de Saint-Amour et la polémique universitaire parisienne 1250–1259* (Paris 1972).

Dygo, M. 'The Political Role of the Virgin Mary in Teutonic Prussia in the Fourteenth and Fifteenth Centuries', *Journal of Medieval History*, xv (1989), 63–80.

Einhorn, J.M., 'Franziskus und der "Edle Heide"', *Text und Bild. Aspekte des Zusammenwirkens zweier Künste in Mittelalter und früher Neuzeit*, ed. C. Meier and U. Ruberg (Wiesbaden 1980), 630–50.

Emery, R.[W.], *Heresy and Inquisition in Narbonne* (Studies in History, Economics and Public Law 480; New York 1941).

The Friars in Medieval France. A Catalogue of French Mendicant Convents 1200–1550 (London and New York 1962).

Felten, J., *Papst Gregor IX.* (Freiburg i.Br. 1886).

Fine, J.V.A., *The Bosnian Church: A New Interpretation. A Study of the Bosnian Church and its Place in State and Society from the 13th to the 15th Centuries* (East European Monographs 10; London and New York 1975).

Förg, L., *Die Ketzerverfolgung in Deutschland unter Gregor IX. Ihre Herkunft, ihre Bedeutung und ihre rechtlichen Grundlagen* (Historische Studien 218; Berlin 1932).

Freed, J.B., *The Friars and German Society in the Thirteenth Century* (The Medieval Academy of America Publications 86; Cambridge, Mass. 1977).

Gallen, J., *La province de Dacie de l'ordre des Frères Prêcheurs. I. Histoire générale jusqu'au Grand Schisme* (Dissertationes Historicae; Institutum Historicum Fratrum Praedicatorum Romae ad Sa. Sabina 12; Helsingfors 1946).

Gatto, L., *Il pontificato di Gregorio X* (Istituto Storico Italiano per il Medio Evo. Studi Storici 28–30; Rome 1959).

Gnegel-Waitschies, G., *Bischof Albert von Riga. Ein Bremer Domherr als Kirchenfürst im Osten (1199–1229)* (Hamburg 1958).

Golubovich, G., *Biblioteca Bio-bibliographica della Terra Santa e dell'Oriente Francescano* (1st ser.), 5 vols. (Ad Claras Aquas (Quaracchi) 1906–27).

Goñi-Gaztambide, J., *Historia de la Bula de la Cruzada en España* (Victoriensia 4; Vitoria 1958).

Goodich, M., 'The Politics of Canonization in the Thirteenth Century: Lay and Mendicant Saints', *Church History*, xliv (1975), 294–307.

Vita Perfecta: The Ideal of Sainthood in the Thirteenth Century (Monographien zur

Bibliography

Geschichte des Mittelalters 25; Stuttgart 1982).

Gottlob, A., *Die Kreuzzugssteuern des 13. Jahrhundert. Ihre rechtliche Grundlage, politische Geschichte und technische Verwaltung* (Heiligenstadt 1892).

Gwynn, A. and Hadcock, R.N., *Medieval Religious Houses. Ireland* (London 1970).

Hageneder, O., 'Die päpstlichen Register des 13. und 14. Jahrhunderts', *Annali della Scuola speciale per archivisti e bibliothecari dell'Università di Roma*, xii (1972), 45–76.

'Die Häresie des Ungehorsam und das Entstehen des hierokratischen Papastums', *Römische Historische Mitteilungen*, xx (1978), 29–47.

Hampe, K., 'Papst Innocenz IV. und die sizilianische Verschwörung von 1246' (Sitzungsberichte der Heidelberger Akademie der Wissenschaften. Phil.-hist. Klasse 8; Heidelberg 1923).

Herlihy, D., *Pisa in the Early Renaissance. A Study of Urban Growth* (Yale Historical Publications Miscellany 68; New Haven 1958).

Hinnebusch, W.A., *The History of the Dominican Order*, 2 vols. (New York 1965, 1973).

Hintze, O., *Das Königtum Wilhelms von Holland* (Historische Studien 15; Leipzig 1885).

[A] History of the Crusades, ed.-in-chief K.M. Setton [in progress] (Philadelphia and Madison 1969ff).

Hoogeweg, H., 'Die Kreuzpredigt des Jahres 1224 in Deutschland mit besonderer Rücksicht auf die Erzdiözese Köln', *Deutsche Zeitschrift für Geschichtswissenschaft*, iv (1890), 54–74.

Housley, N., *The Italian Crusades. The Papal-Angevin Alliance and the Crusades against Christian Lay Powers 1254–1343* (Oxford 1982).

'Politics and Heresy in Italy: Anti-Heretical Crusades, Orders and Confraternities, 1200–1500', *Journal of Ecclesiastical History*, liii (1982), 193–208.

The Avignon Papacy and the Crusades 1305–1378 (Oxford 1986).

Jackson, P., 'The Crisis in the Holy Land in 1260', *English Historical Review*, xcv (1980), 481–513.

'The Crusade Against the Mongols (1241)', *Journal of Ecclesiastical History*, xlii (1991), 1–18.

Jordan, W.C., *Louis IX and the Challenge of the Crusade. A Study in Rulership* (Princeton 1979).

Kaeppeli, T., 'Heidenricus von Kulm (t.1263). Der Verfasser eines Traktates *De Amore S. Trinitatis*', *AFP*, xxx (1960), 196–205.

Scriptores Ordinis Praedicatorum [in progress] (Rome 1970ff).

Kedar, B.Z., 'The Passenger List of a Crusader Ship, 1250: towards the History of the Popular Element of the Seventh Crusade', *Studi Medievali (third series)*, xiii (1972), 267–79.

Crusade and Mission. European Approaches toward the Muslims (Princeton 1984).

Kempf, F., 'Das Romersdorfer Briefbuch des 13. Jahrhunderts', *Mitteilungen des Österreichischen Instituts für Geschichtsforschung Ergänzungsband*, xii (1933), 502–71.

Kennan, E.T., 'Innocent III, Gregory IX, and Political Crusades: A Study in the

Bibliography

Disintegration of Papal Power', *Reform and Authority in the Medieval and Reformation Church*, ed. G.F. Lytle (Washington 1981), 15–35.

Kluger, H., *Hochmeister Hermann von Salza und Kaiser Friedrich II. Ein Beitrag zur Frühgeschichte des Deutschen Ordens* (Quellen und Studien zur Geschichte des Deutschen Ordens 37; Marburg 1987).

Knowles, D. and Hadcock, R.N. *Medieval Religious Houses. England and Wales* (London 1971).

Köhler, H., *Die Ketzerpolitik der deutschen Kaiser und Könige in den Jahren 1152–1254* (Jenaer Historische Arbeiten 6; Bonn 1913).

Köhn, R., 'Die Verketzerung der Stedinger durch die Bremer Fastensynode', *Bremisches Jahrbuch*, lvii (1979), 15–85.

Kolmer, L., *Ad Capiendas Vulpes: Die Ketzerbekämpfung in Südfrankreich in der ersten Hälfte des 13. Jahrhunderts und die Ausbildung des Inquisitionsverfahrens* (Pariser Historische Studien 19; Bonn 1982).

Koudelka, V.J., 'Zur Geschichte der Böhmischen Dominikanerprovinz im Mittelalter II. Die Männer- und Frauenklöster', *AFP*, xxvi (1956), 127–60.

Kroppmann, H., *Ehedispensübung und Stauferkampf unter Innozenz IV. Ein Beitrag zur Geschichte des päpstlichen Ehedispensrechtes* (Abhandlungen zur mittleren und neueren Geschichte 79; Berlin 1937).

Kucynski, K., *Le Bienheureux Guala de Bergame de l'Ordre des Frères Prêcheurs. Évêque de Brescia, Pacaire et Légat Pontifical (t.1244)* (Estavayer 1916).

Lambert, M.D., *Franciscan Poverty. The Doctrine of the Absolute Poverty of Christ and the Apostles in the Franciscan Order* (London 1961).

Lampen, W., 'Joannes van Diest, O.F.M., Hofkapelaan van Graaf Willem II en eerste Nederlandsche Bisschop uit de Minderbroedersorde', *Bijdragen voor de Geschiedenis van het Bisdom van Haarlem*, xliv (1926), 299–312.

Langlois, C.V., *Le Règne de Philippe III le Hardi* (Paris 1887).

Laurent, J.C.M., *Wilbrands von Oldenburg Reise nach Palestina und Kleinasien* (Hamburg 1859).

Laurent, V., 'La croisade et la question d'Orient sous le pontificat de Grégoire X', *Revue historique du Sud-Est européen*, xxii (1945), 105–37.

Lemmens, L., 'De Sancto Francisco Christum Praedicante coram Sultano Egypti', *AFH*, xix (1926), 559–78.

Linehan, P., *The Spanish Church and the Papacy in the Thirteenth Century* (Cambridge Studies in Medieval Life and Thought (3rd. series) 4; Cambridge 1971).

Lloyd, S.D., *English Society and the Crusade 1216–1307* (Oxford 1988).

Loenertz, R.J., 'La vie de S. Hyacinthe du lecteur Stanislas envisagée comme source historique', *AFP*, xxvii (1957), 5–38.

Lopez, A., *La Provincia de España de los Frailes Menores. Apuntes Histórico-Críticos sobre los orìginos de la Orden Franciscana en España* (Santiago 1915).

'Cruzada contra los Sarracenos en el Reino de Castilla predicada por los Franciscanos de la Provincia de Santiago', *Archivo Ibero-Americano*, ix (1918), 321–7.

Lunt, W.E., 'A Papal Tenth Levied in the British Isles from 1274 to 1280', *English Historical Review*, xxxii (1917), 49–89.

Bibliography

Papal Revenues in the Middle Ages, 2 vols. (Records of Civilization. Sources and Studies 19; New York 1934).

Financial Relations of the Papacy with England to 1321 (Studies in Anglo-Papal Relations during the Middle Ages 1; Cambridge, Mass. 1939).

Maccarrone, M., *Studi su Innocenzo III* (Italia Sacra, Studi e Documenti di Storia Ecclesiastica 17; Rome and Padova 1972).

Macquarrie, A., *Scotland and the Crusades 1095–1560* (Edinburgh 1985).

Manselli, R., 'S. Domenico, I Papi e Roma', *Studi Romani*, xix (1971), 133–43.

Maschke, E., 'Die Herkunft Hermann von Salzas', *Zeitschrift des Vereins für Thüringische Geschichte. Neue Folge*, xxxiv (1940), 372–89.

Millares Carlo, A. and Ruiz Asencio, J.M., *Tratado de Paleographia Española*, 3 vols. (Madrid 1983).

Moolenbroek, J.J., 'Signs in the Heavens in Groningen and Friesland in 1214; Oliver of Cologne and Crusading Propaganda', *Journal of Medieval History*, xiii (1987), 251–72.

Moorman, J.H.R., *A History of the Franciscan Order from its Origins to the Year 1517* (Oxford 1968).

Medieval Franciscan Houses (Franciscan Institute Publications. History Series 4; New York 1983).

Morgan, M.R., *The Chronicle of Ernoul and the Continuations of William of Tyre* (London 1973).

Morris, C., *The Papal Monarchy. The Western Church from 1050–1250* (Oxford 1989).

Oncken, H., 'Studien zur Geschichte des Stedingerkreuzzuges', *Jahrbuch für die Geschichte des Herzogtums Oldenburg*, v (Schriften des Oldenburger Vereins für Altertumskunde und Landesgeschichte 14; Oldenburg 1896), 27–58.

Painter, S., *The Scourge of the Clergy. Peter of Dreux, Duke of Brittany* (Baltimore 1937).

'The Crusade of Theobald of Champagne and Richard of Cornwall 1239–1241, *A History of the Crusades*, ii, 463–85.

Panagopulos, B.K., *Cistercian and Mendicant Monasteries in Medieval Greece* (Chicago 1979).

Pasztor, E., 'San Francesco e il Cardinale Ugolino nella "questione Francescana"', *Collectanea Franciscana*, xlvi (1976), 209–39.

Patschovsky, A., 'Zur Ketzerverfolgung Konrads von Marburg', *Deutsches Archiv für die Erforschung des Mittelalters*, xxxvii (1981), 641–93.

Paulus, N., *Geschichte des Ablasses im Mittelalter vom Ursprung zur Mitte des 14. Jahrhunderts*, 3 vols. (Paderborn 1922, 1923).

Pfeiffer, N., *Die Ungarische Dominikanerprovinz von ihrer Gründung 1221 bis zur Tatarenverwüstung 1241–1242* (Zürich 1913).

Pixton, P.B., 'Die Anwerbung des Heeres Christi: Prediger des Fünften Kreuzzuges in Deutschland', *Deutsches Archiv für die Erforschung des Mittelalters*, xxxiv (1978), 166–91.

Planzer, D., 'De Codice Ruthenensi miscellaneo in Tabulario Ordinis asservato', *AFP*, v (1935), 5–123.

Poschmann, B., *Penance and the Anointing of the Sick*, transl. and revised by F.

Bibliography

Courtney (Freiburg i.Br. and London 1964).

Powell, J.M., 'The Papacy and the Early Franciscans', *Franciscan Studies*, xxxvi (1976), 248–62.

'Francesco d'Assisi e la Quinta Crociata. Una Missione di Pace', *Schede Medievali*, iv (1983), 68–77.

Anatomy of a Crusade, 1213–1221 (Philadelphia 1986).

Powicke, F.M., *Stephen Langton* (Oxford 1927).

Pryor, J.H., *Geography, technology, and war. Studies in the maritime history of the Mediterranean, 649–1571* (Cambridge 1988).

Purcell, M., *Papal Crusading Policy. The Chief Instruments of Papal Crusading Policy and Crusade to the Holy Land from the Loss of Jerusalem to the Fall of Acre 1244–1291* (Leiden 1975).

Quétif, J. and Echard, J., *Scriptores Ordinis Praedicatorum Recensiti*, 2 vols. (Paris 1719, 1721).

Renard, J.-P., *La formation et la désignation des Predicateurs au début de l'ordre des Prêcheurs 1215–1237* (Freiburg i.Ue. 1977).

Richard, J., *Le Royaume Latin de Jerusalem* (Paris 1953).

Saint Louis. Roi d'une France féodale, soutien de la Terre Sainte (Paris 1983).

Riley-Smith, J.S.C., *The Crusades. A Short History* (London 1987).

Rodenberg, C., *Innocenz IV. und das Königreich Sizilien 1245–1254* (Halle 1892).

Röhricht, R., *Geschichte des Königreichs Jerusalem (1100–1291)* (Innsbruck 1898).

Roncaglia, M., 'Fonte Arabo-Muselmana su San Francesco in Oriente?', *Studi Francescani*, l (1953), 258–9.

Roquebert, M., *L'épopée Cathare*, 3 vols. (Toulouse 1970–1986).

Roscher, H., *Papst Innocenz III. und die Kreuzzüge* (Forschungen zur Kirchen- und Dogmengeschichte; Göttingen 1969).

Rosenberg, B., 'Marienlob im Deutschordenslande Preussen. Beiträge zur Geschichte der Marienverehrung im Deutschen Orden bis zum Jahre 1525', *Acht Jahrhunderte Deutscher Orden in Einzeldarstellungen*, ed. K. Wieser (Bad Godesberg 1967), 321–37.

Rother, A., 'Johannes Teutonicus (von Wildeshausen). Vierter General des Dominikanerordens', *Römische Quartalschrift für Christliche Alterthumskunde und für Kirchengeschichte*, ix (1895), 139–70.

Rüdebusch, D., *Der Anteil Niedersachsens and den Kreuzzügen und Heidenfahrten* (Quellen und Forschungen zur Geschichte Niedersachsens 80; Hildesheim 1972).

Rusconi, R., 'De la prédication à la confession: Transmission et contrôle de modèles de comportement au xiiie siècle', *Faire Croire. Modalités de la diffusion et de la réception des messages religieux du xiie au xve siècle* (Collection de l'École Française de Rome 51; Rome 1981), 67–85.

Russell, F.H., *The Just War in the Middle Ages* (Cambridge Studies in Medieval Life and Thought (third series) 8; Cambridge 1975).

Sambin, P., *Problemi Politici Attraverso Lettere Inediti di Innocenzo IV* (Istituto Veneto Scienze Lettere ed Arti. Memorie classe di Scienze Morali e Letterare 31, fasc. 3; Venice 1955).

Scheeben, H.C., 'De Bullario quodam Ordinis Praedicatorum saeculi XIII', *AFP*,

Bibliography

vi (1936), 217–66.

Beiträge zur Geschichte Jordans von Sachsen (Quellen und Forschungen zur Geschichte des Dominikanerordens in Deutschland 35; Vechta i.O. 1938).

Schmitt, C., 'Der Anteil der Franziskaner an den Kreuzzügen (13.–15.Jh.)', *800 Jahre Franz von Assisi. Franziskanische Kunst und Kultur des Mittelalters. Niederösterreichische Landesaustellung Krems-Stein*, ed. Amt der Niederösterreichischen Regierung (Kulturabteilung) (Katalog des Niederösterreichischen Landesmuseums. Neue Folge 122; Vienna 1982), 213–20.

Schmugge, L., 'Zisterzienser, Kreuzzug und Heidenkrieg', *Die Zisterzienser. Ordensleben zwischen Ideal und Wirklichkeit*, ed. K. Elm *et al.* (Schriften des Rheinischen Museumsamtes 10; Cologne 1980), 57–68.

Schneyer, J.B., *Geschichte der Katholischen Predigt* (Freiburg i.Br. 1969).

Repertorium der Lateinischen Sermones des Mittelalters für die Zeit von 1150–1350, 10 vols. to date (Beiträge zur Geschichte der Philosophie und Theologie des Mittelalters 43; Munich 1969ff).

Schumacher, H.A., *Die Stedinger. Beitrag zur Geschichte der Weser-Marschen* (Bremen 1865).

Segl, P., '"Stabit Constantinopoli". Inquisition und päpstliche Orientpolitik unter Gregor IX.', *Deutches Archiv für die Erforschung des Mittelalters*, xxxii (1976), 209–20.

Selge, K.-V., 'Franz von Assisi und die Römische Kurie', *Zeitschrift für Theologie und Kirche*, lxvii (1970), 129–61.

'Franz von Assisi und Ugolino von Ostia', *S. Francesco nella ricerca storica degli ultimi 80 anni* (Atti del Centro di studi sulla spiritualità medievale 9; Todi 1971), 157–222.

'Die Ketzerpolitik Friedrichs II.', *Probleme um Friedrich II.*, ed. J. Fleckenstein (Vorträge und Forschungen 16; Sigmaringen 1974), 309–43.

Setton, K.M., *The Papacy and the Levant (1204–1571)*, 4 vols. (Memoirs of the American Philosophical Society 114; Philadelphia 1976–1984).

Sevesi, P.M., 'Documenta Hucusque Inedita Saeculi XIII pro Historia Almae Fratrum Minorum Provinciae Mediolanenis', *AFH*, ii (1909), 561–74.

Siberry, E., 'Missionaries and Crusaders, 1095–1274: Opponents or Allies', *Studies in Church History*, xx (1983), 103–10.

Criticism of Crusading 1095–1274 (Oxford 1985).

Smalley, B., 'John Russel, O.F.M.', *Recherches de Théologie Ancienne et Médievale*, xxiii (1956), 277–320.

Southern, R.W., *Robert Grosseteste: The Growth of an English Mind in Medieval Europe* (Oxford 1986).

Spence, R., 'Gregory IX's attempted expeditions to the Latin Empire of Constantinople: the Crusade for the Union of the Latin and Greek Churches', *Journal of Medieval History*, v (1979), 163–76.

'Pope Gregory IX and the Crusade on the Baltic', *The Catholic Historical Review*, lxix (1983), 1–19.

Strayer, J.R., 'The Political Crusades of the Thirteenth Century', *A History of the Crusades*, ii, 343–75.

Bibliography

'The Crusades of Louis IX', *A History of the Crusades*, ii, 487–518.

Tangl, G., *Studien zum Register Innocenz' III.* (Weimar 1929).

Thomson, W.R., *Friars in the Cathedral. The First Franciscan Bishops 1226–1261* (Pontifical Institute of Mediaeval Studies, Studies and Texts 33; Toronto 1975).

'The Image of the Mendicants in the Chronicles of Matthew Paris', *AFH*, lxx (1977), 3–34.

Throop, P.A., *Criticism of the Crusade. A Study of Public Opinion and Crusade Propaganda* (Amsterdam 1940).

Tuilier, A., 'La Révolte des pastoureaux et la querelle entre l'université de Paris et les ordres mendiants', *La Piété Populaire au Moyen Age* (Actes du 99e Congrès National des Sociétés Savantes (Besançon 1974). Section de philosophie et d'histoire jusqu'à 1610; Paris 1977), 353–67.

Tyerman, C., *England and the Crusades 1095–1588* (Chicago and London 1988).

Urban, W., *The Baltic Crusade* (De Kalb 1975).

The Prussian Crusade (Lanham 1980).

Van Caenegem, R.C., *Guide to the Sources of Medieval History* (Europe in the Middle Ages Selected Studies 2; Amsterdam, New York, Oxford 1978).

Van Cleve, T.[C]., *The Emperor Frederick II of Hohenstaufen. Immutator Mundi* (Oxford 1972).

Van den Wyngaert, A., 'Frère Guillaume de Cordelle O.F.M.', *La France Franciscaine*, iv (1921), 52–71.

Van Moolenbroek, J.J., 'Signs in the Heavens in Groningen and Friesland in 1214: Oliver of Cologne and Crusading Propaganda', *Journal of Medieval History*, xiii (1987), 251–72.

Vaughan, R., *Matthew Paris* (Cambridge Studies in Medieval Life and Thought 6; Cambridge 1958).

Verci, G.B., *Storia della Marca Trivigiana e Veronese*, 20 vols. (Venice 1786–91).

Vicaire, M.-H., *Histoire de Saint Dominique*, 2 vols. (Paris 1957).

'Les clercs de la croisade, l'absence de Dominique', *Paix de Dieu et guerre sainte en Albigeois au xiiie siècle* (Cahiers de Fanjeaux 4; Toulouse 1969), 260–80.

Von Bippen, W., *Geschichte der Stadt Bremen*, 3 vols. (Bremen 1892–1904).

Von Walther-Wittenheim, G., *Die Dominikaner in Livland im Mittelalter. Die Natio Livoniae* (Institutum Historicum Fratrum Praedicatorum Romae ad S. Sabinam Dissertationes Historicae 9; Rome 1938).

Wakefield, W.F., *Heresy, Crusade and Inquisition* (London 1974).

Welter, J.T., *L'"Exemplum" dans la littérature religieuse et didactique du Moyen Age* (Paris and Toulouse 1927).

Wendelborn, G., *Franziskus v. Assisi. Eine historische Darstellung* (Leipzig 1977).

Winkelmann, E., *Kaiser Friedrich II.*, 2 vols. (Leipzig 1889, 1897).

Wolff, R.L., 'The Latin Empire of Constantinople, 1204–1261', *A History of the Crusades*, ii, 187–232.

Zarncke, L., *Der Anteil des Kardinals Ugolino an der Ausbildung der drei Orden des hl. Franz* (Beiträge zur Kulturgeschichte des Mittelalters und der Renaissance 42; Berlin and Leipzig 1930).

Bibliography

UNPUBLISHED STUDIES

Cook, B.J., 'The Transmission of Knowledge about the Holy Land through Europe 1271–1314', 2 vols. (unpublished Ph.D. thesis; Manchester University 1985).

Spence, R.T., 'Pope Gregory IX and the Crusade' (unpublished Ph.D. thesis; Syracuse University 1978).

INDEX

ab. = archbishop; ad. = archdiocese; adn. = archdeacon; adny. = archdeaconry;
b. = bishop.; c. = count; cd. = cardinal; cp. = crusade preacher; d. = diocese; g. = guardian;
k. = king; m. = minister; mc. = money collector; p. = prior; p.l. = papal legate pp. = pope;
OM = Franciscan; OP = Dominican; OT = Teutonic Knight; OTe = Templar; s. = saint

Aachen, siege of, 66–7, 72, 152
Achilles, OM, cp., 81
Acre, 9, 93
Adam, OM (m. of Bologna,) 100–1
Adolf II, c. of Dassel, 48
Agen, adn. of, 143–4
Aigues Mortes, 99, 142
Aimerico, OM (g. of Gerona), mc., 131
Aix-les-Bains, d. of, 96
Alain of Lille, 112
Alberigo da Romano, 116–17
Albert, OM, b. of Marienwerder, 92
Albert the Great, OP, cp., 80, 96, 103, 106
Albert (Surbeer), b. of Üxküll and Riga,
    ab. of Prussia and Livonia, 44–6,
    65–6, 78
Albert Behaim, adn. of Passau, p.l., 63
Albertus Magnus see Albert the Great
Albi, b. of, 70
Albigensians see heretics, Albigensian
Alexander, OM, mc., 130
Alexander IV, pp., 126–7
    and crusade propaganda, 72, 77, 84–5,
    88–90
Alfonse, c. of Poitiers, 68, 70–1, 81, 141–3
Alfonso X, k. of Castile-Leon, 82–3
al-Kamil, sultan of Egypt, 8, 10–16, 35,
    46, 162, 174
Altenesch, battle of, 54
Amalrich of Montfort, c., 40–1
Ancona, 9
Andrew II, k. of Hungary, 58
Angers
    d. of, 42, 127
Anjou, c. of, 85–7
Anselm, OM (g. of Lake Constance), 60
Appingedam, 55

Apulia, 28
Aragon, 86, 131
Arles
    ad. of, 33
Arnold, OP, 72
Arnold of Burgende, 170
Arnold of Diest, 73
Arnsberg, c. of, 57
Arsuf, 157
Assisi, 27
    church of St Francis, 49
Auch, ab. of, 70
Augsburg, b. of, 60
Augustinian Hermits, 94
Austria, 88
Autun, d. of, 62
Auvillars, 68
Avignon, 130
    b. of, 71
    d. of, 130

Baibars, 80
Baldwin, ab. of Canterbury, 106, 108, 111,
    115–16
Baldwin II, Latin emperor, 37, 41–3, 78,
    84, 124
Baltic, 117
    see also crusades: to the Baltic
Barcelona, 170
Bartholomew of Bohemia, OM (m. of
    Austria), cp., 88–90
Bartholomew of Trisulto, p.l., 58
Basel, 111, 116
Bavaria, duke of, 75
Bedfordshire, 120
Bela IV, k. of Hungary, 37–8
Belleville, abbot of, 127

Index

Bern, 121
Bernard Gui, OP, 18
Bernard of Clairvaux, s., 4, 161, 174
Bernard of Nimphia, mc., 146
Bernard of Oporto, cd., p.l., 87, 104
Bernard the Treasurer, 11
Berthold of Regensburg, OM, cp., 75, 80, 96, 103, 107
Besançon, ad. of, 96
Beverley, 95
Blanche of Castile, 154–5
Blancus, OM, mc., 130
Bohemia, 43, 50, 80, 88–92, 94, 97–8
Bologna, 101, 104
    church of St Nicholas, 24
    university, 23, 162
Bonaventure, s., OM, 12–14, 16
Bosnia, 58
    b. of, 33, 38, 58–9
Bourges
    ab. of, 70, 86
    ad. of, 41
Brabant, 62
    c. of, 65
Brandenburg, c. of, 57, 91
Braga, ad. of, 83, 130
Breda, c. of, 54
Bremen
    ab. of, 44, 52–5
    ad. of, 49, 53–4
    dean of, 53
Brescia, 30
    b. of, 30
Breslau see Wroclaw
Brittany, 42, 71
Brunswick, duke of, 57
Burchard, c. of Oldenburg-Wildeshausen, 48, 53
Buckinghamshire, adny. of, 104
Burgos, 103
Burgundy, 42, 71, 130

Caesar of Heisterbach, 137–8, 172
Caesarea, 157
Cambrai, d. of, 65, 96, 152
canonization, 26–8
canon law, 3, 15, 118–19, 136, 159
Canterbury, ab. of, 71, 106, 111, 115–16
Carcasonne, b. of, 18
Casimir, duke of Cujavia, 88
Casimir, duke of Masovia, 45
Catalonia, 34
Ceslaus of Cracow, OP, 24
Ceuta, b. of, 83

Chanson de Roland, 11
Charlemagne, emperor, 11
Charles, c. of Anjou, k. of Sicily, 85–7
Charles, c. of Valois, 86
Chelmno (Kulm), 50
    b. of, 89–90
Chichester, b. of, 71, 152
Christburg, treaty of, 78
Christian, b. of Prussia, 44, 50, 52
Chur, b. of, 77
Cistercians, 156
    as crusade propagandists, 4, 92
Clarus of Sesto, OP, 24
Clement IV, pp., 80–2, 85–7, 92, 102–3, 156
Clermont, 116
Cleve, c. of, 54
Cologne, 120
    ab. of, 57
    ad. of, 90, 96, 152
Coloman, k. of Ruthenia, 37, 58
confraternities against heretics, 76
Conrad, b. of Hildesheim, 56–7
Conrad, OT, cp., 92
Conrad IV, k. of the Romans, 59, 73, 103
Conrad, landgrave of Thuringia, 57
Conrad of Höxter, OP (p. of Germany), 24, 57
Conrad of Marburg, 56–7, 167–8
Conrad of Urach, p.l., 32
Conrad Tors, OP, 56
Conradin of Hohenstaufen, 86
Constance, b. of, 60, 104
Constantinople, 37, 41, 43, 78, 84
    conquest of, 1, 37
    Latin patriarch of, 79
    Orthodox patriarch of, 37
Cordobà
    court of the caliph of, 10–11
Corsica, 95
Councils of the Church
    Lateran IV, 3, 103
    Lyons I, 62, 64, 84
    Lyons II, 93, 132
Courland, 74, 78, 90–2
    b. of, 65, 73, 89–90
Cracow,
    b. of, 87
    duke of, 87
Croatia, duke of, 58
crusade(s)
    against heretics in Hungary, 33, 52, 76
    against heretics in Germany, 5, 55–8, 76
    against Peter of Aragon, 86–7, 104

Index

against the Albigensians, 9, 17–19, 46,
  76, 161, 170–1
against the Drenther, 52, 54, 167–8
against the Romano brothers, 76–7, 111,
  116–17
against the Hohenstaufen, 5–6, 63–8,
  72–7, 79, 85–7, 96, 103, 145, 149, 152,
  154, 164
against the Mongols, 59–60, 84–5, 91,
  104
against the Muslims at Lucera, 171
against the Stedinger, 33, 52–8
Childrens', 173
for the conquest of Majorca, 33, 82
for the defence of the Latin Empire,
  33–4, 37–43, 69–70, 72, 78–9, 84,
  101–2, 124–7, 145, 163
Fifth, 8–9, 14, 16, 108, 111, 136–8. 157
Fourth, 1, 37
in Spain, 82
liturgy, 1–3, 60
movement, 1–4, 6, 7, 135, 162
naval support for, 83–5, 94, 110
of the Shepherds, 152–4, 166, 173
Third, 1
to North Africa, 82–4
to the Baltic, 4–5, 43–52, 59, 72, 77–8,
  85, 87–93, 97–8, 105, 163
to the Holy Land, 1, 4, 29, 31–7, 39–40,
  42, 46, 48, 50, 56, 61–3, 65, 67–72,
  78–82, 84–5, 91, 93–9, 101–2, 105,
  108, 114, 124–30, 133, 139–45, 150–5,
  157–8, 163
see also finance of crusades, crusade
  preachers, crusade sermons
crusade preachers
  authority of, 105–6, 157
  number of, 4, 94–5, 98–9, 164
  plenary indulgence for, 102
  quality of, 4, 98, 115, 165
  quarrels between, 89, 98
  right to celebrate mass during interdict
    for, 106
  seals of, 100, 106
  subdelegates of, 103–4, 106
crusaders (crucesignati)
  as pilgrims, 2
  familiy of, 118–19, 173
  female, 139, 173
  privileges, 1, 2, 35, 56, 80, 103, 118, 139,
    149
  spiritual benefits for, 1, 64, 108 see also
    indulgence
crusade sermons, 111–22

by Baldwin of Canterbury, 116
by Eustace of Flay, 111, 120
by Fulk of Neuilly, 120
by Henry of Strasbourg, 111, 116
by Innocent III, 111, 116
by Martin of Pairis, 111, 116
by Oliver of Cologne, 111, 120
by Philip of Ravenna, 114–15, 117
by Urban II, 116
exposition of relics during, 109
locations for, 106–7, 113, 165
miracles and visions during, 119–20, 173
powers to convoke people for, 106
special dates for, 107–9, 112–14
see also indulgences: for the attendance
  of crusade sermons, sermons,
  preaching of the cross
crusading chansons, 157–9
Cujavia, duke of, 88
Culm see Chelmno
Culmerland, 45

Dalmatia, 9, 138
Damietta, 8–11, 14, 16, 172
Daniel, prince of Galicia, 87
Danzig see Gdansk
Dassel, c. of, 48
Demnark, 44, 62 see also Scandinavia
Desiderius, OM, mc., 131
Dietrich of Kiwel, 88
Dominic Guzmàn, s., OP, 8–9, 17–19,
  23–5, 161
Dominicans
  as papal judge delegates, 31
  as inquisitors, 69–70, 76–7, 168–9
  at Antwerp, 96, 152
  at Barcelona, 33
  at Basel, 108
  at Beverley, 106
  at Bolgna, 23–5, 29
  at Bremen, 53, 55, 97, 169
  at Brescia, 29
  at Bristol, 155
  at Brno (Brünn), 97
  at Chelmno (Culm), 47, 88
  at Colonge, 25
  at Cracow, 97
  at Elblag (Elbing), 88
  at Freiberg, 97
  at Friesach, 169
  at Gdansk (Danzig), 47
  at Halberstadt, 97
  at Hamburg, 97
  at Hildesheim, 97

Index

Dominicans (*cont.*)
  at Kamien Pomorski (Cammin), 47
  at Kulmbach, 88
  at Lancaster, 106
  at Lausanne, 133
  at Leipzig, 97
  at Lübeck, 97
  at Louvain, 96, 152
  at Magdeburg, 52, 97
  at Marseille, 98, 126
  at Olomouc (Olmütz), 97
  at Paris, 25, 42, 98
  at Pontefract, 106
  at Prague, 24, 97
  at Regensburg, 97, 169
  at Scarborough, 106
  at Sigunta, 100
  at Strasbourg, 33, 169
  at Tallinn (Reval), 47
  at Toulouse, 69
  at Vienna, 60, 97
  at Visby, 97
  at Wroclaw (Breslau), 47, 97
  at Würzburg, 169
  at Yarm, 106
  at York, 106
  female convent at Rome, 29
  general chapter, 4–5, 29, 72, 99–100, 118
  governmental structure, 4–5, 97, 109–10, 118
  ideal of poverty, 128, 131, 133, 148–9, 161, 165
  in Austria, 26, 63, 88
  in Bohemia, 26, 51, 77, 84, 88
  in Corsica, 86
  in Cyprus, 26
  in Dalmatia, 26
  in England, 26, 35, 71, 79, 81, 94, 125, 129
  in Flanders, 73
  in France (general), 26, 43, 72, 80–1, 86, 126
  in France (northern), 42, 51, 71, 96, 102, 124, 163
  in France (southern), 23, 62, 69, 79, 99, 101, 105, 125, 133
  in Germany, 5, 24, 26, 36, 49, 60, 63, 67, 71, 73, 80–1, 84, 88, 95, 97–8, 100, 102–3, 143, 168
  in Germany (northern), 47, 77
  in Greece, 26, 43, 129
  in Holland, 73
  in Hungary, 24, 26, 38, 58–60

  in Ireland, 26, 71, 94
  in Italy (general), 26, 77, 86
  in Italy (northern), 23, 80, 94–5, 125
  in Italy (southern), 76, 94–5
  in Moravia, 84
  in Poland, 24, 26, 51, 60, 77, 84, 88, 97, 126
  in Pomerania, 77
  in Portugal, 26, 81
  in Sardinia, 86
  in Scandinavia, 24, 26, 51, 77, 81, 88, 95, 97, 100, 126
  in Spain, 24, 26, 81–3
  in the Ad. of Bremen, 49
  in the Ad. of Embrun, 82
  in the Ad. of Gran, 38
  in the Ad. of Magdeburg, 49
  in the Holy Land, 26
  in the March of Ancona, 86, 94
  in Tuscany, 35
  master general, 4, 25, 32, 47, 50, 102, 106, 158
  privileges against commissions, 66, 128–9, 131
  provincial chapters, 100, 133, 156
  training of preachers, 4
Drenther, 52, 54
Dublin, ab. of, 132

Eberhard, OP, cp., 100
ecclesiastical censures, 54, 65, 74, 88–9, 106, 125
Edward I, k. of England, 94, 132
Egypt, 16, 70, 157
Elizabeth of Thuringia, 56
Elstow, nunnery of, 113
Ely
  b. of, 173
  d. of, 147
Embrun, d. of, 96
Emo, 55–6
England, 42, 62, 72, 81, 111, 124, 127, 129–31, 139, 146–52
  bishops of, 35, 42, 148, 156, 159
enquêteurs, 126
Epirus, 37
episcopal endorsement of papal commissions, 104–5, 110
episcopal registers, 85, 159
Ernoul, 11, 13
Essex, adn. of, 152
Estonia, 51
Eudes (Rigauld), OM, ab. of Rouen, cp., 85, 107, 142

194

Index

Eudes of Châteauroux, cd., p.l., 62, 64, 85, 101, 112, 119, 142, 170, 173
Eustace of Flay, 111, 120
Evreux, b. of, 71, 142–3
excommunication, 27, 30, 50, 52, 60, 63, 73, 88–9, 102–3, 125, 145
exempla, 13–16, 120–2, 137–8
 as preaching aids, 111, 118, 120
 by Caesar of Heisterbach, 137–8, 172
 by Stephen of Bourbon, 172–3
 by Thomas of Cantimpré, 173
Exeter, b. of, 71
Ezzelino da Romano, 76–7, 117

Fabriano, 94
Fanjeaux, 18
Ferrara, 115, 117
finance of crusades, 1, 34, 40
 collection of subsidies, 2, 67–8, 74, 78, 80, 123–60, 165–6
 collectors, 124, 126–132
 subcollectors, 127, 131
 storage of money, 123, 132–3
 taxes, 2, 36, 83–4, 128–9, 131–3, 137, 140–1, 149
 testamentary bequests, 67, 102, 119–20, 123, 125–7, 140, 145–8
 unlawfully acquired money, 123, 125–6
 usurious interest, 102, 125–6
 see also redemption of crusade vows
Finland, 51
Fivelgo, 55
Flanders, 42, 74, 81, 97
Florence, 21
Fulk of Neuilly, 120, 161
France, 31, 34, 37, 39, 42–3, 65, 71–2, 81, 84, 86, 94, 96, 98, 124, 126, 129–30, 136, 139–43, 154, 164
 bishops of, 35, 39, 130, 141
Francis of Assisi, s., OM, 8–17, 21, 26–8, 49, 161–2, 174
Franciscans
 as inquisitors, 69, 76–7
 at Anduze, 61
 at Basel, 81
 at Beverley, 106
 at Bologna, 87, 101, 104, 156
 at Constance, 60, 103
 at Doncaster, 106
 at Limoges, 68
 at Marseille, 94, 98, 156
 at Nottingham, 106
 at Périgeux, 101
 at Perugia, 86

at Preston, 106
at Richmond, 106
at Torun (Thorn), 88
at Verona, 100
at Worcester, 127
at York, 106
cardinal-protector, 21, 27, 49
general chapter, 4–5, 9, 12, 21–2, 27, 49, 99, 118
governmental structure, 4–5, 22, 97, 109–10, 118
ideal of poverty, 49, 128, 131, 133, 148–9, 161, 165
in Austria, 35
in Bohemia, 23, 84, 91
in Corsica, 86
in England, 23, 35, 71, 79, 81, 94, 99, 104, 109, 125, 129
in Flanders, 73
in France (general), 21, 22, 72, 80–1, 86
in France (northern), 70–1, 96, 99
in France (southern), 69, 79, 105, 125
in Frisia, 67
in Germany, 5, 22, 48–9, 60, 63, 71, 73, 80–1, 84, 95, 98, 102, 143
in Greece, 23
in Holland, 73
in Italy, 22, 77, 86, 94–5
in Ireland, 23, 35, 71, 94
in Hungary, 21, 23, 59–60
in Lombardy, 35, 99–100, 125
in Moravia, 84, 91
in Northern Africa, 23
in Poland, 60, 84, 91
in Pomerania, 91
in Portugal, 81
in Sardinia, 86
in Scandinavia, 80
in Spain, 20–1, 23, 81–3, 103
in the Ad. of Magdeburg, 90–1
in the D. of Foligno, 86
in the Holy Land, 21, 23
in the March of Ancona, 86, 94–5
in the Province of Bologna, 95, 100–1, 104
in the Province of Rome, 86
in the Province of St Francis (Umbria), 86, 95, 98
in the Province of St James, 103
in Tuscany, 87, 104
minister general, 4, 62, 158
training of preachers, 4
Frankfurt, 57
Frederick (Visconti), ab. of Pisa, 85, 171–2

Index

Frederick I (Barbarossa), emperor, 48
Frederick II, emperor, 27–32, 35–6, 44–6,
  49–50, 63–6, 79, 101, 103, 105,
  129–30, 138, 142, 152, 162, 167–9
Freiburg i. Br., 102
Frisia, 64–8, 71–3, 98, 107, 111, 141–2,
  167, 172
  b. of, 64
Fulk of Neuilly, 4

Ganelon, 11
Gascony, 42, 83, 130
Gdansk (Danzig), duke of, 77
Genoa, 12
  ad. of, 83
Geoffrey, OM, mc., 127
Geoffrey of Argentan, 41, 140
Geoffrey of Belmont, p.l., 86
Gerald, OP, mc., 128
Gerard of Fracheto, OP, 18–19, 32
Gerard, c. of Mâcon, 173
Gerhard II, ab. of Bremen, 52–5
Gerhard Lützelkolb, OM, 56–7
Germany, 34, 43, 45, 51, 59–60, 62, 67,
  72–3, 75, 77, 80, 91–2, 96–7, 120, 130,
  152, 154, 163, 167–9, 172
  bishops of, 35, 59–60, 168
Gilbert of Tournai, OM, 5, 109, 156–7,
  171
Gnesen, b. of, 88
Godfrey, OP, , mc., 130
Godfrey of Bredal, 73
Gotland, 49
Gotzewia, 89
Gran, ab. of, 59
Greece see Latin Empire
Gregory IX, pp., 20–31, 87, 138–9, 142,
  162, 167–8
  and crusade propaganda, 4, 34–62,
  78–9, 84, 95, 99, 108, 124–5, 163
  cardinal-protector of the Franciscans,
  21, 27
  household of, 25, 30, 34, 139
Gregory X (Tedaldo Visconti), pp., 80, 93
Groningen, 55
Guala of Bergamo, OP, b. of Brescia,
  29–31
Guelders, c. of, 54, 65, 167

Hartwig II, ab. of Bremen, 44
Hattin, battle of, 1, 14
Heidenreich, OP (p. of Leipzig and
  Poland), b. of Chelmno, cp., 89–90
Henry I, b. of Constance, 60, 104

Henry, OM, b. of Courland, cp., 89–90
Henry, b. of Strasbourg, 111, 116
Henry II, c. of Oldenburg-Wildeshausen,
  48
Henry III, c. of Oldenburg-Wildeshausen,
  53
Henry VI, emperor, 48
Henry III, k. of England, 62–3, 71, 107–8,
  127, 130, 132, 148, 150–1, 155
Henry VII, k. of the Romans, 36, 168
Henry (Raspe), landgrave of Thuringia,
  57, 60, 64–5, 129
Henry, marquess of Minden, 57
Henry de Spinis, OT, cp., 92
Henry of Avranches, OM, 10
Henry of Bar-le-Duc, c., 40
Henry of Cologne, OP (p. of Cologne), 25
Henry of Lützelburg, OM, b. of
  Courland, cp., 65, 73
Henry of Montfort, OP, b. of Chur, cp.,
  73, 75–6
Henry of Segusio see Hostiensis
Herard of Chancenai, 39
Hereford, episcopal registers of, 159
heretics, 33, 36, 53, 56–9, 69–70, 76–7,
  167–9
  Albigensian, 8, 17–19
  see also crusades: against heretics
Hermann II, c. of Lippe, 52
Hermann of Salza, 46–8
Hildesheim, b. of, 56–7
Holland, 68, 98
  c. of, 54, 167
Holstein, 49, 91
Holy Land, 16, 23, 31, 35, 65, 85, 117, 142
  as patrimony of Christ, 2
  St Francis's journey to, 9
  transmission of knowledge about, 6, 80,
  118–19
  see also crusades: to the Holy Land
Honorius III, pp., 3, 29, 44, 105
Honorius IV, pp., 87
  and crusading propaganda, 59
Hostiensis (Henry of Segusio), 119
Hugh of St Cher, 119
Hugh of Turenne, OM (g. of Limoges),
  cp., 68, 144
Hugh IV, c. of Rodez, 143–5
Humbert of Beaujeau, 40–2, 127
Humbert of Romans, OP (master-
  general), 33, 43, 106, 109, 114–15,
  118, 171
Hungary, 37, 58–9, 94
  b. of, 35, 38, 58

Huon of St Quentin, 157
Hydus, OP (p. of Germany), 67

Ile d'Oléron, 42
Illuminatus, OM, 12–14, 16
indulgence, 35, 52, 56, 72, 80, 87, 102–3,
    108, 118, 149, 168, 173
  authority to issue, 2
  for crusaders' families, 118–19
  for the attendance of crusade sermons,
    35, 50, 54, 73, 102, 106
  partial, 2, 54, 87, 123, 136–7, 139, 147
  plenary, 2, 43, 54–5, 64, 76, 82, 102,
    118, 120, 123, 137, 146–7, 155–6
Innocent III, pp., 2–3, 107, 111–12,
    116–18, 136–7, 166
Innocent IV, pp., 125, 129–31, 140–3, 145,
    151, 156
  and crusading propaganda, 52, 62–79,
    83–5, 87, 95, 107, 119, 163
Innocent V, OP, pp., 83, 103
inquisition, 55–6, 67–8, 70, 167–9
  recruiting crusaders, 69–70, 76–7, 164
Iohanninus, OM, cp., 101
Ireland, 131
Israel, OP (lector of Sigunta), 100
Italy, 9, 21, 23, 26, 29–31, 31, 85–6, 94,
    162, 164, 168
Ivo of Ayr, OP, mc., 128

Jacob of Praeneste, cd., p.l., 58
Jacek of Ople, OP, cp., 50–1
James I, k. of Aragon, 33, 82
James Pontaléon, adn. of Liège, patriarch
    of Jerusalem see Urban IV, pp.
James of Vitry, 10, 26, 109, 119, 170
Jatwingians, 87
Jerusalem, 14, 16, 31
  patriarch of, 31, 80
Jews, 125–6
João Martins, OM (g. of Lisbon), cp., mc.,
    83, 130–1
John, c. of Brandenburg, 57
John Asen, ruler of Bulgaria, 37–8, 78
John Balistar, OM, cp., 101–2
John Sarracenus, mc., 146
John de Canter, OM, mc., 127–8
John le Romeyn, ab. of York, 95, 108
John of Abbeville, 170
John of Béthune, 43
John of Brienne, Latin emperor, 27, 37,
    39, 41
John of Darlington, OP, mc., ab. of
    Dublin, 131–2

John of Diest, OM, b. of Sambia and
    Lübeck, cp., 73–5, 96, 152
John of Gorze, 10–11
John of Limoges, OM, mc., 127, 140, 143
John of Piano Carpini, OM, 172
John of St Albans, 25
John of St Arnulf, 10
John of Vincenza, OP, 24
John of Wildeshausen, OP (master-
    general), b. of Bosnia, cp., 32–3, 38,
    48, 53, 57–8, 107
John Russel, OM, 112, 172
John the Englishman, OM (m. of
    Provence), mc., 130, 151
John Vatatzes, Byzantine emperor, 37–8,
    41, 78
Jordan, river, 14
Jordan of Giano, OM, 72
Jordan of Saxony, OP (master-general),
    17, 25, 47–8, 50
Julian of Speyer, OM, 10

Knights of Dobrin, Order of the, 44
Kolocsa, b. of, 58
Kulm see Chelmno

Languedoc, 8, 17–19, 143
Las Navas de Tolosa, battle of, 1
Latin Empire, 117, 129
  see also crusades: for the defence of the
    Latin Empire
Latvia see Livonia
Le Mans, b. of, 41
Leo, OM, 12, 16
Leo of Perego, OM (m. of Lombardy),
    100
Leon, b. of, 103
Leonard, mc., 128
Le Puy, d. of, 41
Lethowia, 89
Levant, 21, 68
Liège
  adn. of, 75, 91, 93
  d. of, 96
Lille, 87
Limoges, 102
Lincoln
  adn. of, 146
  b. of, 104, 146–8, 151–2
  d. of, 146
  episcopal registers of, 159
Lithuania, 87–9
  b. of, 89
Lithuanians, 77, 87, 90

Index

Livonia, 44–50, 77–8, 89, 91
  ab. of, 65–6
local church *see* secular clergy
London, 109, 128, 146
Lombard League, 30
Lombardy, 167–8
Looz, countess of, 57
Lope, OM, b. of Ceuta, cp., 83
Lotharingia, 42
Louis VII, k. of France, 174
Louis IX, k. of France, 62, 64–6, 68, 70–1,
  78–9, 81, 83–4, 93, 99, 125–6, 129–30,
  140–3, 150–1, 153–4, 157
Louvain
  b. of, 65
  d. of, 65
Lucera, 86
Lübeck, b. of, 52, 54–5, 75
Lund, 100
  ab. of, 51
Lyons, 66–7, 129, 151
  ad. of, 96

Mâcon
  c. of, 173
  d. of, 40
Magdeburg
  ad. of, 49
Maguelonne, b. of, 105
Mainz, 57
  ab. of, 56–7, 60, 64, 66
  ad. of, 90
Manfred of Hohenstaufen, 85–7, 145
Mansuetus, OM, mc., 127–8
Mansurah, battle of, 153–4
Marseille, 85, 98
  b. of, 85
  d. of, 85
Marsile, k., 11
Martin, OM, mc., 131
Martin IV, pp., 86–7
Martin of Pairis, 111, 116
Master of Hungary, 153
Matthew Paris, 35–6, 72, 118, 123–4,
  129–30, 139, 141–2, 147–51, 154
Melfi, constitutions of, 168
Menko, 66
Menzano, abbot of, p.l., 88
Metz, d. of, 65, 96
Michael VIII (Palaeologus), Byzantine
  emperor, 84
Middlesex, adn. of, 127
Mindaugas, k. of Lithuania, 77–8,
  90–1

Minden
  b. of, 54–5
  d. of, 54
  marquess of, 57
mission, 8, 47, 51, 161
missionaries, 9, 11
Moneta of Cremona, OP, 24
Mongols, 38, 59–60, 63, 78, 84–5, 91, 104,
  172
Montfort, c. of, 17–19, 70
Moravia, 49, 88, 91
Münster
  b. of, 54
  d. of, 54
Murbach, abbot of, 173
Muret, battle of, 18
Muslims, 2, 9–17, 36, 80, 162
  in North Africa, 9, 82–4
  in Spain, 1, 9, 82
  of Lucera, 86

Narbonne, 70
  ab. of, 70, 86
  ad. of, 33, 61
Navarre, 71
negotium crucis *see* crusades: movement
negotiom Terrae Sanctae, *see* crusades: to
  the Holy Land
Nevers, b. of, 40
Nicholas, b. of Riga, 51
Nicholas of Lund, OP, 24
Nicholas, papal chamberlain, 144
Nicholas IV, OM, pp.
  and crusading propaganda, 59, 85, 93–4,
  99
Nicea, 37
Novgorod, 77
Norway, 71, 98, 143

Oldenburg-Wildeshausen, c. of, 48, 53–4
Oliver Sutton, b. of Lincoln, 104
Oliver of Cologne, 4, 107, 111, 120, 138,
  172
Olmütz *see* Olomouc
Olomouc (Olmütz), b. of, 89
Opizo of Menzano, abbot, p.l., 78
Osnabrück
  b. of, 54
  d. of, 54
Otto II, b. of Utrecht, 167
Otto, c. of Brandenburg, 57
Otto II, duke of Bavaria, 75
Otto, duke of Brunswick, 57
Otto I, emperor, 10

Index

Otto of St Nicholas, cd., p.l., 33, 53
Oxford, 148, 170
  adny. of, 104

Padua, 31
Paderborn
  b. of, 54
  d. of, 54
Palestine *see* Holy Land
papal chamberlain, 144
papal chaplain, 33, 75, 86, 128, 130–1
papal legate
  and crusade propaganda, 3, 32, 45,
    86–7, 103–4, 111, 116–17, 121–2, 142,
    164, 173
  in Bosnia, 58
  in Denmark, 53, 65
  in England, 124,140
  in France, 61, 64, 101, 106, 156
  in Germany, 32–3, 53, 63, 65, 67, 103
  in Italy, 65, 86–7, 104, 111
  in Languedoc, 8
  in Livonia, 45
  in Lombardy, 24, 105, 116
  in north eastern Europe, 88
  in Poland, 65
  in Prussia, 39
  in Scotland, 140
  in Spain, 65
  in the Balkans, 33, 38
  in the Baltic, 78, 91
  on the Fifth Crusade, 11
papal penitentiariy, 33–4, 39, 53, 75, 143
papal registers, 7
papal state *see* Patrimony of St Peter
Paris, 24, 141, 170
  b. of 141
  university, 23–5, 112, 162
Passau, adn. of, 63
Patrimony of St Peter, 76
Paul of Hungary, OP (p. of Hungary), 24
Pedro of Tarragona, OM, mc., 131
Penitents of Jesus Christ, order of, 133
Peter, k. of Aragon, 86–7
Peter (of Dreux), duke of Brittany, 41–2,
  127
Peter de Philistiim, OM, mc., 127
Peter Garcia, 68, 70
Peter of Seila, OP, 69–70
Peter of St George, cd., p.l., 67, 103
Peter of Vaux-de-Cernai, OP, 18
Peter (the Martyr) of Verona, OP, s., cp.,
  76
Peter the Hermit, 161

Petrizolo, of Aposa, OM, cp., 100
Perugia, b. of, 38
pilgrims, 40, 48, 139
  see also crusaders: as pilgrims
Pisa
  ab. of, 85
  ad. of, 83
Philip of Marerio, 145
Philip, c. of Montfort, 70
Philip of Oxford, 114
Philip of Ravenna, p.l., 114–15, 117
Philip the Chancellor, 170
Poitiers
  c. of, 68, 70–1, 81, 141–3
  d. of, 42, 127, 140
  treasurer of St Hilary, 141
Poland, 43, 49, 77, 87–91, 94–5, 98, 130
  nobility of, 87–8
Pomerania, 49
Ponce of Lesparre, OP (p. of Provence),
  62, 101
Ponsa, OP, b. of Bosnia, 59
Portugal, 81, 130–1
  k. of, 81
preaching of the crusade(s)
  handbooks for, 43, 109, 114–16, 165, 172
  preaching aids for, 111–22, 165 *see also*
    exempla, sermons
  recruitment areas for, 96–8
  unauthorized, 51, 138, 141
  by individuals, 3, 4, 33–4, 61, 73, 162
  by papal legates *see* papal legates: and
    crusade propaganda
  by secular clergy, *see* secular clergy: and
    crusade propaganda
  for individual crusades *see under* crusades
  see also crusade sermons
Premonstratensians, 92, 128
Prouille, 17–18
Provence, 130, 168
  march of, 71, 85, 98, 143
Prussia, 44–6, 51–2, 77–8, 87–8, 91
  (a)b. of, 44, 50, 52, 65–6
Prussians, 44, 50, 77–8, 87, 90
public notary, 104, 144

Raimon Gaucelm of Béziers, 157
Rainer of St Mary, cd., 72
Ratzeburg
  b. of, 54–5
  d. of, 54
Ravenna, 169
Raymnd of Amiliavo, adn. of Agen,
  143–4

Raymond of Nogaret, 131
Raymond of Penyafort, OP (master-
    general), cp., 24, 33, 82
Raymond VII, c. of Toulouse, 68, 70,
    143–5
Raymund, ab. of Seville, 83, 103
Reconquista *see* crusades: in Spain
recruitment of crusaders
    by diplomatic negotiation, 65, 73–6
    by personal talks, 114
redemption of crusade vows, 2, 40–2,
    49–50, 60, 69, 78, 82, 96, 106, 119–20,
    123–8, 133, 135–60
    conditions for, 135–7
    distribution of money from, 40–1,
        139–40
    forced, 139–40
    frauds concerning, 50, 138–40, 139–41,
        145, 150, 152, 157, 172
Reginald of Orleans, OP, 23–5
Regno, 27–8, 30, 49, 63–4, 87, 168
relic(s), 108
    of St Mary Magdalene, 108
    of St Paul, 108
    of St Peter, 108
    of the True Cross, 14
Renold, OM, cp., 67
Rheims
    ab. of, 40, 70
    ad. of, 40–1
Richard, earl of Cornwall, 124, 146, 150
Ricaut Bonomel, OTe, 157
Riga, 45, 48
    (arch)b. of, 44–5, 47, 51, 92
Ripon, 95
Robert I (of Courtenay), Latin emperor,
    37
Robert Curzon, 136, 139
Robert Grosseteste, b. of Lincoln, 146–8,
    151–2
Robert of Château Roussillon, 33
Rodez
    b. of, 144
    c. of, 143–5
Roger of Lewes, OM, cp., 120
Roger of Salisbury, 171
Roland of Cremona, OP, 24
Rome, 23, 27, 108, 138, 168
Rostand, mc., 127
Rottum, 55
Rouen, ab. of, 70, 85–6, 127, 140, 142
Rutebeuf, 158–9

Saladin, sultan, 14

Salimbene, OM, 62, 105, 107, 115
Sambia, b. of, 74
Samogitia, 78, 90
Samogitians, 77
Santiago de Compostela, 20
Sardinia, 95
Sayn, c. of, 57
Saxony, duke of, 75
Scandinavia, 51, 77, 163
Schoolen, c. of, 55
Scotland, 62, 128, 130, 140
secular clergy, 22, 40, 129, 133, 166
    and crusade propaganda, 3–4, 34, 42,
        51, 54, 57, 59, 61, 64–5, 70–1, 73, 75,
        82–3, 85–7, 90–1, 94–5, 103–5,
        110–11, 120–2, 165
Semgallia, 78, 92
Senlis, b. of, 71, 142–3
Sens
    ab. of, 39–41, 70, 140
    ad. of, 40
sermons
    as preaching aids, 111–16, 165
    by Aldobrandinus Toscanelli, 113
    by Antonio Arazo de Parma, 113
    by Allain of Lille 112
    by Bonaventure, 113
    by Eudes of Châteauroux, 85, 112, 119,
        171
    by Frederick Visconti, 171
    by Gilbert of Tournai, 109, 171
    by Henricus de Friemar, 113
    by Humbert of Romans, 171
    by James of Lausanne, 113
    by James of Vitry, 109, 119, 170
    by John of Abbeville, 170
    by John Russel, 112, 172
    by Martinus Strebus, 113
    by Nicholas of Biard, 113
    by Philip the Chancellor, 170
    by Roger of Salisbury, 171
    by Stephen Langton, 170
    by William Peyraut, 113
    for feastdays of the Cross, 112–13
    for Lent, 113–14
    for the preaching of the cross, 111–12
    production at Paris, 112
    see also crusade sermons, preaching of
        the cross
Seville, ab. of, 83, 103
S. Germano and Ceprano, peace of, 30,
    44, 46, 168
Siboto, b. of Augsburg, 60
Sicily, 28, 94

Index

kingdom of *see* Regno
Siegfried, ab. of Mainz, 56–7, 60, 64, 66
Simon, c. of Montfort, 17–19, 161
Simon of Sta. Cecilia, cd., p.l., 61, 86
Simon of St Martin, cd., p.l., 86
Simon of Sweden, OP, 24
Slutter, 55
Solothurn, 133
Southwell, 95
Spain, 81, 83–4, 130–1, 172
Speyer, dean of, 136
St Albans, abbey of, 148
Sta. Maria in Valle Viridis, order of, 133
St David's, b. of, 71
Stedinger, 52–6
Stephen of Bourbon, OP, 172
Stets, 55
St Hyacinth *see* Jacek of Ople
Strasbourg, 111
  b. of, 111, 116
St Thomas of Torcello, Cistercian abbey
  abbot of, 38, 43
Suravia, 49
Swabia, 75
Swantopelk, duke of Gdansk, 77, 87
Swietopelk, duke of Pomerania, 47
Swordbrothers, Order of, 44–5, 50–1

Tarantaise, d. of, 96
Tavistians, 51
Tedaldo Visconti, adn. of Liège, *see*
  Gregory X, pp.
Templars, 128
Teutonic Order, 43, 45–7, 49–52, 59,
  77–8, 87–93, 163
Theodore Dukas, ruler of Epirus, 37
Thibald IV, c. of Champagne, 39–42,
  124–5
Thibald II, k. of Navarre, 81
Toledo, ad. of, 131
Thomas, OTe, mc., 139
Thomas of Cantimpré, OP, 155–6, 173
Thomas of Celano, OM, 10–13
Thomas of Marly, 42
Thuringia, landgraves of, 48, 57, 60, 64–5,
  129
Toul, d. of, 65, 96
Toulouse
  b. of, 105, 144
  c. of, 68, 70, 143–5
  county of, 71, 143
  inquisition at, 69–70
  siege of, 18
Tournai, d. of, 152

tournaments, 107, 165
Tours, ad. of, 41
Treviso, march of, 31
Trondheim, ab. of, 105
troubadours, 157–9
Tuscany, 34
Tzurulum, 38

Üxküll, b. of, 44
Ugolino of Ostia, cd. *see* Gregory IX, pp.
Ulrich, OM (g. of Lake Constance), 103
Ulrich, c. of Würtemberg, 75
Urban II, pp., 116
Urban IV (James Pontaléon), pp., 92, 126
  and crusade propaganda, 80, 84–5, 91,
    105, 158
  while still adn. of Liège, 75, 91
Utrecht
  b. of, 52, 167–8
  canon of, 25

Valois, c. of, 86
Venice, 31, 79, 105, 116
  doge of, 39
  fleet of, 94
Verden
  b. of, 54
  d. of, 54
Verdun, d. of, 65, 96
Vienne, ad. of, 96
Virgin Mary, 23, 47, 153
Vistula, river, 50
vows
  crusade vows, 27–8
  commutation of crusade vows, 2,
    37–40, 50, 65, 67, 82, 89, 142
  see also redemption of crusade vows

Wales, 108, 111, 115
Walter Cantilupe, b. of Worcester,
  147–8
Walter de Langele, OM, cp., 104
Walter Giffard, ab. of York, 104
Walter of St Martin, OP, 31
Whithorn, 128
William Longsword, 62
William Miannani, public notary, 144
William of Cordelle, OM, cp., 33–4,
  39–41, 107, 124, 126–7, 139–40
William of Holland, k. of the Romans,
  65–6, 72–3, 96, 152
William of Maaseik, OP, cp., 73–5, 152
William of Modena, p.l., 45–8
William of Monteils, OM, cp., 81

William of Montferrat, OP, 25
William of Oléron, OP, cp., 41–2, 127, 139
William of Sabina, cd., p.l., 78
Willibrand, OM, cp., 66–7
Willibrand, b. of Utrecht, 52, 54, 167–8
Winchester, 107
Wladislaw, duke of Poland, 50–1
Worcester, b. of, 147–8, 151

Wroclaw (Breslau), b. of, 88–9
Würtemberg, c. of, 75

York, 95
  ab. of, 71, 95, 104, 106, 108
  ad. of, 104

Zagreb, b. of, 58
Zeeland, 68, 98

Cambridge studies in medieval life and thought
Fourth series

Titles in the series

1 The Beaumont Twins: The Roots and Branches of Power in the Twelfth Century
  D. B. CROUCH
2 The Thought of Gregory the Great*
  G. R. EVANS
3 The Government of England under Henry I*
  JUDITH A. GREEN
4 Charity and Community in Medieval Cambridge
  MIRI RUBIN
5 Autonomy and Community: The Royal Manor of Havering, 1200–1500
  MARJORIE KENISTON MCINTOSH
6 The Political Thought of Baldus de Ubaldis
  JOSEPH CANNING
7 Land and Power in Late Medieval Ferrara: The Rule of the Este, 1350–1450
  TREVOR DEAN
8 William of Tyre: Historian of the Latin East*
  PETER W. EDBURY AND JOHN GORDON ROWE
9 The Royal Saints of Anglo-Saxon England: A Study of West Saxon and East Anglian Cults
  SUSAN J. RIDYARD
10 John of Wales: A Study of the Works and Ideas of a Thirteenth-Century Friar
  JENNY SWANSON
11 Richard III: A Study of Service*
  ROSEMARY HORROX
12 A Marginal Economy? East Anglian Breckland in the Later Middle Ages
  MARK BAILEY
13 Clement VI: The Pontificate and Ideas of an Avignon Pope
  DIANA WOOD
14 Hagiography and the Cult of Saints: The Diocese of Orléans, 800–1200
  THOMAS HEAD
15 Kings and Lords in Conquest England
  ROBIN FLEMING
16 Council and Hierarchy: The Political Thought of William Durant the Younger
  CONSTANTIN FASOLT
17 Warfare in the Latin East, 1192–1291*
  CHRISTOPHER MARSHALL
18 Province and Empire: Brittany and the Carolingians
  JULIA M. H. SMITH
19 A Gentry Community: Leicestershire in the Fifteenth Century, c. 1422–c. 1485
  ERIC ACHESON

20 Baptism and Change in the Early Middle Ages, *c.* 200–1150
   PETER CRAMER

21 Itinerant Kingship and Royal Monasteries in Early Medieval Germany, *c.* 936–1075
   JOHN W. BERNHARDT

22 Caesarius of Arles: The Making of a Christian Community in Late Antique Gaul
   WILLIAM E. KLINGSHIRN

23 Bishop and Chapter in Twelfth-Century England: A Study of the *Mensa Episcopalis*
   EVERETT U. CROSBY

24 Trade and Traders in Muslim Spain, 1000–1250
   OLIVIA REMIE CONSTABLE

25 Lithuania Ascending: A Pagan Empire in East-Central Europe, 1295–1345
   STEPHEN C. ROWELL

26 Barcelona and its Rulers, 1100–1291
   STEPHEN P. BENSCH

27 Conquest, Anarchy and Lordship: Yorkshire, 1066–1154
   PAUL DALTON

28 Preaching the Crusades: Mendicant Friars and the Cross in the Thirteenth Century
   CHRISTOPH T. MAIER

*Also published as a paperback.